The Ultimate in Anti-Highrise Handbooks

● The world's first comprehensive study of the true costs of skyscrapers, done by a special Guardian task force scouring every San Francisco neighborhood and every city department for every piece of evidence.

● A horrifying look at what lies in store for each San Francisco neighborhood in the next ten years — with an arsenal of legal ways for sniffing out, then snuffing out skyscrapers invading your turf.

● A blow-by-blow description of how citizen pressure folded up U.S. Steel's plan for highrising the Waterfront — and what's being cooked up for us after the hubbub dies down.

● Also: a no-holds-barred introduction by Chamber of Commerce Enemy No. 1, Alvin Duskin . . . Louis Dunn's cartoons (the nastiest since David Levine nailed Lyndon Johnson) . . . an eyeful of fascinating tables and graphs . . . medical advice . . . acerbic architectural critiques . . . a list of highrises most likely to fall in the next earthquake . . . and much, much more . . .

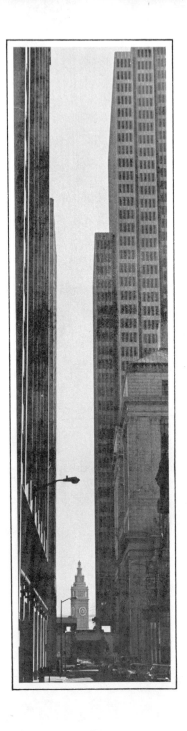

THE ULTIMATE HIGHRISE

San Francisco's
Mad Rush Toward the Sky...

Editors: Bruce Brugmann,
Greggar Sletteland
Art Director: Louis Dunn
Graphics Director: Marion Dibble

Waterfront Case Study: Richard Reinhardt
Foreword: Alvin Duskin

San Francisco Bay Guardian Books

"The Ultimate Highrise" is published by the San Francisco Bay Guardian, an independent newspaper founded in San Francisco in September, 1966. The Guardian specializes in investigative reporting, reviewing the arts and reporting on San Francisco and the Bay Area.

In 1971, the American Society of Planning Officials, the national organization of professional planners, gave a special planning award to the Guardian and cited the newspaper for "the immensely useful role it plays in digging into areas where the big dailies apparently fear to tread: its stories reflect a great deal of research and careful documentation."

For subscription information, a list of back Guardians and special Guardian publications, write or call:

The San Francisco Bay Guardian
1070 Bryant St.
San Francisco, Calif. 94103
415-861-9600

Table of Contents

81598

Foreword

By Alvin Duskin

I stumbled onto the Ultimate Highrise for the first time in the battle over the fate of Alcatraz Island. I was new to the conservation movement and I thought that what my friends and I were doing was simply pointing out that the plan for the commercialization of the island was a bad one and that, given time, someone might come up with a better one. What I didn't see was that the plan for Alcatraz gave us a clue to what was planned for San Francisco. Half of the island would be a towering monument to our technology — a representation of the Apollo 8 moon rocket — and the other half would be a monument to our past — a "re-creation of Victorian San Francisco."

The Texan who had all these plans for Alcatraz was introduced to the politicians and to the business community of San Francisco by the director of the Greater San Francisco Chamber of Commerce.

And what did the Chamber want for San Francisco? I didn't see at the time that it was exactly what they wanted for Alcatraz. A highrise side that would be a monument to technology, industry and finance, and a side that would re-create what we once had but lost. The new San Francisco would have an expanding Manhattan-style core of highrise office buildings. The old residential neighborhoods with their spacious flats and Victorians would be "redeveloped" (bull-dozed) into highrise apartments for middle income people without children. And then there would be the city of the tourists — Union Street, Ghirardelli Square, Fisherman's Wharf, Grant Avenue. The plan doesn't make much sense for San Francisco — tourists come here to get away from what we would become; but that isn't as easy to see in the City as a whole as it was on Alcatraz.

The battle to save Alcatraz was won very quickly because 8,000 people who live here suddenly realized that it was *their* island and *they* could decide what it should become. Who else should decide? The Chamber of Commerce? A developer from Texas? The Mayor? The Board of Supervisors? The developers and our elected officials all agreed on the Apollo 8/Re-created Victorian San

Francisco Plan which we would have to look at for the rest of our lives! Anyway, I think that the Alcatraz victory re-awakened in San Francisco the idea that when our politicians betray the trust of the voters, the people of the City can still win.

The next confrontation with the Ultimate Highrise was a kind of backwards one. I had become involved in the fight over the California Water Plan, the plan to move our water to Southern California just before it enters the Bay-Delta system. It was an easy step because it wouldn't do much good to save Alcatraz if the Bay was going to die.

The governor and a lot of people in Sacramento thought that we Northern Californians were being irresponsible. We claimed that it was *our* water and if we wanted it to keep our rivers flowing freely and our Delta and Bay alive with fish and birds, then the water should stay here. The governor said that the whole thing had been decided by the fact that a majority of the voters of the state wanted the California Water Plan and that was that.

Actually, most of the voters hadn't any idea of the damage the Water Plan would cause, and the Southern California real estate interests spent fortunes to distort the issues and confuse everyone. So we started a series of lawsuits against the state that have, so far, helped foul up the completion of the Water Plan, particularly the Peripheral Canal.   The essence of the lawsuits is that the majority rules only when the decision of the majority conforms with the law and the Water Plan violates all kinds of Federal and State environmental laws.

The strangest part of all this was that we found support where we never expected it. All kinds of business and industry groups in Contra Costa County were speaking out and spending money to defend the migrating salmon of the Delta, the waterfowl of the Suisun marshes, etc. One of the first rules of political action is to know what your allies *really* want — before you get into bed with them. I couldn't believe that the Chamber of Commerce of Contra Costa County had been converted by the arguments of the Sierra Club. And it turned out that although it was good to have them on our side against the Peripheral Canal, the Chamber wasn't all that interested in birds and fish. The real story was that just as San Francisco was going to be a new Manhattan, Contra Costa County was going to be another Newark. And to bring in new steel mills and glass mills and oil refineries they needed to have deep water access for the current generation of super tankers. To do that they were pushing through a plan to dig something called the Baldwin Channel, a deep trench that would start by cutting through the sand-bar outside the Golden Gate. From there they would dig a deep channel past Angel Island, to the refineries of Richmond and then on up to Pittsburg and Antioch, and then to Stockton.

But you couldn't make the Baldwin Channel work very well unless there was a lot of fresh water coming in all the time to keep it flushed out. And to get the fresh water, the industrialists had to join the Sierra Club, Friends of the Earth and Trout Unlimited in the fight against the water coalition of Southern California!

What worried me most about the Baldwin Channel problem was that I had never heard anything about it. And no one else, except a few activist kids over in Contra Costa County — who no one paid any attention to — seemed to know anything about it either. But the planning had been going on for years, and legislation in Congress was moving along to bring in the money for the project. There had been, of course, some public hearings. But not many people attended and those who did had little political weight. And the Baldwin Channel would let super tankers full-to-the-brim with Alaskan oil into the Bay. Did we want that? And what else was going on that we hadn't heard anything about? And if there were a lot of destructive things going on that we haven't even heard of, how did we decide what to do next?

I was planning on letting people know about the Baldwin Channel when — another crisis. U.S. Steel announced a 550 ft. highrise on the waterfront. And all the environmentalists and urban conservationists rushed into another ad-hoc, stop-the-latest-outrage campaign. I rushed too, but it was strange to be forgetting the Baldwin Channel. I felt there must be a way to get at both U.S. Steel and the Baldwin Channel. So I dropped out of things for a while and did a little research to find out how it all started.

It all began, I think, about 30 years ago. And not accidentally but with a plan.

In 1942 the war in the Pacific was going badly for America and we weren't helping much here in the Bay Area. The problem was that everything seemed to be in the wrong place. The workers lived far from the shipyards and could spend hours every day getting to work. The materials for war came in to the wrong places and would get tied up on their way to the factories. Nothing moved as it did at, say, the Brooklyn Navy Yard, and the Defense Department was talking about not sending any more rush contracts into the Bay Area.

So the business men and the leaders of industry did a very sensible thing. They sat down together and tried to figure out a way to make some regional plans to speed things up, to organize the entire Bay Area in such a way that the people were in the right places, industry was where it should be and the services of the business community were centralized where everyone could get at them. And who could quarrel with that? If you are going to win a war, you need order, control, centralization. If you are going to beat the Axis Powers you don't bother to hold a public hearing to decide whether or not you are going to build a road, a building or a freight depot.

And of course they made it work just like the generals at the Pentagon made it work, and we can be very happy that they did. But the problem is that like the generals, our business leaders didn't want to stop. So they kept going with an organization called the Bay Area Council, a kind of super Chamber of Commerce to make decisions that no one else thought of making.

In the late 1940's the Bay Area Council started talking about a regional plan for transportation as the key to the orderly growth of the Bay Area. There would have to be, it said, a freeway system that would link things up so that people and goods could move to all parts of the system with maximum speed and efficiency. Part of the freeway system would be new bridges across the Bay; one linking San Rafael and Richmond, another a southern crossing of the Bay that would connect San Francisco and Alameda.

By the early 1950's they were already talking about an electrically driven rapid transit system that would bring office workers to the high density core of the area.

The Bay Area Council commissioned a study in the early 1960's called BATS (Bay Area Transit Study) that was the largest planning study of its kind ever done anywhere. It cost about $5,000,000 and in it you can see emerging the shape of the Ultimate Highrise. The land of the Bay Area, the study said, should be developed in an increasingly orderly manner. Mixed zoning of land — housing and businesses and open space in the same neighborhood — was inefficient and would be phased out.

People would raise their families in the residential suburbs like Walnut Creek or Burlingame or Mill Valley. Industry should be outside of the city in places like Emeryville or the industrial parks of the Peninsula. Refineries in Richmond, some open space in Tilden Park, Tamalpais, etc., and the headquarters for all this, the place where pencils would be put to paper, would be San Francisco. All linked up by the new rapid transit system, the new freeways and the new bridges.

It all sounded good and in fact it is good if you want to win a war against a real enemy or an economic competition against some other region. If you are not thinking about winning, you might decide that you want open space in your own neighborhood as well as on the top of a mountain. You might want certain factories in the neighborhoods so that minorities will have a better chance of finding jobs.

You might want to have people living downtown next to the banks and the insurance companies so that when the offices close at five o'clock the neighborhoods will stay lively. You might not want to forge ahead because you might not want to give up whatever it takes to win the race to grow faster than anyone else is growing. Because you can't win without losing something.

To win a shooting war you have to lose a great many lives. The Bay Area Council was not preparing for another shooting war, but what they had in mind was to be the control center for the development of the Western United States and the furtherance of American economic power throughout the Pacific. You needed a Wall Street of the West to do what the Wall Street of the

East had done to develop the Eastern United States and fashion our economic ties with Europe.

So San Francisco was going to become the headquarters city for the western states and for the Pacific. Winning that meant giving up what San Francisco was — a city of people who lived here, who raised their children here and who spent a lot of time playing, eating, walking, living in the city. And winning at headquarters city of the Pacific meant — because San Francisco is so much smaller in land area than New York — building an even more concentrated city: the Ultimate Highrise.

As the Bay Area Council said many years ago, "San Francisco can surpass New York." Can it? Do a little homework and see. First, compare the rate of growth of the central business district with the rate of growth of New York. (New York is bigger, like an adult is bigger than a child, but we are growing and they have almost stopped.) Next, compare the total number of people, potential customers, on the Pacific side of the United States with the total number on the Atlantic side. (The news is that President Nixon is going to China, not Europe.) Then compare the available supplies of raw materials that are west of San Francisco with the stock east of New York.

By the time the kids who are in nursery school now are looking for houses for their own families, where will the greatest number of business transactions be made? Perhaps still in New York, but if Japan continues on its present course, and if China begins to take an active part in world trade, and if India begins to move, then what?

The leaders of business and industry in the Bay Area have asked these questions for a long time. Their answer has been to start the construction of the Ultimate Highrise in San Francisco. And perhaps the further expansion of American economic interests into Asia and the continued industrial growth of the western United States is a good thing. But if it is, we should at least know what it is costing. Will it make us happier to live in a World Headquarters City? Will it cost us less to live here? Would we rather raise our children in San Francisco as we know it or in the Ultimate Highrise? Where would we rather have lunch? Walk? Work? Can we do anything to change direction?

I think the answer is that environmentalists and urban conservationists have to confront the master plan for the growth and development of Northern California in its entirety. We have spent our time stopping a building here and saving a few choice acres there while Northern California as a whole is a less and less healthy and happy place to live. If we can win on key regional issues like the Baldwin Channel (without losing on the Peripheral Canal) and if we can win on the Vote on High-Rise Initiative, then we will have moved a good part of the way towards the time when the people of this area will be ready to make a basic decision on where it's all going.

Particularly on the Vote on High-Rise Initiative in November—Vote Yes on

T! — we have a good chance of severely setting back the master plan. If the people assert their right to vote on highrise projects it is doubtful developers will be able to build World Headquarters City here. That would mean that world headquarters might be Seattle or Los Angeles. (It won't be Portland because the people of Oregon seem to have decided that they don't want endless growth.)

There is, of course, the possibility the people of Los Angeles and Seattle won't choose World Headquarters City either. Because the lesson of this book, *The Ultimate Highrise,* is that the people of a city or a region always have to give up more than they get. The higher taxes that always accompany growth are the least of the problem. Giving up clear air and clean water, peace, happiness and the pace of life as it is lived here are even more important.

Alvin Duskin
October 19, 1971
San Francisco

Welcome to San Francisco
JOSEPH L. ALIOTO, MAYOR

1.

A City of Skyscrapers

By Greggar Sletteland

38 Manhattanization Clues

"Only 15 or so years ago, the city was still comparatively uncluttered and open. The skyline had a decent proportion — graceful and light. When you look at photos of the skyline of 1957 and compare it with today's it is hard to believe you are looking at the same city, which of course you aren't. The old city grew beautiful by accident, the new one is growing ugly by design." — Herb Caen (S.F. Chronicle 10/10/71)

"A plan to organize the sprawling San Francisco region into one efficient package is slowly emerging . . . . The rapid growth of the cities clustered around the broad, land-locked basin known as the San Francisco Bay is.awakening them to mutual needs and problems. The Bay Area Council has been the first concrete manifestation of this . . . In fact, San Francisco Bay communities are beginning to think *big.*" (Christian Science Monitor, 1949)

"We work with banks, railroads, utilities and other business groups, as well as with local Chambers of Commerce and industrial development associations, in endeavoring to develop the kind of business climate which will be conducive to the growth of existing industry and which will be attractive to new industry. We tell the story of the entire region." — Stanley McCaffery, Bay Area Council president (*Saturday Review,* 1/8/66)

"Corporations heavily involved in the Bay Area's political economy dominate the BAC's Board of Trustees, which includes executives from Bank of America, Crocker-Citizens Bank, Wells Fargo Bank, Ampex, Levi Strauss, PG&E, Bechtel, Kaiser Industries, Del Monte, Utah Con-

---

"The whole San Francisco skyline is going to change — though not all at once, of course. We're going to have a great building wave. Money is going to ease up. We're going to become a second New York."

—*Ben Swig, from* Ben Swig: The Measure of a Man, 1955

Commercial land-usage in S.F. is expanding 3% per year, mostly for more downtown office skyscrapers. (See "Economics," page 45.)

struction and Mining and Hewlett-Packard." (*Leviathan*, Fall 1969)

"The Bay Area can move forward boldly and profitably to intensive and prosperous competition with areas like New York, while resolving the transportation problems which until now have threatened to stifle and choke off its economic greatness. In this challenging venture, a sensible halt is being called to the economic Balkanization of the Bay Area." — Edgar Kaiser, president of Kaiser Industries, Bay Area Council Director (S.F. Chronicle, 3/24/59)

The Largest Single Act of Urban Design

"Rapid transit is the only practical way. Certain financing, banking industries, want to be centralized, want to have everyone near each other . . . . The big city is naturally a center to which everyone comes . . . BART will make it possible to bring all the people in here. The new construction it will generate will be of great improvement for San Francisco." — Adrian Falk, Bay Area Council founder, former president of the California State Chamber of Commerce, Executive Director of BART 1958-1968.

"The leaders, bankers and corporate officials of San Francisco were banded together (starting in 1950) in a private organization called Citizens for Rapid Transit. It was headed by Kendric B. Morrish of the Wells Fargo Bank, Mortimer Fleishhacker Jr. of the Wells Fargo Bank, and Carl Wente of the Bank of America. The first three highrise buildings which went up in conjunction with BART construction were the Wells Fargo Bank, the Bank of America, and the Crocker-Citizens Bank." (S.F. Bay Guardian, 6/1968)

"[BART] is more than transportation. It's the largest single act of urban design currently underway in the United States." — James Bailey, editor of *Architectural Forum*, 1968.

> ". . . this loveliest of American cities is in mortal danger of total disappearance. There is the remorseless brutalization of the uniquely delicate skyline, and the obliteration of everyone's view. All that clean air is filling up with Big Black Specks from pollution, and the famous clarity of the light is fading away forever. . . . San Francisco is the last civilized outpost in the U.S.A., and damn well worth conserving, *now*, before hell strikes it. And . . . it is past time for San Franciscans to wipe those smug smiles off their cheerful faces and work harder at preserving their fragile birthright. Who are we to say it? New Yorkers, that's who. And we ought to know."
> —The Editors of Holiday Magazine

A Pat on the Ego

"The juggernaut rolls on . . . . San Francisco is ceasing to be a self-contained city. Day by day it is being converted into the Manhattan of the West, the Central Business District of an unnamed supercity encompassing the whole Bay Area." — Nicholas von Hoffman (*Holiday*, 3/70)

"The value of highrises built [in downtown S.F.] between 1965 and 1968 totaled $255.7 million — seven times the value of all highrises built during the entire decade of 1950-1960." (*Wells Fargo Report*, 1970)

"Montgomery Street is the pulsating artery of San Francisco's financial community. Decisions made on the seven prime blocks of Montgomery Street effect all of California, the West, and often the nation or the world." (*S.F. Business*, 1969)

"There aren't many pure local and regional firms left in the Pacific Coast Stock Exchange since the New York boys moved in." — Palmer York, president of York Securities (*S.F. Business*, 2/69)

"The prime directive here has been Manhattanization: dense office and residential construction in complement . . . creation of a white collar city with an army of white collar employees working in hygienic filing cabinets by day and filed away in hygienic highrisers by night." — Dick Nolan (S.F. Examiner, 5/27/71)

"It looks like a graveyard — and, as is the custom, the richer the dead, the bigger the gravestone." — Bernard Baruch Zakheim, Sebastopol Artist, upon seeing the S.F. skyline for the first time in many years (S.F. Chronicle, 9/24/71)

". . . a team of Soviet architects, touring the country, said that we have 'too many tall buildings' and that they preferred St. Louis. My God, St. Louis! We always took it for granted — as we took the Bay, the hills and the views for granted — that visiting Europeans would

---

"BART will also transform the residential profile of the Bay Area. Land values which are rising rapidly are spurring landowners to maximize economic use of their land. Single-family dwellings are being replaced by multi-family units. By 1980, a large percentage of BART riders will be living in apartments. San Francisco is second to Manhattan Island in population density. But because it has only 6% of the land (in the Bay Area) and 16% of the population, it logically is the first to undergo extensive demolition of its single-family housing stock into multi-family highrise units."

—San Francisco Business, *October 1970*

---

name San Francisco as their favorite American city. Now we can no longer count on that pat on the ego." — Herb Caen (S.F. Chronicle, 10/10/71)

Queen Borough of the New New York

"The luxuriant growth of highrise c .e structures encouraged by large-scale public Redevelopment and .. iss transit expenditures will result in land-use densities comparable only to downtown Chicago and Manhattan Island." (*Wells Fargo Report*, 1970)

"I think it's absolutely inevitable that San Francisco will become another New York. I see the same signs of it. I lived in New York for eight years. San Francisco can't be as bad as Manhattan, but they're making a good start at it." — Stanford N. Sesser, urban affairs expert for the Wall Street Journal (11/6/70)

"The change-over into its new role as the queen borough of the new New York will be hastened when the BART subway is finished . . . . This subway was sold as an anti-traffic, anti-smog device, but what it really does is provide an efficient way for skillions of employees and shoppers to get to the new high buildings just as the subways of New York do." — Nicholas von Hoffman (*Holiday*, 3/70)

"Obviously, our buildings are going to be higher than in the past, but I don't know of any city that has more open space all around it. There's no more beautiful land so close to so many people in any other city in the world." — Mayor Joseph Alioto (Wall Street Journal, 11/6/70)

"Highrises are essential. San Francisco's future as a business-management center must have the kind of buildings that that type of enterprise requires." — Dick Pearce, Director of Editorial pages, S.F. Examiner (*S.F. Magazine*, 9/71) .

"[If San Franciscans don't want their city converted into Manhattan,] then let 'em go someplace else. But don't keep complaining about it, because that's what is going to happen, and nobody can stop it." — Roger Lapham, Jr., president, North Waterfront Associates (S.F. Bay Guardian, 6/68)

"Frank Lloyd Wright used to say that only a city as beautiful as this can survive what we're doing to it. But I don't think you can go on justifying the ruin of a city indefinitely using an economic basis as a yardstick." — Herb Caen (S.F. Chronicle, 3/71)

Giant, Hungry New Markets

"Geographically, San Francisco is a natural gateway for this country's ocean-going and airborne commerce with the Pacific area nations. Trade with Asian nations is gaining in importance especially relative to Europe. The most important stimulus to San Francisco's economic base has been the increasing involvement in this century in Asian geo-politics with the concurrent buildup in armament production . . . and large gains in foreign trade." (*Wells Fargo Report*, 1970)

"There is no more vast or rich area for resource development or trade growth in the world today than this immense region, and it is virtually our own front yard . . . Were we California businessmen to play a more dynamic role in helping trade development in the Pacific rim, we would have giant, hungry new markets for our products and vast new profit potentials for our firms." — Rudolph Peterson, president, Bank of America (*California Business*, 9/68)

"From 1964 to 1968 domestic exports through the San Francisco Customs District jumped by 61% to Japan, 80% to Australia, 300% to the Republic of Korea, 171% to Thailand, 35% to the Philippines." (*Wells Fargo Report*, 1970)

Urban Disaster Plan from the Department of Highrise Planning

"In rapid and uncontested votes, the San Francisco City Planning Commission yesterday adopted the Nation's first Urban Design Plan and implemented it with sweeping emergency zoning laws throughout the city." (S.F. Chronicle, 8/27/71)

"A hundred years ago they created 'spot' highrise zones in the boroughs of New York City, fully confident that the major highrise development would be limited to Manhattan. It wasn't." — Anthony P. Kilroy, president of San Francisco Tomorrow (9/16/71)

"This is just what the business community wants 'planning' to be, for the men who are building what People's Architecture has called 'the Imperial Control Center of the Pacific Rim' have nothing to fear from townscape." — John Kenyon (S.F. Chronicle, 8/29/71)

"The Urban Design Plan provides for a developer's free-for-all in the downtown. One-hundred-story blockbusters as bulky as the Bank of America would easily fit within the plan's 'height and bulk guidelines . . . . Virtually every neighborhood in the city is opened up for 'medium' high-rise, high-density development (88 to 240 feet)." (S.F. Bay Guardian, 9/71)

"The general ease with which key concepts and principles of master plans are subverted for reasons of political expediency leaves us with little confidence that this one will fare any better . . . it is especially vulnerable to the kind of irresponsible political tinkering that has been so destructive in recent years." — Anthony P. Kilroy, president of S.F. Tomorrow (9/16/71)

"Ten public members of San Francisco's Urban Design Advisory Committee resigned in a group today to protest approval by the City Planning Commission of a proposed 25-story Holiday Inn here . . . the group complained that the Holiday Inn, as approved, would rise far above the 160 foot limit set in the recently adopted Urban Design Plan, which was worked out by the committee." (S.F. Examiner, 10/13/71)

"The new Urban Design Plan is for open space and gardens and plazas and fountains in the downtown area. And it has the teeth to insure that the developers will develop a more beautiful city for the people — not just more profitable projects for themselves." — Chamber of Commerce ad published two weeks after Planning Commission approval of the Holiday Inn (S.F. Chronicle, 9/12/71)

Small and Delicate Ways

"There is a general and reasoned conviction that growth and progress are ruining a city its inhabitants love with a zeal unmatched anywhere else. For them, San Francisco is built; it needs no renewal program to make it liveable, no massive spending of money to attract people back to it; it needs only to be preserved and perfected, but perfected in small and delicate ways — not by chomping, clomping and uprooting." — Nicholas von Hoffman (*Holiday*, 3/70)

" 'Who owns the city?' asks Alvin Duskin, a driving force behind the citizens' initiative for a six-story height limit, 'the highrise interests or the people? Do the people decide or do the elite few? I think the few decide what's in their interest and we all pick up the tab'." (*Holiday*, 3/70)

THE CHAMBER'S SECRET PLAN TO BLITZ SF NEIGHBORHOODS

March 18, 1970: the Chamber of Commerce calls 50 leading SF bankers to the posh Bohemian Club. Purpose: to gain financial backing for the Chamber's horrendous scheme to build 400-unit highrise housing enclaves for the rich in 10 SF neighborhoods (choice spots: Sutro Baths, John Muir Drive, N. Waterfront, Sunset Reservoir, see map, p. 24). The bankers' pledge: $100 million in low-interest loans to get the project started.

May 5, 1970: the Chamber calls together top City Hall politicians, unveils its plan and asks for 1) power of eminent domain "to overcome holdouts;" 2) five years' full tax forgiveness; 3) some city-owned property such as that at Fort Mason for a nominal fee. "If you can house buffaloes in Golden Gate Park, I don't see why you can't put people in there," James E. Stretch (Chamber VP for Planning; Met. Life President) adds ominously.

The planning process: first, the chamber comes up with a blockbuster plan, then to the bankers, then to their politicians. The people who live here, the people who will subsidize the plan, haven't been consulted and, until they read this, won't know about it.

They'll know only when it's a fait accompli.

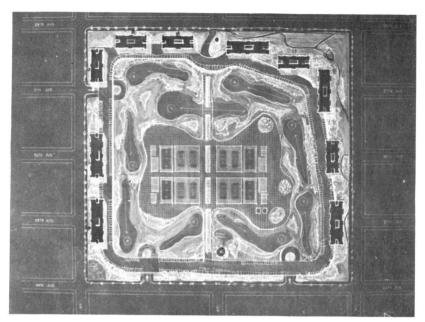

The Chamber's plans for Sunset Reservoir (top) include ten 14-story buildings, and a 9-hole golf course. Another prospective site (below): untouched land along John Muir Drive, near Lake Merced.

TWO CITIZENS' TRIUMPHS

Until the skyscraper boom of the 1960's, San Francisco neighborhood groups often proved more than a match for ambitious developers and the powerful downtown growth-at-any-price bloc. Two triumphs: 1) N. Waterfront/Aquatic Park residents were stunned by the sudden appearance in 1961 of a developer's scaffolding for the massive, view-blocking Fontana apartments ("Bayfront buckteeth," one opponent derisively called them--left). It was too late to stop the Fontanas, but residents organized to win a 40-foot height limit which barred further monstrosities from the area. 2) The world-famous "freeway revolt" of the late 1950's forced the city to shelve its plans for six new commuter freeways and halted the Embarcadero Freeway in its tracks (below). An unprecedented coalition of neighborhood groups beat back the freeways, but dissolved shortly afterward. Individual groups soon exhausted themselves battling the onslaught of skyscrapers--sometimes winning skirmishes, but decisively losing the war to save San Francisco from high-density overdevelopment.

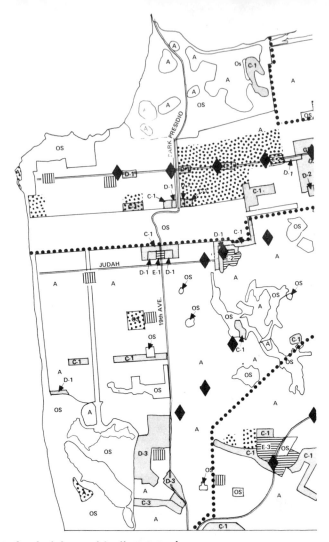

Interim districts for height and bulk controls

HEIGHT CONTROLS

Map Symbol	Maximum Height Permitted Without Review (in feet)	Maximum Height That May Be Permitted By City Planning Commission After Review (in feet)
OS	O (open space)	40
A	40	no greater height to be permitted
B	40	300 (by special review of point towers)
C	40	88
D	88	160
E	160	240
F	240	240
G	240	Unlimited, but tapering toward outside edges of district
H	400	Unlimited

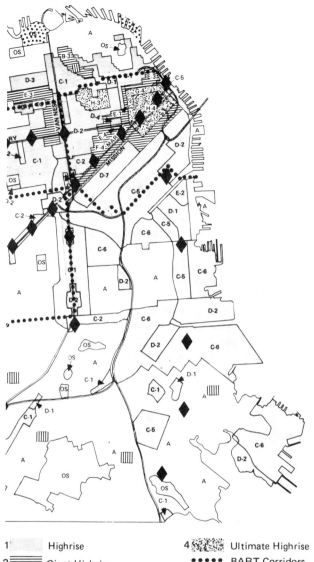

1 ░░░ Highrise

2 ≡≡≡ Giant Highrise

3 ||||||||||| "Defining" Highrise

4 ▒▒▒ Ultimate Highrise

●●●●● BART Corridors

◆ BART Stations

▒▒▒ The Chamber's Unannounced Highrise Housing Enclaves

1. Map symbols C and D
2. Map symbols B, E and F
3. In preparing this map, the City Planning Department perhaps inadvertently neglected to include the controversial 300-foot towers called for by the Urban Design Plan to "define" neighborhoods throughout the city. So that readers might gain a better sense of what the planners envision as desirable for San Francisco is the way of highrise construction, we have added the locations for these towers to the map.
4. Map symbols G and H

81598

Neighborhoods

Today Russian Hill, tomorrow the entire city. The people who brought San Francisco BART, the Bank of America building, Rockefeller Center West, the Transamerica pyramid, the twin Russian Hill towers and a long list of similar upcoming horrors — these people don't wish San Francisco residents to know it, but their high-density schemes don't stop at the boundaries of the downtown or the inner core neighborhoods.

In the next ten years, every neighborhood in the city — possibly excepting those with height limits or Planning Commissioners in residence — will experience stunning changes on the same scale as the 1960s skyscraper boom in the downtown. By 1980 or thereabouts, the cherished diversity and uniqueness of San Francisco's neighborhoods will be as obsolete as trees and back yards on Russian Hill.

Sounds far-fetched? It's all laid out in excruciating detail in a massive document called the "Comprehensive Plan for San Francisco" — prepared by the City Planning Department and duly incorporated into the city's Master Plan by the Planning Commission. Among the components of the "Comprehensive Plan" are the "Transportation Plan," the "Improvement Plan for Residence" and the ballyhooed "Urban Design Plan." Hidden away inside the glossy pages of these reports, behind the public relations cosmetics, are the unpublicized facts outlining what's in store for·San Francisco neighborhoods. Before listing some of the more outrageous details, several notes:

1) At no time have *any* of the changes codified in these plans been approved by San Francisco voters — nor will they be presented to voters in the future. Passage of the "Comprehensive Plan" by the Board of Supervisors — which must consider it before late 1973 — is virtually assured by political influence of the Chamber/Downtown Association/SPUR/Bay Area Council bloc.

2) The "Comprehensive Plan" inevitably understates the changes in prospect for San Francisco. Its major function is to justify and prettify for the public (with highly flexible "design concepts," clouds of planning jargon, idealized drawings and expensive, slick production) the development decisions already taken or about to be taken by private interests. That's why these plans must be "up-dated" every 10 to 20 years — and why they're usually obsolete the day they're published.

3) When it comes to the crunch, the "Comprehensive Plan" is meaningless anyway. Legally, it is only "advisory"; it can be over-ridden at any time (and frequently is) by the Planning Commission, the Board of Permit Appeals and the Board of Supervisors — all dominated by development interests. (See politics section.)

Which means: developers will do with San Francisco pretty much what they want to do with it. The items listed below indicate only those neighborhood developments so certain that they have already been written into the "Comprehensive Plan" for San Francisco.

1. The Mission/Bayshore Corridor

Inner Mission: BART stations at 16th and 24th Streets plus proximity to downtown and high land values assure massive high-density development; ticketed for highrise white collar apartments; 160-foot height limits around BART stations; Redevelopment planning to apply the kiss of death to low-rent Chicano neighborhoods; E. Mission recommended for FACE (Federally Assisted Code Enforcement) that forces rents up and low-income people out; the E. Waterfront/India Basin area will be fenced off for shipping operations.

Bernal Heights recommended for FACE, but will probably serve as receiving area for low-income people from Inner Mission.

Hunter's Point/Bayshore: "high priority" freeway will disrupt and uglify; BART-airport line will do the same and (if the ghetto gets a station) will drive up land values and rents; 200-300 foot highrise apartments on Bayview Hill; vast Redevelopment schemes for eye-sore industrial parks and "low-income" housing that only middle-income people can afford.

Outer Mission/Ingleside: BART stations at Glen Park and Balboa Park, surrounded by 160-240 foot height limits, will devastate these single-family areas; 300-foot towers at Holly Park, University Mound and Portola; widening of O'Shaughnessy Boulevard for vastly expanded cross-town traffic; 240-foot highrise apartments around City College and up Ocean Avenue (look for a "middle-income" enclave of 3,000 to 4,000 units on the site of the Jewish Orphans home).

2. Twin Peaks/Sunset Corridor

Upper Market/Eureka Valley/Noe Valley: 5-12 story apartment buildings will sprout throughout the area (it's too close to the downtown for single-family homes); 160-foot height limits along Valencia; FACE and Redevelopment will put an end to the current renaissance in Eureka/Noe Valleys.

Haight/Ashbury: "Intensification of residence" (means apartments up to 12 stories, crowding, congestion, zooming rents) along both sides of the Panhandle and the eastern end of the park will spread upwards, leading to demolition of lovely old Upper Haight Victorians; FACE and Redevelopment for E. Haight.

Parnassus Heights: cancerously growing UC Med Center (largest in

N. California) will expand its domination of the area, leading to critical congestion problems; 240-foot limit for Med Center (twice current size); 160-foot luxury apartments for surrounding area, especially along Irving near new BART station; widening and dividing of Laguna Honda into another major cross-town artery; all to be crowned with the 981-foot KRON/KGO/KTVU/KPIX television tower atop Mt. Sutro that will rival Seattle's Space Needle as an architectural monstrosity. It will be visible on clear days from 30 miles away in all directions.

Sunset: BART's arrival in the mid-70's will signal the Sunset's death as a single-family area; 20-story highrises at 19th and Judah; 16-stories at 19th and Irving, on Sloat across from the zoo, along Lake Merced Boulevard, possibly at Sunset Boulevard and Judah; Noriega and Taraval converted to "multiple use" areas for 5-12-story apartments; highrise complexes along John Muir Drive and over the Sunset Reservoir (if the Chamber of Commerce gets its way, and it usually does); 300-foot towers in Merced Heights and near Sunset Reservoir; Muni/BART line along Sunset Boulevard; 5-12 story apartments along Lincoln Way bordering Golden Gate Park and also along the Great Highway; undergrounding of 19th Avenue at Irving and Judah, possibly under the park: the Sunset will become a vast white collar apartment/highrise area.

3. Western Addition/Richmond corridor:

Western Addition: Redevelopment has already worked its highrise/high-density taxpayer-supported magic on this area; expect more of the same spreading along Fillmore in both directions, extensive demolition of fine old Victorian homes for 5-12 story apartments; Alamo Square with its 160-foot height limits and marvelous views will be a prime target.

Richmond: will rival Inner Mission as the city's most drastically changed area; 160-foot limits around BART stations on Geary at Arguello, 11th, 25th; 240-foot limit at Masonic/Geary/California; entire length of Geary scheduled for conversion to multiple use with 12-story limits; entire Inner Richmond eyed by FACE, Redevelopment, Chamber of Commerce for huge middle-income highrise enclave; "Intensification of Residence" — up to 12 stories — entire length of Arguello, lengthy stretches of Fulton bordering Golden Gate Park; 160-foot highrises at Fulton and Park Presidio; 300-foot towers in the vicinity of 35th and Anza and 41st and Geary; luxury 14-story apartments marring Sutro Baths and the Ocean Beach/Playland area; Sunset Boulevard tunnelled under Golden Gate Park, making it yet another fuming cross-town artery.

4. Marina Corridor

North Waterfront/Aquatic Park/Russian Hill: fate still undecided because of stand-off between intense citizen pressure and determined SPUR/Chamber/DA/BAC forces, but look for a trade-off: mostly low-rise tourist-oriented commercialization on N. Waterfront for super-highrise from Broadway past Ferry Building to Pier 22; intensive sky-scraper apartment development is a certainty for Russian Hill.

Marina/Pacific Heights: Marina population density will remain relatively low because of height limit, except for possible luxury highrise enclave on Fort Mason; undergrounding of freeway along Broadway with a tunnel under Fort Mason; one-way controls on Bay and North Point; 160-240 foot highrises (and possibly larger) along Van Ness, Franklin and Polk above Washington all the way to Market; entire Pacific Heights area from Franklin to Steiner will intensify its current high-rise apartment rush, up to 240 feet and possibly higher.

2.

Economics of Highrise

By Greggar Sletteland

"The sky's falling in on us in the cities," San Francisco Mayor Joseph Alioto testified in Washington in April, 1971. "We've had six cops killed in San Francisco since I took office. We need jobs and money for the poor and have neither. Our people are trying to put a Maginot line around the suburbs and zoning them. We can't go on like this. Even the capitalistic system's not going to survive, the way we're going."

Yet even as the sky was falling in on Alioto's San Francisco, a spectacular building boom was reaching sky-high in the downtown. In less than a decade the amount of office space increased almost 50%. Thirty-one new skyscrapers sprouted between 1966 and 1971, and at least that many more were planned for the next five years. The Chamber of Commerce proclaimed the advent of a commercial miracle that would soon convert the city into a "Wall Street of the West."

Downtown interests took dead aim at those who dared to see a link between the building boom and the budget bust. "The one economically viable thing you have in San Francisco," warned skyscraper wheeler-dealer Walter Shorenstein, "is what's happening in the office buildings."

Mayor Alioto himself put it even more succinctly while praising a 40-story U.S. Steel monolith proposed for the waterfront: "We need tall buildings," Alioto said, "because they give us jobs and taxes."

But then on Oct. 19, 1970, a full-page ad signed by conservationist Alvin Duskin in the S.F. Examiner and Chronicle challenged this conventional wisdom. "Skyscrapers are economically necessary," Duskin said, "but only if you own one." He proposed a city-wide height limit that would require voter approval on all buildings taller than 72 feet.

Economics of Highrise

The supposed economic benefits of skyscrapers have long been virtually a matter of faith to architects, politicians, businessmen and skyscraper owners. Their argument for viewing San Francisco simply as a choice piece of real estate to be exploited for private gain runs, in brief, something like this: As we build more, the city enjoys increased revenues (from property taxes on new buildings), lower taxes for residents, more jobs, and therefore less crime in the streets, less welfare, etc. — you've heard it all before.

Brandishing several authoritative academic studies to support his case, Duskin argued that, on the contrary, highrises cost more in municipal services than they pay in tax revenue, drive up taxes for homeowners, lose jobs for city residents and help foment the urban chaos currently threatening every major American city.

If skyscrapers were so great, Duskin added, how did you explain Manhattan?

To check out the facts about San Francisco's highrise boom and its impact on city residents and taxpayers, the Bay Guardian gathered a team of experienced investigative reporters and urban affairs experts headed by Tom Lehner of Berkeley's School of Public Policy. Then, aided by 30 volunteer researchers, we spent six months examining city, state and federal records.

What we came up with will not sit well with the Aliotos and Shorensteins:

1) Far from "subsidizing" the municipal budget, as claimed by real estate interests, the downtown highrise district in 1970 actually contributed $5 million *less* than it cost.

2) Property tax payments from the downtown, instead of providing relief for homeowners through assessments on expensive new highrises, actually *declined* by 16% as a proportion of the city total over the decade of the skyscraper boom.

3) Head-spinning growth in downtown land values "rippled out" to all San Francisco neighborhoods, causing assessment increases as high as 380% and leading, in many cases, to destruction of a neighborhood's original character.

4) Changing patterns of land-use and other highrise-related phenomena drove 100,000 middle-income San Franciscans to the suburbs and mauled the city's delicate demographic balance.

5) Highrises not only failed to provide new white collar jobs for San Franciscans, but caused the loss of 14,000 blue collar jobs.

6) Highrises were the prime villains in tripling the city's welfare costs over the decade.

7) Transportation facilities to service skyscrapers cost taxpayers a staggering $5 *billion* over a ten-year period.

31

8) Police costs for protecting the downtown highrise district averaged at least ten times the cost for protecting the rest of the city.

9) Highrises caused vast amounts of air and water pollution which will cost the city close to $1 *billion* to clean up.

The most disturbing finding can't be quantified—but it should be shouted to the heavens. It is this: unless the city of San Francisco reverses past practice and immediately enacts an ironclad land-use policy such as Duskin's proposed height limit, the long-scoffed-at "Manhattanization" of the entire city is a surefire, 100%-guaranteed inevitability.

1. Who Subsidizes Whom

A very small part of San Francisco contains most of the city's highrise buildings. The City Planning Department's massive Sanborn Map Books show that, of 783 buildings in the city over 72 feet tall, 495 of them, or 64%, can be found in an area that comprises just 3.4% of the developable land. What's more, 94% of the buildings over 15 stories high cluster in this same area.

The U.S. Bureau of the Census calls this area the Central Business District (CBD). We enlarged the CBD's boundaries slightly to sim-

The waterfront 1971: the ferry building, a crane and a wrecking ball.

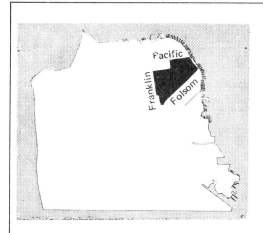

SF'S DOWNTOWN HIGHRISE DISTRICT

3.4% of developed land
9% of residential population
50% of peak-hour population
64% of highrise buildings

plify data-collecting procedures and changed its name to the Central Highrise District (CHD).

Not all buildings in the CHD are over 72 feet, of course. Highrise buildings are essentially huge machines, and like all huge machines they require many specialized smaller machines nearby to operate efficiently (an automobile engine, for instance, needs a battery, starter, windshield wipers, jack, etc.). Most buildings smaller than 72 feet in the CHD either furnish support to highrises — parking garages, print shops, factories containing various business services — or derive sustenance from them: high-priced department stores and shops, luxury town-houses for executives, etc.

What's more, City Planning Department maps show the entire area is zoned for highrises. The City Assessor is required by law to increase the assessments of undeveloped or lightly developed properties where highrises could be built. This means that from the perspective of municipal revenues, all property within the CHD is highrise property.

Before attempting to assess how much the CHD district contributes to — and takes from — the city budget, we armed ourselves with a methodology provided by a 1962 Urban Land Institute study of the Central Business District in Charlotte, North Carolina. The U.L.I. methodology required only minor adjustments before it could be applied to San Francisco (See box, page 36) Next, a Guardian task force of 30 researchers interviewed city officials and dug into city account books to come up with figures for all San Francisco revenues — there are 17 main ones — and all expenditures by the various city departments (see charts, pp. 34–35).

The results:

The 250-block Central Highrise District in fiscal 1970 contributed 25.2% of all locally-generated revenues — a substantial proportion indeed.

But it cost even more: 27.9%.

Put another way: the downtown contributed $62.9 million, but it cost $67.7 million. This means for every $10 the downtown produced, it cost $11.06.

Or: each downtown block received an average of $270,000 in city services, all other blocks just $25,000.

What the Downtown costs: $67.7 million (A summary of expenditure apportionments for San Francisco's Central Business District)			
Apportionment by expenditure source [6]	total city '69-'70	apport- ionable to CBD	CBD's %
A. SERVICES TO PROPERTY[1]			
1. Police protection	$31.5m	$9.5m	30%
2. Fire protection	23.7	5.4	23%
3. Engineering and administration	1.9	.6	31%
4. Streets, sanitation	3.6	.47	13%
5. Sewers, sewage treatment	3.9	.98	25%
6. Municipal railway deficit	19.0	12.45	65%
7. Retirement[2]	28.6	8.6	30%
8. Unaccounted (storm drains & street lights)	9.8	3.2	31%
TOTAL	122.0	41.3	31%
B. COMMUNITY- WIDE SERVICES[3]			
1. General[4]	37.81	9.19	25%
2. Welfare	45.24	7.33	16%
3. Debt services	15.73	3.81	25%
TOTAL	98.78	20.33	21%
C. GENERAL ACTIVITIES[5]			
TOTAL	21.66	6.04	28%
TOTAL	242.44	67.68	27.9%

4. These include Corrections, Sheriff's Office, Parks and Recreation, Courts, Library, Community Promotion, Health, Elections, Law Library, and Miscellaneous.
5. These include Board of Supervisors, Mayor's Office, Chief Administrative Officer, County Clerk, Controller, Treasurer, and City Attorney.
6. Figures from fiscal 1970 State Controller's Report

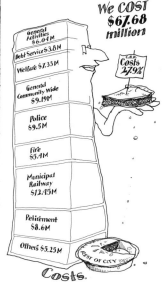

We COST $67.68 million

General Activities $6.04 M
Debt Service $3.8 M
Welfare $7.33 M
General Community Wide $9.19M
Police $9.5M
Fire $5.4M
Municipal Railway $12.45M
Retirement $8.6 M
Others $5.25 M

C.B.D. Costs 27.9%

REST OF CITY

Costs.

Who Subsidizes Whom

In short: city taxpayers subsidized the Central Highrise District that in real estate rhetoric was subsidizing them.

What's more, this appears to have been happening for years. The city does not keep itemized records of expenditures going back more than 12 months, so we couldn't check cost figures for past years. But revenue figures are another matter. These show that the proportion of the city's property taxes paid by the downtown has been declining steadily over the past two decades:

● In fiscal 1970, $39.3 million of $161.8 million raised by the property tax came from the CHD. That's 24.3%.

What the Downtown brings in: $62.9 million			
(A summary of revenue apportionments from San Francisco's Central Business District)			
Apportionment by revenue source 6	total city '69-'70	apport-ionable to CBD	CBD's %
1. Property taxes	$161.8m	$39.3m	24%
2. Sales and use taxes	23.8	7.6	32%
3. Hotel occupancy tax	3.9	3.1	80%
4. Business gross receipts tax	9.0	2.9	32%
5. Parking meter and lot revenue	1.3	1.2	93%
6. Construction permits	1.1	.9	80%
7. Real property transfer tax	.4	.1	24%
8. Rents and concessions	.6	.5	83%
9. Franchises	.6	.4	67%
10. Vehicle code and other fines	5.5	1.4	25%
11. State liquor license fee	1.0	.3	30%
12. State property tax relief	4.3	.2	5%
13. State inventory tax relief	1.3	.3	23%
14. State cigarette tax	3.8	.8	20%
15. State motor vehicle tax	9.1	.5	5%
16. State gasoline tax	9.2	.5	5%
17. Earnings from interest	12.1	3.0	25%
TOTAL	249.0	62.9	25.2%

1. Services which can be apportioned to areas of the city where the actual work is performed.
2. Computed on the basis of contributions to retirement on behalf of city employees who service the downtown area.
3. Services whose benefit is felt by the community as a whole and only indirectly by any particular area of the city.

We contribute $62.9 million

C.B.D. Revenue 25.7%

Property Taxes $39.3M

Sales and Use Taxes $7.6M

Business Gross Receipts $2.9M

Hotel Occupancy Tax $3.1M

Earnings from Interest $3.0M

Others $7.1M

CITY OF CITY

Revenue.

How We Found
That Highrises Cost the City More than they Pay

The Guardian research team followed a methodology laid out in "A Cost Revenue Study of the Central Business District," a published dissertation by Raymond J. Green of the Urban Land Institute, on file at the Institute of Government Studies, Berkeley.

Revenues

In fiscal 1970, the latest year for which complete figures were available, total city and county revenue exclusive of school districts was $406.3 million. Federal and State grants accounted for $94.6 million of this, charges for current services and user fees another $61.6 million. The remainder, $250.1 million, came from 17 local sources. We investigated each of these to determine the amount which came from the Central Highrise District. Examples:

● Gross receipts tax and sales and use tax: we established the percentage of the city's retail sales which occur in the CHD (31.3%) by consulting Department of Commerce distribution charts.

● Parking meter and lot revenue: we compiled revenue totals from Police Department account books on the 7,300 CHD meters (51% of the city total) and nine CHD off-street garages (100% of the total).

Expenditures

Green's study proved an invaluable guide for hacking through the dense jungle of city expenditures. Following Green's method, we divided city expenditures into three categories and computed them as follows:

● Services to property (police, fire, sewage, etc.): we determined these by painstaking examination of the accounts of all city departments engaged in such services and extensive personal interviews with 30 key city officials.

● Community-wide services (health, elections, etc.): we apportioned these according to the only available financial measure of a district's worth — the assessed valuation of land and improvements in that district.

● General activities (Mayor's Office, City Attorney, etc.): we apportioned these by multiplying each by the sum of services to property and community-wide services accorded to the CHD, expressed as a percentage of the city total.

Important footnote: Since education provides a service which spreads its value over the entire community, each sector of the city, under Green's methodology, receives educational services in proportion to the assessed value of that sector. San Francisco levies taxes to pay for education by this same method (property taxes), and therefore education revenues and costs for each sector of the city are equal by definition. Since, in addition, the Unified School District is a governmental entity separate from the City and County of San Francisco, we did not further consider it in our report.

- In 1960, the downtown contributed $32.2 million. That's 28.2%.
- In 1950, the downtown gave $27.3 million, or 31.1%.

A decline in downtown contributions from 31% to 28% to 24% during the years of the highrise boom: this is hardly evidence for those who defend skyscrapers on the grounds that they pay for services to the rest of the city.

Even Mayor Alioto has attacked downtown interests for their diminishing tax contributions. Speaking to the Homeowners Tax Control Association on March 3, 1971, he blamed "big business interests" for the city's climbing tax rate. He harked back to the infamous bill AB 80, which passed the state legislature in 1967 and equalized tax assessment practices for all city properties in 1968. "Big business interests including the San Francisco Chamber of Commerce waged a successful fight," Alioto said, "to tax your home on the same basis as an industrial plant, a refinery, a big office building or a huge apartment."

Alioto had the right villains — but he was wrong in pinning the blame solely on AB 80. This bill caused an immediate increase in homeowners' assessments of approximately 50% for all city residential properties between 1967 and 1968, and its impact should not be underestimated. But it only emphasized a process that had been going on for years. This is clearly shown by the fact that the downtown's proportion of property tax payments fell 3% in the decade *before* AB80.

2. The Bigger We Get, the Poorer We Become

The reason the Central Highrise District costs so much is, in a word, density. According to a man who should know, Mayor John M. Lindsay of New York, "Density is responsible for inevitably higher costs for almost every conceivable service."

A disturbing study by the League for Industrial Democracy supports Lindsay's view. Based on Census and Department of Commerce figures, it shows that the per capita cost of operating a city in the 0-499,999 population range is $144.80; of a city of 500,000 to 999,999, $208.60; and of cities over one million, $444.40.

The upshot of this is a variant of the rich-get-richer slogan: the bigger our cities get, the poorer their residents become.

Highrise buildings, of course, increase a city's population density enormously. This happens because of the efficiency business gains by "clustering" large numbers of offices and people in a small area. As economic consultant Claude Gruen concludes in his anti-Duskin report produced for the San Francisco Chamber of Commerce,

HOW PER CAPITA CRIME RATES AND MUNICIPAL COSTS INCREASE WITH CITY DENSITY

1. CRIME RATES[1]

Pop. size	Pop. density/ sq. mile	Number of crimes per 100,000 per year			
		Murder	Rape	Robbery	Assault
over 250,000	7100	6.8	15.2	117.6	154.1
100,000-250,000	4271	5.6	7.6	56.5	83.3
50,000-100,000	3910	3.3	5.5	36.6	58.9
25,000-50,000	2810	2.9	4.7	22.6	39.9

2. MUNICIPAL COSTS[2]

Pop. size	Pop. density/ sq. mile	Per capita expenditures				
		Welfare	Hospitals	Police	Health	Total
1,000,000 or more	14,000	$88.50	$34.80	$44.20	$11.80	$444.40
500,000-999,999	9,500	25.30	17.50	31.90	7.90	$208.60
0-499,999	4,100	5.50	5.60	19.40	2.20	$144.80

1 source: Kenneth Watt, Environmental Systems, Davis, Cal. (1960 figures)
2 source: Dept. of Commerce, Bureau of the Census (1960 figures)

"The Tax Foundation, which is the most prestigious organization in the U.S. doing studies of tax structures, confirms . . . that high-density development does not lower taxes. What it does is 'shrink the tax base,' says the foundation, meaning that the people best able to afford the taxes leave, and everyone else pays more."--Vancouver Sun, 6/24/71 "the clustering of economic activities [in downtown skyscrapers] does provide very sizable benefits to the firms within the cluster."

But the public costs of producing business efficiencies and "sizable benefits" fall back on city taxpayers, who must pick up the tab for vastly expanded municipal services in such areas as transportation, sanitation, safety and health. Moreover, as the effects of high-density development spread throughout the city, they cause rends in the social fabric which demand costly municipal patchwork.

The worst kind of high-density development brings large numbers of commuters into a city. Commuters create a special, deadly form of density — peak-hour density — which radiates outward from downtown offices to afflict every homeowner inside city boundaries with staggering municipal tax increases.

From the homeowner's perspective, commuters swarm into the city at the worst possible time: during the working day, when most "free" city services are available for the commuter's use. Transportation systems, parking, police, sewer systems, power-producing capability, water delivery — to say nothing of libraries, city offices, hospitals and courts: all must expand substantially to keep the commuter happily working at top efficiency. But the commuter is taxed where he sleeps, not where he works.

Because San Francisco's population density has for many years run second in this country only to Manhattan's, the expenses of government here have been relatively high. But even a decrease in residential density between 1960 and 1970, from 16,306 to 15,763 per square mile, has not prevented the situation from drastically worsening over the past decade. The reason is simple: during the same period the commuter swarm has doubled.

Currently commuters swell the city's population by 300,000 for nine to 10 hours five days a week. This means the 715,000 residents of San Francisco must pay the costs of a city of more than one million.

City officials are the first to agree, when it is politically expedient to do so, that commuters cost San Francisco a fortune. Testifying on behalf of his ill-fated commuter tax proposal in 1968, Mayor Alioto said the tax was "justified on the basis of the Controller's estimate that it costs $44 million to provide them [commuters] with health, safety, sanitation and transit services during their working days in the city." (Chronicle, 7/4/68)

Because of the current height limit controversy, neither the Controller nor the Mayor will comment on the 1968 estimates of commuter costs or provide up-dated figures. It's safe to assume, however,

that 30,000 new commuters added to the peak-hour population since 1968, rising salaries and inflation have boosted the bill well over $50 million. Now recall the amount which the Central Highrise District contributed to municipal coffers in 1970 property taxes: $39.3 million.

When the commuter swarm reaches such proportions that downtown property taxes don't even cover *its* costs, to say nothing of the much greater expense caused by *total* downtown high-density demands, real trouble lies in store for city homeowners and taxpayers.

3. How Highrises Breed More Highrises

If you own a small soda shop and someone builds a factory containing 5,000 thirsty workers next door, your shop suddenly becomes much more valuable. In fact, the value of your property shoots up even if it's vacant — because it could become a soda shop. This is basically why assessments in San Francisco neighborhoods have increased as much as 380% over the past 20 years. It also explains why even outlying areas of the city face an imminent invasion of highrise developers.

How Highrises Breed More Highrises

Start with the downtown. Between 1950 and 1970, the skyscraper boom drove up the full assessed valuation of the Central Highrise District by $780 million (that's three-quarters of a *billion* dollars). This immense increase also hiked the price of land to well over $100 per square foot in the Financial District, with other parts of the CHD not far behind.

Land values, of course, grow with density. Chamber of Commerce consultant Gruen confirmed this in his anti-Duskin study with an emphatic certainty that must have had downtown realtors dancing in the marble canyons. "The filling up of each new multi-storied office building," Gruen wrote, "feeds back to make its own and neighboring sites still more valuable. In San Francisco the feedback whereby the increase of work density at one location makes locations within walking distance more desirable for the development of still more work space has continued strong since the late 1950's." (For more on the Chamber reports, see p.**156**, 166.)

In other words, skyscrapers breed more, and bigger, skyscrapers. With each increase in downtown density caused by a new 30- or 40-story building, land values rise in surrounding blocks. Tenants in older 6- to 15-story highrises flock to the new "prestige" offices, leaving the older buildings a smaller profit margin to apply against taxes on the increasingly valuable land beneath them. The land, as realtors say, "demands a higher use." Which means: another blockbuster skyscraper.

Another anti-Duskin report for the Chamber, this one by architect Gerald McCue, shows exactly how this works. The rising cost of land, plus the cost of demolishing the old building (there is no vacant land in downtown San Francisco), plus the cost of lost rent during construction, demand that new buildings be at least twice the size of the old ones — and in some cases four times as large:

* A 10-story building in the Tenderloin-Civic Center area must become 20 stories.

* A 10-story building in the financial district must become 30 stories.

* A 3-story building South of Market must become 12 stories. (See chart, page 44.)

Thus the two Chamber reports, in their eagerness to describe the economic benefits of skyscrapers to downtown businesses and landholders, actually confirm the very fear they were commissioned to allay: Manhattanization of downtown San Francisco is inevitable. Or, as the Wall Street Journal put it, with its usual sober un-

THE RIPPLE EFFECT . . . .

	1950		1970	
	Assessed value land (000)	A.V. Improvements (000)	A.V. land (000)	A.V. improvements (000)
downtown highrise district	2553.6	2118.4	2936.0	4878.4
Inner Arc				
Chinatown	590.1	744.9	1783.0	1711.2
* Telegraph Hill	244.1	314.2	1114.6	1509.1
* Aquatic Park	227.4	313.0	1151.4	909.2
Western Addition	233.9	290.7	609.5	1037.0
Inner Mission	405.5	519.6	709.2	745.8
Average	340.2	436.5	1073.5	1182.4
Middle Arc				
* Marina	242.4	523.1	955.1	1312.0
Pacific Hts.	251.7	302.8	653.4	901.9
Richmond	194.5	390.4	665.3	1136.6
Alamo Sq.	202.6	404.1	468.9	1173.1
Haight	300.9	412.6	933.3	809.8
Eureka Valley	134.3	177.0	499.8	517.7
Average	221.1	368.3	682.6	975.2
Outer Arc				
Sunset	126.7	415.6	544.1	810.3
Portola	110.0	238.6	398.4	584.2
Ingleside	64.5	267.6	341.4	848.4
Bayshore	66.7	119.0	310.9	327.0
Hunter's Pt.	64.1	50.4	264.6	238.4
Potrero Hill	51.6	101.8	306.0	360.1
Average	80.6	198.8	360.9	526.1
Entire City	338.5m.	468.4m.	739.2m.	1177.7m.

   This chart emphatically and categorically refutes claims by downtown interests that the skyscraper boom has "broadened the tax base" and lightened tax loads on homeowners in the neighborhoods. The crucial figures are in the two columns on the far right: they show that the downtown's assessed valuation increased just 67% between 1950 and 1970.

   Assessments in the neighborhoods shot up a stunning 197%. Equally important, the chart shows how these whopping boosts in assessments "rippled out" from the downtown. Over 20 years, downtown assessments increased by $3.14 million; neighborhoods in the inner arc by $1.47 million; in the middle arc by $1.06 million; and in the outer arc by $.61 million. That is, assessed valuation increased in inverse proportion to distance from the downtown.

   Other points of interest:

   1) Areas with height limits (*) showed uncharacteristically large increases. This is because, in a city of great and growing population density, neighborhoods protected from high-density growth by height

. . .how downtown construction drives up neighborhood taxes

	1950 Total assessed value (000)	1970 Total assessed value (000)	Absolute increase (000) 1950- 1970	% increase
downtown highrise district	4672.0	7814.4	3142.4	+ 67%
Inner Arc				
Chinatown	1335.0	3494.2	2159.2	+161%
* Telegraph Hill	558.3	2623.7	2065.4	+370%
* Aquatic Park	540.4	2060.6	1520.2	+280%
Western Addition	524.6	1646.5	1121.9	+214%
Inner Mission	925.1	1455.0	530.0	+ 57%
Average	776.7	2255.9	1479.2	+191%
Middle Arc				
* Marina	765.5	2267.1	1501.6	+196%
Pacific Hts.	554.5	1555.3	1000.8	+180%
Richmond	584.9	1801.9	1217.0	+208%
Alamo Sq.	606.7	1642.0	1035.3	+171%
Haight	713.5	1743.1	1029.6	+144%
Eureka Valley	311.3	1017.5	706.2	+227%
Average	589.4	1657.8	1068.4	+190%
Outer Arc				
Sunset	541.3	1354.4	813.1	+148%
Portola	348.6	982.6	634.0	+182%
Ingleside	332.1	1189.8	857.7	+258%
Bayshore	185.7	637.9	452.2	+243%
Hunter's Pt.	114.5	503.0	388.5	+341%
Potrero Hill	153.4	666.1	512.7	+335%
Average	279.4	887.0	608.6	+218%
Entire City	806.9m.	1916.9m.	1110.0m.	+137%

limits become the most valuable of all.

2) Neighborhoods where 1970 land value exceeded $600,000 (column three) are ripe for highrise, high-density development. Re-development bulldozers are ticketed for neighborhoods whose 1970 land values equaled or exceeded 1970 improvements values (excepting the politically influential Aquatic Park area).

3) Guardian experts figure that legislative bill AB80, passed in 1967 after strenuous lobbying by downtown interests, accounted for 42% of the rise in neighborhood assessments. It should be stressed, however, that AB80 only emphasized a trend that ran continuously throughout the 20 years. Thus, even after discounting AB80's effect, assessments in the neighborhoods zoomed 114% over the 20 years--twice the downtown's rate of increase.

(Land and Improvement assessment figures represent totals obtained from the City Assessor's Block Total Books for average four-block areas in each neighborhood.)

Minimum Heights of New Buildings

Area	Estimated Height of Existing Building[2]	Total Floor Space in Building	Cost of Land[3]		Estimated Value of Existing[4] Building	Cost of Demolition[5]	Rent per sq. ft. per year[6]
			per sq. ft.	Total			
North Beach	3 stories 30 feet	48,000	$13.81	$ 276,200	$ 360,000	$ 16,800	$ 1.80
Financial District	10 stories 100 feet	160,000	96.98	1,939,000	2,400,000	112,000	12.00
Central District	10 stories	160,000	73.89	1.477,800	1,800,000	112,000	3.60
South of Market	3 stories	48,000	11.04	220,800	600,000	33,600	2.40

Area	Loss of Income During New Construction[7]	Cost of Vacant Site		% Increase Over Original Land Cost	Minimum Increase in Density for Economic Feasibility[8]	Economic Height of New Bldg.[9]
		per sq. ft.	Total			
North Beach	$ 172,800	$ 40.00	$ 825,800	190%	190%	6 stories
Financial District	3,840,000	404.00	18,291,000	310%	310%	30 stories
Central District	1,152,000	227.00	4,541,800	200%	200%	20 stories
South of Market	230,400	59.00	1,184,800	440%	440%	12 stories

1. Short-run only. Assumes land values will remain constant for a short time regardless of height restrictions.

2. Typical height of older buildings in area.

3. Calculated using median value of land sales in area given by Wells Fargo Bank. Assume each lot is 200' x 100' = 20,000 sq. ft. with 80% coverage allowed.

4. Present cost of replacement less 50%. Current construction costs: Wood frame - $15 per sq. ft. (North Beach); Steel frame - $30 per sq. ft. (Financial District); Steel frame - $25 per sq. ft. (Central District); Steel frame - $20 per sq. ft. (South of Market). Construction estimates based on recent data collected by McCue Boone Tomsick for San Francisco Bay Area.

5. San Francisco Redevelopment Agency estimate, June 1971: $.35 per sq. ft. for Wood frame; $.70 per sq. ft. for concrete block & steel frame.

6. Based on Wells Fargo Bank Study (1970) and informal survey of local realtors.

7. Assume time from vacating old building to opening new is two years.

8. Assuming rents to remain about the same as in the old building.

9. Providing current land values remain the same.

Source: "Tall Buildings and San Francisco: The Relationships between Building Height and Traffic, Economic Vitality, and Environmental Quality," McCue Boone Tomsick, 1971 derstatement: "The construction of more and more skyscrapers in downtown San Francisco seems nearly certain " (11/6/70).

Gruen's analysis shows that the downtown skyscraper glut will continue expanding not only upwards but, equally important, outwards. Yet another Chamber report, this one published in the January, 1969 issue of San Francisco Business, confirms this. The report predicts that land in the city used for commercial purposes (more office buildings) will expand at the rate of 3% per year through 1985, while residential land will decrease at roughly the same rate.

Still more important, the expansion of highrise, high-density development will not be restricted to land bordering the downtown. Basically, this is because the land-value feedback caused by increasing population density extends much further than the "walking distance" mentioned by Gruen. In fact, it sends out waves of rising land values and assessments that wash all the way to the city limits.

Analysis of property tax assessments in the period between 1950 and 1970 demonstrates this "ripple out." For an average four-block area in the CHD, assessments increased over that period by $3.14 million; in the inner arc of neighborhoods by $1.47 million; in a middle arc by $1.07 million; and in the neighborhoods furthest away from the CHD by $.61 million. As might be expected, the size of increases is inversely proportionate to distance from the downtown. (See chart, page 42-43.)

The meaning of the "ripple out" to taxpayers jumps into focus when we view these figures as percentages:

● The CHD, which started out with the largest base, shows the second lowest percentage increase in the entire city — just 67%.

● Assessments in the city as a whole have risen much more — an average of 137%.

● To balance the small CHD increase, assessments in the neighborhoods have increased at a far higher rate than the city average — over 300% in some areas.

These figures explain and confirm an observation made earlier: While the downtown's proportion of the city's tax bill has been steadily decreasing over the past 20 years, homeowners and taxpayers in the neighborhoods have picked up an increasingly larger share of the downtown's high-density bill.

Incidentally, exceptions to the land-value "ripple out" should give pause to those who assert a city-wide height limit would reduce downtown assessments. Telegraph Hill, Aquatic Park and the Marina all show uncharacteristically large assessment increases —

and all three have height limits. This could only mean that in a city of such great and growing population density, land values grow fastest in areas which are protected from high-density development. (If the height limit were city-wide, of course, these areas would no longer receive special protection and their land values would grow normally.)

The "ripple out" also shows up as large increases in rents and market prices of homes. Statistics released by the U.S. Bureau of the Census show that the value of a median house in San Francisco has climbed over the past ten years from $17,200 to $28,100 — an increase of 63%. This rate of increase is 20% greater than that for the state as a whole. During the same period, rents in San Francisco shot up at a rate 40% greater than the state-wide average. That the rates of increase in San Francisco so greatly exceed statewide averages must primarily be a reflection of higher-than-average land value increases.

The most crucial consequence of "ripple out" has yet to be mentioned. As residential land in the neighborhoods becomes too valuable for single-family homes, developers snap it up, demolish the houses and throw up apartment buildings. But for such development to be profitable, the apartment building must be much larger than the original house. Just as in the downtown, high land costs, demolition costs and lost rents during construction dictate that new buildings exceed the height of the ones they replace by factors of 100% and more.

What this means is that virtually all new construction in the arc of neighborhoods immediately surrounding the CHD, and also in some areas in the middle and outer arcs, must be highrise. Russian Hill, Chinatown, Inner Mission, Haight, Pacific Heights, North Beach, Inner Richmond, Western Addition: all face imminent highrising. With rapid increases in land values flowing out from the downtown, the others, excepting only those with height limits, will soon follow suit.

The implications of this are frightening. Growing population density drives up the value of land — which can then be developed profitably only by building highrise and driving up population density still more.

Seen in this light, land values rippling out from the CHD become not the boon they may first appear to be, but a deadly radiation that kills off residential neighborhoods and induces in their place concrete-and-steel high-density jungles. In a restricted land area as small as that in San Francisco — whose 22 square miles of developable land exactly equals the size of Manhattan Island — Manhattanization of the entire city, not just the downtown, is a virtual certainty.

4. Density and Demographics

Given the raging tax hikes and wide-spread disruptions in land-use patterns caused by highrises, it's scarcely surprising that the city's demographic character — the age and racial distributions of its population — has undergone extensive changes in the past decade. The rash of new skyscrapers has not only increased population density: it has also changed the kinds of people who make up that density.

Altogether an estimated 100,000 middle-income people left San Francisco between 1960 and 1970. During this same period, census figures show the number of children under the age of 15 in San Francisco dropped by 24,473, or 14%. The loss of children under age 5 was even more dramatic: 15,548, or 27%.

This means families with young children who can afford to leave the city — and who aren't prevented from doing so by racial barriers — are moving to the suburbs. They take with them their tax-paying ability, leaving larger burdens for those who are left.

In addition to open spaces, greenery, absence of congestion and other city hazards — in fact, *because* of these low-density characteristics — suburbs can offer a further important advantage: better education. For example, contrast the way San Francisco and surrounding suburbs use their taxes: suburbs on the average spend 70% more than San Francisco for education and 70% less for density-related services.

Taxpayers in the San Mateo county suburb of Atherton, for instance, paid $3.03 cents per $100 for services in fiscal 1970, while San Franciscans paid $7.53. But for education Atherton spent $8.43, San Francisco just $4.71. The combined tax rates for the two were nearly equal: $13.06 in Atherton, $12.82 in San Francisco.

As middle-income families flee the city to gain the low-density advantages of the suburbs, low-income families fill their places. Real estate investors buy aging inner core homes left behind by the new suburbanites and (temporarily, waiting for Redevelopment bulldozers and highrise profits) convert the houses into apartments packing in large numbers of renters, who thereby share costs of amortizing the land.

As time passes and taxes rise still more, the landlord must increase rents, squeeze more people in or cut back on the building's upkeep — in time, perhaps, all three. In this way aging neighbor-hoods quickly become slums.

The availability of such "low-income housing," combined with suburban discrimination, attracts low-income minority people to San Francisco. Thus in the past decade, the city's minority popu-lation has increased by 48%.

Highrise development effects the demographic balance in a third major way: it increases the number of singles and elderly people living in highrise apartments.

While the city's population dropped from 740,316 to 715,674 be-tween 1960 and 1970, the number of households, according to PG&E statistics, actually *increased* by 20,000. A 1970 Wells Fargo report on downtown growth explains why: "There was a new shift to centralization [in housing patterns], stimulated largely by Re-development and the attendant construction of large apartment complexes."

Currently, 215,000 San Franciscans live in multi-unit apartments, and the number is increasing each year. More than 90% of new construction permits issued over the past 10 years have been for multi-unit apartment houses. The current city-wide vacancy rate— 1.2%, the lowest in the country — assures continued demand for more highrise apartments.

However, families with young children shun living in these apart-ments. The rents are too high, and there is not enough room for children. A survey done by ITT Levitt & Sons, the world's largest home-builders, confirms that rent increases and birth of children are two of the four main reasons (the others being "desire to own a home of their own," and "desire to escape the congestion and hazards of city life") that young families living in city apartments bail out for the suburbs. "In fact," according to ITT director Don Salvetti, "the majority of Levitt home-buyers are [inner city] apart-ment dwellers purchasing their first home."

The apartments go instead to young singles and older people who have already raised their children. As a result, San Franciscans in the 15-24 age group have increased by an astounding 36% over the past decade. Residents over 65 have increased by 6.5%. All other age groups have declined.

The over-all result of these density-related population shifts is not promising for San Francisco. They aggravate three forms of po-larization: young-old, rich-poor, and white-non-white. Social fric-tion is bound to increase under such circumstances, driving up municipal costs still more. And meanwhile the middle class has shifted its taxpaying abilities to the suburbs.

5. The Rising Cost of Less Law and Order.

"In general, we have no data," according to former San Francisco Police Chief Al Nelder, "to establish that highrise structures per se have necessitated the assignment of additional police manpower." (San Francisco Magazine, September, 1971)

But no less an authority on San Francisco crime than former Chief Nelder himself has contradicted this pattern. In a signed letter dated Dec. 9, 1970, to Lloyd A. Pflueger of the Downtown Association, Nelder writes: "The total square feet of ground space occupied by a highrise office building will increase the population density in that area proportionately to the height of the building. It is not the height of the building that increases the need for police services, it is the concentration of people in large numbers that creates an increased need for police services." The fact that Pflueger never received the letter — Nelder withheld it for political reasons arising from the highrise controversy, according to a department source —only underscores its accuracy.

Of course it's not the highrise structure *per se* that brings in additional police, as Nelder knows perfectly well — it's the people (and the traffic) attracted by highrises. In a growing high-density city it's all police can do to hold this year's increase in the crime rate to what last year's increase was.

U.S. Bureau of the Census figures confirm that per capita police costs increase dramatically with population density. Cities in the 0-499,999 range pay $19.40 per capita for police; cities of 500,000-999,999 pay $31.90 per capita; and cities over 1,000,000 pay $44.20. (See chart, page 38.)

A block-by-block analysis of police records of non-traffic crimes clearly shows the relation of density and crime in San Francisco. No fewer than 30% of the city total of these crimes in 1970 occurred in the 250-block Central Highrise District. Ten per cent of all robberies in the entire city occurred in a 26-block area roughly approximating the Financial District. That's 10% of the robberies in 0.3% of the developed land area—or 30 times the average.

But it's not just downtown crime that increases with density. Like land values, increased crime "ripples out" to the entire city, and especially to those areas where land-use changes have created ghettos and low-income "troubled" areas teeming with the unemployed. This helps explain why police costs have more than doubled in the past ten years.

A second component of safety costs is fire protection — and here it's much the same story. Modern glass-and-steel skyscrapers, far, from being "fireproof" as claimed by developers, present serious fire hazards that are a matter of mounting concern to insurance companies and fire department officials across the country. (See page 148.)

Assignment of San Francisco fire-fighting personnel and equipment reflects this concern and also the grim reality that many older highrises are firetraps. In 1970, 408 of the Fire Department's 1,768 fire fighters guarded the Central Highrise District, along with 25.5% of the engines and 50% of the salvage companies. On a per-man basis, the CHD, with its 3.4% of the city's developable land, required 22.9% of the total Fire Department budget.

6. Employment and Unemployment

To say that downtown office skyscrapers provide jobs, as downtown interests never tire of doing, is akin to saying that freeways provide transportation: it's true by definition. The purpose of high-density development is to enable business to pile more workers onto the same amount of land. But highrise defenders rarely raise the important questions about the employment impact of the downtown skyscraper boom: 1) What kind of jobs does it create? 2) Who gets the jobs? and 3) What's the impact on non-highrise employment in the city?

In a 1961 study for the Real Estate Research Program, Paul F. Wendt accurately predicted the course on which high-density development would lead San Francisco: "The role of San Francisco is clear and established," Wendt wrote, "that is, to serve as the administrative, shopping and entertainment capital of Northern California . . . public policy [should] be directed toward maximizing this role for San Francisco and permitting the outlying areas [suburbs, East Bay industrial parks] to absorb the bulk of future residential, wholesale, warehousing and industrial development."

U.S. Department of Commerce statistics confirm the accuracy of Wendt's prediction. Between 1960 and 1970, the total labor force in San Francisco jumped by 60,400, or 11.2%, to 536,300. During the same period white collar jobs increased by 28%, or 44,000. That is, white collar jobs accounted for almost three-quarters of the net employment increase for the decade.

Who gets the white collar jobs? The Wells Fargo report supplies an emphatic answer: between 1963 and 1968, the report shows, jobs held by commuters in the Central Highrise District vaulted

28%, while jobs held by San Franciscans in the same area increased just 1%. "The skills most in demand by the city's employers," according to the California Department of Human Resources, "are not generally possessed by residents seeking work . . . . [White-collar] jobs require education or experience which most of the city's underemployed do not have. The employers draw their employees from labor supplies in surrounding communities."

But the growth of white collar businesses in downtown sky-scrapers has had a far more profound effect upon San Francisco employment. "Quite systematically," writes Dick Nolan in the Examiner (5/27/71), "factories, warehouses, and even the old produce market have been driven out of town. The market site is given over to high-rising development. The mattress factory becomes a stores-restaurants-apartments complex. The printing industry is scattered. And so on . . . ." The 1971 Area Manpower Review says it more bluntly: "The industries where many low-skilled and unskilled job-seekers find work are declining in San Francisco."

Statistics support these observations. From 1960 to 1970, employment in trades in San Francisco declined by 2,000 to 110,000 and manufacturing fell from 69,000 to 57,000. A Chamber of Commerce survey conducted in 1968 indicated that, at that time, one of every five blue collar industries in the city was formulating plans to leave — and for each one with plans, probably two or three more were thinking about it.

In 1968, Chamber economic consultant David Bradwell reported a "steady drain" of 100 or so blue collar industries from the city each year. Current PG&E records show the "steady drain" has become a flood. According to PG&E, there are 5900 fewer commercial and industrial PG&E customers in the city than there were just ten years ago — an astounding 15% drop.

The reasons for this loss are complex (Peter Petrakis explores them thoroughly in Chapter Three). But the most significant factor is, of course, high-density development. Rising land values and taxes, according to the Wells Fargo report, are the primary reason blue collar industries leave town. Beyond this, when a highrise office building or apartment house goes up, or when an area is cleared for Redevelopment (which stresses high-density rebuilding, as we shall see), numerous small businesses are torn down. Because many of these are "marginal operations," small and presumably family-owned, their mortality rate is high. The growing expense of commercial property in the city leaves them no place to relocate.

The devastation of blue collar industry wrought by high-density development produces several ironic and expensive effects for San Francisco residents and taxpayers:

1) As Dick Nolan puts it: "The jobs go where the people are not, and the people teem where there are no jobs. Welfare costs go through the roof." Zooming taxes increase the number of people living on fixed incomes who must turn to the city for relief. Rising land values change housing patterns and attract more low income people to the city. Giant downtown highrises provide thousands of new jobs — but they go to commuters. The result: costs of providing welfare in San Francisco (roughly one-third of which are paid by local taxpayers) have more than tripled in a decade, from $31 million in 1960 to $109 million in 1970.

2) Another myth given wide circulation by downtown interests maintains that commuters working in skyscraper offices support the city's retail industry with lunch-hour spending. Yet during the years of the highrise boom, retail sales in the CHD declined steadily as a percentage of city-wide sales (by 1970, the CHD share had fallen to less than a third: 31.3%), just as city-wide sales dropped as a proportion of Bay Area retail business. The downtown may have gained some sales from commuters, but mushrooming downtown congestion frightened away much more business (the decline would have been still greater except for large boosts in tourist spending). Over all, retail employment in San Francisco fell 1% between 1960 and 1970.

3) Highrise advocates like the Chamber of Commerce's Gruen admit that white collar jobs in skyscrapers go to commuters, but claim that highrise "support" industries have provided thousands of new service jobs for San Franciscans. These advocates show no regret that low-skill workers should have to exchange blue collar jobs with decent income and some hope for the future for low-paying, dead-end service jobs (messenger boys, bellhops, retail clerks, etc.). But in any case, Gruen's claim is greatly exaggerated. Of the 27,-000 new service jobs created in San Francisco over the past decade, more than half have resulted from a 67% increase in tourism and another substantial proportion from massive growth in medical and other health services. Business services account for less than a quarter of the new jobs. (Incidentally, another Gruen claim — that growth in white collar jobs and loss of blue collar jobs in San Francisco reflects Bay area trends — is flatly false. While fall-

ing off in San Francisco by 12%, manufacturing employment rose 28% in the Bay Area over the past decade — exactly the figure for white collar growth in San Francisco.)

4) Many San Francisco unions have shortsightedly opposed limitations on highrise development because of the loss of union construction jobs which they believe would ensue. But, according to Gruen, highrise construction provides the equivalent of only 2,400 year-round jobs for construction workers (most of them going to out-of-town workers) — whereas the loss of manufacturing and trades jobs, most of them union, has amounted to 14,000 over the past decade alone.

5) In 1969, the city of San Francisco enacted a payroll tax, supposedly to compensate for the loss of taxes from commuters. But the city then turned around and exempted the 40% of the city's work force employed by banks, insurance firms, federal, state and city agencies — that is, white collar commuters working in highrises. As a result, the payroll tax fell most heavily on blue collar industries and added new ammunition to their economic rationale for leaving the city.

7. Development and Redevelopment

Not many people clearly realize what Redevelopment is. The most prevalent notion envisions a vast federal agency that builds cheap ghetto housing and restores aging neighborhoods.

Actually, the San Francisco Redevelopment Agency is a part of city, not federal, government, and its primary accomplishments over the past decade have been the development of massive new highrise office building complexes in the downtown and the destruction of several neighborhoods — all at the city taxpayer's expense.

The 1970 Wells Fargo report states that "government subsidies benefitting the downtown business district have emanated primarily from the federal government Redevelopment activities. It is in commercial and industrial areas that Redevelopment has been most successful." According to the report, 58% of the total of 8,000,000 square feet of office space built in the last decade is situated in the downtown Golden Gate and Yerba Buena Redevelopment projects.

Redevelopment has also served as the opening wedge for expanding highrise zones into new neighborhoods. Both the Yerba Buena and Golden Gateway projects have been built in former industrial and residential areas. Concerning the $100 million Western Addition project directly west of Van Ness Avenue, the Wells Fargo report states: "The high locational value of this district, be-

ing immediately adjacent to the downtown and comprising the central core portion of a core city in a metropolitan area of four million persons, should result in a total rebuilding and renovation."

As for Redevelopment's concept of "rebuilding and renovation," the report goes on: "As in other areas of the city, there is a trend to high density with many single residences being demolished to make way for highrise apartments. The majority of the [demolished] structures are old Victorians. Most of the new dwelling units constructed since 1960 are in apartments of five units or more."

Nor does Redevelopment rid the city of "blighted" areas. As M.I.T. economist Jay Forrester points out in *Urban Dynamics*, (M.I.T. Press, 1970) "Decaying regions move . . . . Past programs [such as Redevelopment] that try to rebuild the physical area without integrating the underemployed into an economic revival merely shift the troubled area to a new location."

The Neighborhood Legal Assistance Foundation's "Shame of San Francisco" reports that Redevelopment "has destroyed over 5,000 more low-income units than it has produced." When Redevelopment strikes, low-income people move into aging neighborhoods gradually being abandoned by middle-income San Franciscans. These neighborhoods, of course, become the new "troubled" areas targeted for Redevelopment's bulldozers and highrise developers, and the cycle repeats itself — all at the taxpayer's expense.

So far, Redevelopment's highrise schemes have consumed $274 million in taxpayers' money — with $91 million of that provided by San Francisco taxpayers. Most of the money has gone to buy condemned land which the Agency then assembled into handy large-scale parcels and resold at much less than the going rate to wealthy investors to make high-density development "attractive."

8. Density and Congestion

By no coincidence, the first waves of skyscraper development in this country appeared shortly after Henry Ford married the assembly-line to the automobile. The availability of cheap, fast, flexible transportation enabled ever-greater numbers of people to travel large distances each day to gather in a single small area. At a single stroke, the mass-produced automobile ignited both the urban high-density boom and the rush for the suburbs.

For large corporations and white collar workers, the skyscraper/auto way of doing business has been highly beneficial. But for city taxpayers stuck with the costs of providing roads and parking facilities as well as unravelling nightmarish traffic snarls, it's been disastrous.

Start with the most obvious and direct — and the smallest — costs of congestion in downtown San Francisco. In 1970, municipal expenditures for road-repair, road-widening, traffic lights, streetlights, signs, conversion of streets from two-way to one-way, street-cleaning, etc., in the Central Highrise District topped $1 million. In the same year, 136, or 48%, of 303 police personnel assigned to cover traffic in the city were stationed in the CHD. (Huge increases in downtown traffic forced former Chief Nelder to double the number of downtown meter maids in just two years, between 1969 and 1971.) The police department can't provide breakdowns for traffic and non-traffic functions, but on the basis that the 136 CHD traffic personnel constituted 7.5% of the department's 1800 personnel, a rough estimate of $2.3 million might be made for the cost of policing downtown traffic.

Other "minor" costs of downtown congestion don't appear directly in the city budget. Michael Metcalf has shown, for example, that CHD traffic tie-ups force the Municipal Railway to run well below maximum efficiency, adding $3.7 million to its yearly operating cost. (See "The High Cost of Ugliness," page 217.) Numerous other similar examples could be cited: ambulances caught in traffic, municipal employees late to work, wear and tear on city vehicles, and so on. Illegally parked cars prevent sanitation trucks from sweeping the streets and slow down the process of garbage collection, thus raising its cost to the city and to private consumers. (Illegal parking is, fundamentally, a reflection of congestion: legal parking spaces are difficult to find and the cost of garages, if they are not full, is for many people prohibitive.)

The fuming mass of commuter cars (50,000 per day as of late 1970) must pass through other parts of the city on its way to and from the downtown. As Chamber consultant Gerald McCue states, this growing swarm "is increasing . . . traffic congestion on major routes within the city" — and, he should have added, on minor streets as well, since local drivers avoid major routes during rush hours. The city-wide cost of widening and repairing roads, street signs, etc., amounted to $5.5 million in 1970. Also, a significant proportion of the 167 police traffic personnel stationed outside the CHD —police can't say exactly how many — handled commuter traffic.

In addition, the 20,000 units of new highrise apartments built in San Francisco during the past decade have been a major factor in boosting auto registration within the city by 27,000 to a total of 291,000. This works out to twice the number of auto-registrations per square mile as in Manhattan, the nation's second most congested city.

The bite that congestion puts on city residents and taxpayers begins to get more painful when the cost of auto insurance is added in. This cost is based in any particular area on the likelihood of an accident happening there, a factor directly related to auto density. Thus, in super-congested San Francisco a typical family must pay $394 for the most common form of auto insurance ($50 deductible; 25/50 liability). In San Mateo County, the same coverage costs $293; in Marin County, $242. That's a $152 bonus yearly for commuters who flee across the Golden Gate.

Viewed from a city-wide perspective, the immensity of auto insurance costs becomes more readily apparent: car-owners in San Francisco altogether pay $44 *million* more than they would if they paid at Marin's rate. This sum alone is as large as Mayor Alioto's 1968 estimate of the entire municipal cost of providing services to commuters.

Congestion also costs in other ways impossible to measure. A study of San Francisco traffic patterns by sociologists Donald Appleyard and Mark Lintell concluded: "Heavy traffic activity was associated with an increase in the number of apartment buildings [along the street] and decrease in the number of [single-family] homes with children." The study also noted that heavy traffic led to a "drastic decrease in social interaction" and a "withdrawal from the physical environment." In short: congestion drives away those who can afford to leave and diminishes the quality of life for those who stay.

Which brings us to the supreme congestion cost: highways. Expenditures for highways in the Bay Area have been running at the rate of $250 million per year — with 60% of that going for state freeways hooking the suburbs with San Francisco. To correct so-called "deficiencies" in the highway system (read: to make it more efficient for commuters), the BATSC study performed for BART — more on that tax-gobbler in a moment — forecasts the "need" for $3 *billion* or so worth of new highways over the next ten years.

The BATSC study also points out two other "critical" deficiencies: the "need" for a Southern Crossing bridge to relieve the commuter load on the Bay Bridge (minimum cost, not including interest: $350 million, plus $150 million for approach roads) and the "need" for a second deck on the Golden Gate bridge (cost: $80-100 million).

The massive expense of unspooling endless concrete ribbons for commuters is hidden to San Francisco residents because freeways are paid for largely by state and federal gas tax moneys. An average San Francisco driver who travels 10,000 miles per year contributes up to $60 to the gas tax funds. Only a miniscule fraction of this money, needless to say, goes for patching streets in his neighborhood. Most helps build and repair freeways that bring more commuters into San Francisco.

Over the past 10 years, according to the Security Pacific report, automotive traffic entering the city has almost doubled. The 1966 Downtown Parking and Traffic Survey states that the number of cars entering the downtown will continue growing, despite BART, by 18.5% through 1975 (probably a gross underestimate).

An article in Town and Planning Review (Vol. 35) by Professor R. J. Smeed, one of the world's leading traffic systems analysts, reports a disquieting finding about burgeoning commuter traffic. Smeed shows that where there are 10,000 commuters in a city, they require about eight square feet of roadway per person. 100,-000 commuters require 28 square feet of roadway per person. 1,000,000 commuters require 97 square feet per person. Thus the provision of new freeways leading into the city expands the number of commuters, boosting at an exponential rate the demand for new freeways *within* the city — the most expensive and disruptive highways of them all.

It was to break this commuter/freeway cycle — or so the voters of San Francisco were told — that the Bay Area decided nine years ago to underwrite the construction of a rapid transit system.

9. The Ultimate Money-Drain: BART.

The Wells Fargo report describes what BART is intended to do, and who profits from it: BART, says the report, "will invigorate the San Francisco Central Business District resulting in higher land use. The more intensive use will evidence itself through larger real estate density via highrise structures resulting in large increases in non-residential employment in the financial district. The trends toward centralization now evident in the spate of highrise buildings will be accompanied by an attendant rise in the value of real estate . . . ."

It's the same old story. BART will benefit downtown interests, attract thousands of new commuters, and immeasurably worsen all the high-density problems from which the city now suffers: higher cost of municipal services, rising land values and taxes, fewer jobs for residents, middle class exodus, destruction of neighborhoods.

BART will be especially effective in destroying neighborhoods. Stations currently under construction in the Mission district, Glen Park and Balboa Park insure that those areas will shortly switch to high-density land-use patterns. BART extensions scheduled for the Richmond and Sunset districts in the middle 1970's will have the same effect there.

(Richmond and Sunset residents have complained for years because BART service for their areas was postponed, even though they had to pay BART taxes like everyone else. But they might do better to keep quiet. It's now clear that when the Geary and Judah lines are built, residents will pay still more in new high-density costs — in exchange for a two-minute reduction in time a trip to the downtown requires.)

So far, BART's construction costs alone amount to at least $2.2 billion just for the skeleton three-county service scheduled to begin operation in 1972. To understand how large that figure is, keep in mind that it's $300 million greater than the 1970 assessed valuation of the entire city of San Francisco.

In 1970, the average San Francisco home-owner paid $39.90 for BART in his property tax bill. He paid another $50 or so in the one-half cent BART sales tax levy. He paid a still larger amount, difficult to estimate, in high-density costs reflected in the municipal tax rate and assessments — probably several hundred dollars. And, of course, the costs of BART are only beginning to be felt.

That's not the end of it. In 1962, BART was sold to the public as a means of cutting down congestion and smog. It will actually do just the opposite. Even when fully operative, the BART line, according to estimates made by BART engineers, will carry a maximum of only 30,000 commuters per hour. That is, it will handle only 10% of the *current* commuter flood. But the construction of BART has caused a flurry of new downtown development which promises to increase commuters by 30% in just the next three years and by 100% by 1990.

There will be no room for these new commuters on BART. Most will drive smog-belching cars to work, increasing both congestion and pollution.

These estimates, it should be added, are highly optimistic. Essentially, BART is a 1900's mode of transportation too inflexible to meet modern transportation needs. It's designed to handle peak-hour commuter traffic, which occurs only three hours per day, or 600 hours per year. The other 8,160 hours per year much of its equipment will lie idle and unproductive.

What this means is that either the BART-rider must pay an exorbitant charge to compensate for all those idle equipment hours — or the taxpayer must subsidize the system. Even the city's Municipal Railway does not pay for itself (it ran up a $19 million deficit in 1970). BART, which will be much more expensive to run, will probably make those Muni deficits look as quaint and dainty as the nickel fare.

10. Pollution

Urban economists had been cursing traffic and wiping smog-caused tears from their eyes for years before discovering that pollution costs money. So far, the science of pinning cost figures on a particle of carbon monoxide or a gallon of sewage is far from precise. But some indications do exist.

San Francisco is already the single largest polluter of the Bay, dumping some 105 million gallons of inadequately treated sewage there each day. Assuming that what goes into property as water comes out as sewage, it follows that the Central Highrise District, which receives 24.8% of the city's water supply, causes roughly a quarter of the city's water pollution.

To clean up this mess, and also to treat the vast new amounts of sewage which will be created by high-density growth, City Public Works Director S. Myron Tatarian has prepared a "Master Plan for Waste Water Management" which will cost the city up to $864 million. "People will think we are using drugs or something to be talking about $700 million or $800 million for the sewer system," protested Supervisor Terry Francois when the plan was first presented to the Supervisors on Sept. 27, 1971. But the "Master Plan" is neither a hallucination nor a conservationist's dream: it's the minimum cost of meeting current minimal standards required by law. The cost of the new system, disregarding operating costs and interest on bonds, works out to $1,208 for each of San Francisco's 715,000 residents.

The cost of air pollution is much more difficult to ascertain. Until more accurate measures are devised, the best way to get at least a hint is to view air pollution as an important factor in determining the city's overall health. Other congestion-related factors also influence city health costs: the psychological wear and tear of traffic on drivers, pedestrians and people whose homes border heavily-travelled streets; increased social friction; and expansion of those sectors of the populace most likely to need (and least able to afford) hospital care — elderly people and underemployed minorities. Also, high density itself, because it increases each resident's likelihood of encountering an individual who carries a disease, raises the city-wide incidence of infectious diseases. (This is why Gallup polls show flu epidemics strike a greater proportion of the population in large cities.) Finally, city-financed public hospitals in high-density areas must serve large numbers of people, residents and commuters alike, even though construction and maintenance costs are paid only by city taxpayers.

Kenneth Watt's analysis of per capita municipal costs confirms that health costs in large cities vastly exceed those of small cities (see chart, page 38). In San Francisco, city health and hospitals expenditures have leaped 128% over the past decade, from $13.5 million to $30.8 million. Part of this increase can be attributed to inflation (28.6% for the decade) and rising costs of medical services. Most of the rest stems directly from air pollution and other side-effects of high-density growth.

11. Tourism

"The irony," writes Herb Caen in the Chronicle, "is that these build-and-be-damned (the public be jammed) types think of themselves as hard-nosed businessmen. Since tourism is our number one industry, do they ever stop to consider what tourists come here to see? You can bet your bottom dollar that it isn't tall buildings and traffic jams."

For a ten-year period until 1969, tourism in San Francisco grew at almost twice the rate of the city's white collar/skyscraper industry. But in 1969 and 1970 the number of visitors fell off by 8% and then 4%, signalling the beginning of what many observers within the tourist industry believe will be a permanent decline. "No more tourists are coming," according to Richard Swig, brother of Fairmont owner and downtown power Ben Swig (Wall Street Journal, 8/4/71).

Why do tourists visit San Francisco? Advertising in the Visitor and Convention Bureau's *News* brags that what's "special" about San Francisco is its "natural beauty." "Much of this gateway city's charm," reads one ad, "derives from the fact that it refused to fit a mold. It climbed hills while other cities spread out" — and built up, it might be added. But Herb Caen explains the tourist lure much better: "They come here for what San Francisco has always been famous for and what is now being threatened: exhilarating vistas, good food in a variety of little eating places, a way of life that is 'different,' a bit more free and open than their own. Parks, not parking lots. Even topless dancers in preference to topless buildings."

The economic impact of a continuing decline in tourism could be catastrophic for San Francisco. Last year's 4% drop, according to the Visitors and Convention Bureau, destroyed 9,000, or 14.2%, of the city's tourist-related jobs. Because these jobs call for no special skills and pay low wages, they go primarily to the city's underemployed and marginally employed workers — the ones most likely to wind up on the welfare rolls. A drop of 30% in tourism could double the city's welfare bill.

Ignoring ominous signs of a tourist boycott, San Francisco is currently in the midst of a highrise hotel boom that by 1974 will nearly double the 16,000 rooms available in 1970. "We've way over-expanded," Richard Swig notes glumly. The city-wide hotel occupancy rate hovers at 70%, only three percentage points above the generally accepted break-even line. "For every new room being built," warns the Hilton Hotel's Henri Lewin, "an old one will have to close" (Chronicle, 10/11/71).

Even if tourist business expands by 50% — a highly unlikely prospect, to say the least — a large number of the city's older and less prestigious hotels will be driven out of business. Meanwhile, the new hotels will help drive up downtown land values and further devastate the downtown skyline, shaping San Francisco still more firmly into the mold it "refuses to fit."

12. Final Solutions

An army of economists could occupy themselves for years discovering new ways highrise, high-density development costs the residents and taxpayers of San Francisco. The real question is this:

how did we ever let ourselves be deluded into thinking that such a fundamentally inefficient way of organizing our economy could be, of all things, *economically necessary?*

"The sky is falling in on us in the cities," in Mayor Alioto's phrase: the reason is that it simply doesn't make sense, economically or otherwise, to pile people on top of each other in huge numbers in a small area, with each added layer costing more to build than the last. Nor to house hundreds of thousands of workers 20 to 30 miles from their jobs. Nor to gather huge numbers of people without jobs into the decaying areas closest to the giant buildings — which will not employ them.

Highrise buildings are essentially huge machines which have grown rapaciously over the years by feeding on an old industrial age myth: that the economies of scale produced by centralization and specialization create no corresponding *dis*economies of scale. The taxpayers' obliging readiness to pick up the tab for these diseconomies, however outrageous, has encouraged the monster machines to multiply and to carry centralization to freakish and absurd heights — to the point now where the costs of diseconomies have rushed every overgrown urban center in the country to the brink of fiscal and social chaos.

One of the sadder ironies of San Francisco's devastation by highrise buildings is that these immense monuments to economic myths are rapidly approaching the day when they will become obsolete. The 1970 Wells Fargo report notes: "Automation of industrial communication and decision-making tasks could signal a decline in the growth of employment centers in the city core with extreme decentralization. Computer-controlled production processes [cybernation] are already replacing between 2 million and 2.5 million jobs a year [in the U.S.]. The enormous quantity of money and resources which are poured into transportation systems could be reduced by eliminating the need to commute entirely. Theoretically a company employee could transmit his image and voice through electronics and obtain access to information necessary for his work through a home-based computer terminal . . . . The average American currently spends 10-15% of his waking time traveling to work." Like all monstrous creatures that over-specialize, highrises face imminent extinction.

There is little likelihood, however, that the creatures — here or elsewhere — will disappear of their own accord. The reason is simple: costs of developing and operating cybernation systems will fall on business, not on the public. Instead of accepting public underwriting of the cost of delivering a worker to the work-place, a company will essentially have to deliver itself, through electronics, to the worker. But why should a company pay for such an expensive technological feat when the public will deliver the worker to the company for free?

Since highrises won't willingly force their own extinction, city residents might do well to consider what other steps might be taken in the meantime to hurry the process along. One method — not very promising to those who dislike skyscrapers but also place some value on human life — is being tested in New York right now.

There the mad proliferation of higher-and-higher-rises has finally caused something approaching a fatal rupture in the social fabric. By itself, this is of little consequence to highrise developers. But the people who commute from Long Island and New Jersey to work in New York's skyscrapers have raised such a clamor over the difficulties they face that big business has been moving many of its offices to "satellite centers" in the suburbs, there to work the high-density cycle all over again. And the people who rent space in New York's buildings, presented with tax bills so large their profits are threatened, have become concerned enough about New York's social and fiscal problems to move their operations to cities less advanced in the cycle, such as San Francisco.

Some expert observers propose a second kind of remedy: forcing business to adopt the public costs of its high-density centralization. This won't work, however, for two reasons: 1) high-density development has gotten so out of hand that the public costs far exceed the economies gained by business; and 2) business control of the political process (as documented in chapter 3) is so overpowering that even the mildest efforts at reform, such as San Francisco's payroll tax and Urban Design Plan, are either gutted of meaning by "exemptions" and other forms of political payoff, or are ignored by the officials charged with their enforcement.

A third kind of remedy exists in those few states, including California, which permit the voting public itself to make law through the initiative process. That remedy — an ironclad city-wide height limit — is elegantly simple and has worked well enough, economically and socially, in European cities such as Amsterdam, Paris and Geneva. It is San Francisco's only discernible hope for rescuing itself from the ravages of city-wide high-density development.

3.

Politics of Highrise
By Bruce Brugmann

"I knew an aldherman wanst that was honest as th' sun except whin th' sthreet railroad or th' gas comp'ny needed something," said Mr. Hennessy.

"Well, there ye ar're," said Mr. Dooley. "It seems to me that th' on'y thing to do is to keep pollyticians an' business men apart. They seem to have a bad influence on each other. Whiniver I see an aldherman an' a banker walkin' down th' sthreet together I know th' Recording Angel will have to ordher another bottle iv ink." From the *World of Mr. Dooley* by Finley Peter Dunne.

It wasn't the invisible hand of Adam Smith at work that tossed sky-scrapers into San Francisco like Lincoln logs.

It was a concentrated panoply of land and development forces and their power bloc of Bay Area Council/Chamber of Commerce/SPUR/ Downtown Association that successfully promoted the key elements of big development policy: BART to bring commuters in and out, the Downtown Zoning Plan of 1967/the Urban Design Plan of 1971 to grease the way for more and more skyscrapers, highrise Redevelopment that started and then fueled the highrise boom in downtown San Francisco in the early and mid-1960s, Alioto for Mayor.

The crucial point is that the forces making San Francisco the Wall Street of the West have worked hand in hand for years with City Hall.

For example, the city through Redevelopment made high density development of the downtown profitable and inevitable by using emi-nent domain and taking land from smaller businessmen, then handing it over to big developers at a cheap price. This intimacy between city hall and development has been reflected in the sky-is-the-limit devel-opment policies of the city's four development commissions (Planning, Port, Redevelopment, Board of Permit Appeals, see analysis, p. 68) and in the highrise votes of the supervisors (see analysis, p. 66) and the highrise policies of Mayors and the assessors (see analysis of campaign contributions, p. 72).

Thus, when the chips were down, in the 1971 election on the Duskin highrise initiative, not one major candidate for mayor (Alioto, Feinstein, Dobbs), not one supervisor, not one appointed or elected official in City Hall would go up against the BAC/Chamber/DA/SPUR bloc and publicly support the Duskin petition.

However, the Chamber quickly mustered 8 of 11 supervisors (Driscoll, Mendelsohn, Tamaras, Barbagelata, von Beroldingen, Gonzales, Mailliard, Francois) to publicly back its front group, Citizens for San Francisco, and its $400,000 or so full page ads/direct mail-to-each-residence campaign to defeat the initiative. Also: Planning Commissioner Mortimer Fleishhacker, Jr., Mayor Alioto, Chief Administrator Thomas Mellon, Municipal Judge Joseph Kennedy and a host of others.

It's been the operating principle for years in San Francisco: When the Chamber of Commerce spits, City Hall swims.

1. Who approves highrise buildings on the Board of Supervisors?

Compiled by Leslie Waddell

A = AYE
N = NAY
X = EXCUSED
NOT = NOT ON BD. AT TIME

DATES		BARBAGELATA	BLAKE	BOAS	DRISCOLL	ERTOLA	FEINSTEIN	FRANCOIS	GONZALES	MAILLIARD	McCARTHY	MENDELSOHN	MORRISON	PELOSI	TAMARAS	VON BEROLDINGEN
1966	Approve $118 Million Yerba Buena Convention Center.	Not	A	A		A	A	A	A Not	A	A	A Not	N	Not	A	A
5/20/68	Approve 14 to 1 downtown density ratio.*		N	A		N	Not	A	A Not	N	A	A	A	Not	N	N
6/15/68	Approve International Market Center.		A	A		A	A	A	A	A	A	A	N	A	A	A
3/3/69	Approve in principle Candlestick expansion.		A	A		A	A	A	A	A	Not A	A	N	A	A	A
7/28/69	Approve Transamerica Merchant Street closing.		A	A		A	A	A	A	A	A	Not A	N	A	A	A
8/4/69	Approve Alcatraz appraisal for leasing.		A	N		A	A	A	A	A	A	A	N	A	N	A
9/29/69	Approve Lamar Hunt Alcatraz Plan.	A	A	A		N	A	A	A	A	A	N	A	N	A	A
5/18/70	Establish Oceanfront height limit.	A	Not A	Not A		A	A	X	A	A		A	Not	X		
5/25/70	Motion that construction of Peripheral Canal of State Water Project be held in abeyance.	A				A	A	A	A	A		A		X	A	A
6/29/70	Oppose Southern Crossing	A		A		A	A	A				A	X	X	A	A
9/14/70	Motion by Feinstein & Boas to put U.S. Steel on ballot; Needed four Supervisors' signatures-Failed (no vote recorded)															
11/17/70	Delay decision on U.S. Steel for 90 days.**	A		N		A N	A N	A	A	N		A	N	N	A	A
2/16/71	Set 175 foot limit on U.S. Steel waterfront site.	X		A	N	Not A	Not A	N	A	A		A	A	A	N	N
6/6/71	Tishman-Cahill Building-Vote to close Ecker St.	A		X		A	A	A	A	A		A	A	A	A	X
7/19/71	Change Yerba Buena Project to include highrise hotel.	A		A		A	A	X	A	A		A	A	A	A	A
7/26/71	Approve $4 million from hotel tax for Yerba Buena.	A		X		A	A	A	A	A		A	A	A	A	A
8/9/71	Approve appt. of Blumenthal to Housing Authority.	A		A		A	A	A	A	A		A	A	A	A	X
9/13/71	Approve Prop. K doubling the number of signatures need-ed for initiative, Prop. M could override the Duskin initiative	A		A		A	A	A	A	A		A	A		A	A

66

* Aye for 14:1 which, with bonuses, would allow a building to go up to 24:1 and downtown New York/Chicago-style density. Nay held out for 16:1 density which, with bonuses, would allow the densest concrete jungle in the world.

** Aye vote interpreted as a delay move to help U.S. Steel.

Low rise: Morrison.

Medium rise: Pelosi, Feinstein, Boas, all latecomers with the U.S. Steel fight.

Highrise all the way: Mendelsohn, Barbagelata, Driscoll, Francois, Mailliard, Tamaras, von Beroldingen and Gonzales. (All eight nailed down their highrise voting records by allowing their names as "advisory members" of the Chamber's front group to fight highrise, "Citizens for San Francisco." See Chamber p. 156.) All these supervisors, excepting Jack Morrison, got much of their campaign money from land/development/real estate interests. See campaign contribution analysis, p. 72.

Early highrise: McCarthy, Blake.

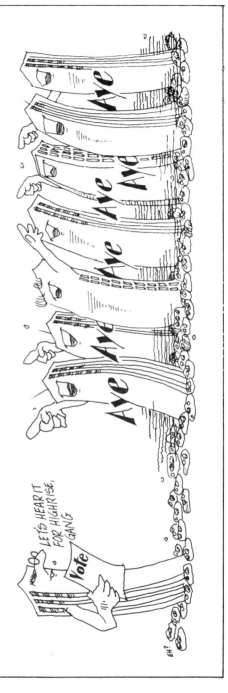

2. Who approves highrise buildings on the four major development-oriented commissions?

All commissions and most commissioners, which means that the development of San Francisco is passed on by an extremely narrow section of the city's business/labor establishment. One result: most favor and very few have questioned sky-is-the-limit development.

Members of the four city commissions most concerned with building and development (Planning Commission, Board of Permit Appeals, Port Commission, Redevelopment Authority) and their addresses and businesses at their time of service.

The residences of commissioners (see map numbers) correspond with numbers on list.

Compiled by A.P. Margaronis

BUSINESS

1. Fred G. Ainslie, 155 Beach St.-Bd. of Permit Appeals; Owner, Fred G. Ainslie Co. (insurance)
2. Victor Atkins, 2815 Vallejo-Redv. Agency; Pres., Doran Co. (manufacturing)
3. Peter Boudoures, 1200 California-Bd. of Permit Appeals; Pres., Olympic Savings & Loan
4. Henry J. Budde, 1050 North Point-Port Comm.; Publisher, S.F. Progress
5. L.M. Cole, 1000 Green St.-Planning Comm.; Pres., Walter Hoey Motors
6. George Y. Chinn, 719 Grant Ave.-Bd. of Permit Appeals; Pres., Six Companies

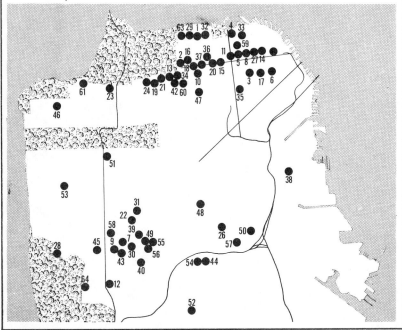

7. Michael Driscoll, 307 St. Francis Blvd.-Redv. Agency; Owner, Driscoll's Mortuary
8. W.M. Davis, 1000 Green St.-Bd. of Permit Appeals; Pres., W.M. Durant Co. (cosmetics)
9. W.A. Ehrhardt, 25 San Rafael Wy.-Bd. of Permit Appeals; Pres., Alta Coffee Co.
10. Mortimer Fleishhacker, Jr., 2600 Pacific-Planning Comm.; Natomas Corp.; Pres., KQED
11. James A. Folger, 1040 Green St.-Redv. Agency; Pres., Folger Coffee Co. (retired)
12. G.B. Gillin, 295 Stratford-Bd. of Permit Appeals; Pres., G.B. Gillin (realty)
13. Everett Griffin, 3277 Pacific-Redv. Agency; Mgr., Chemical Developers Co.
14. Sam J. Husband, 866 Green St.-Port Comm.; Stockbroker, Dean Witter& Co.
15. Walter F. Kaplan, 1875 Broadway-Redv. Agency; Sec./ Treas., Emporium/ Capwell
16. Dan London, 2701 Broderick-Port Comm.; Exec. VP., Western Intl. Hotels; Mgr. Dir., St. Francis Hotel
17. Cyril I. Magnin, 999 California-Port Comm.; Pres., J. Magnin & Co.
18. Max Moore, 2470 Broadway-Bd. of Permit Appeals; Exec. VP., Moore Manufacturing
19. Gardner Mein, 214 Spruce St.-Planning Comm.; Asst. to Pres., Calavaras Cement Co.
20. John L. Merrill, 1940 Broadway-Redv. Agency; Pres., Merrill Co.
21. Walter S. Newman, 3663 Washington-Planning Comm.; VP. (Admin.), J. Magnin & Co.
22. Kevin O'Shea, 50 Allston-Bd. of Permit Appeals; Mission district Insurance broker
23. Ron Pelosi, 18-16th Ave.-Planning Comm.; Partner, Dean Witter & Co.
24. John B. Ritchie, 3955 Washington-Planning Comm.; Pres., Ritchie & Ritchie (realty)
25. Trevor C. Roberts, Atherton (not on map)-Port Comm.; Investment counsellor, Trevor C. Roberts Investments
26. James Rudden, 148 Chenery Ave.-Port Comm.; VP./Treas., Ray Oil Burners
27. M.R. Sullivan, 945 Green St.-Planning Comm.; Bd. Chmn. PT&T; Pres., Perini Land Co.
28. James Silva, 88 Country Club Dr.-Redv. Agency; Mgr., AA Top & Trim (car upholsterers)
29. Roy Scola, 1735 Beach St.-Bd. of Permit Appeals; Pres., John De Martini (grocers)
30. O.W. Willard, 40 San Andreas Wy.-Planning Comm.; VP., Macy's
31. J.W. Walsh, 130 Pacheco-Port Comm.; Acct. Exec., E.F. Hutton & Co.
32. E.L. West, 165 Marina-Bd. of Permit Appeals; Salesman, Walston, Hoffman & Goodwin (investment securities) (retired)
33. Stephen Walter, 2504 Leavenworth-Redv. Agency; Exec. VP., DN&E Walter & Co. (wholesalers, now a holding co.)

PROFESSIONAL
34. Joseph Alioto, 34 Presidio Terr.-Redv. Agency; Atty.
35. Richard Bancroft, 2922 Sacramento-Bd. of Permit Appeals; Atty.
36. Alvin Baum, Jr., 2009 Green-Planning Comm.; Atty.
37. William Brinton, 2434 Broadway-Planning Comm.; Atty.

38. Robert E. Gonzales, 541 Missouri-Bd. of Permit Appeals; Atty.
39. James W. Harvey, 160 Miraloma-Bd. of Permit Appeals; Atty.
40. J.F. Henning, 185 Westwood-Bd. of Permit Appeals; Atty.
41. George T. Rockrise, 468 Vallejo-Planning Comm.; Architect
42. Sherwood Stockwell, 21 Presidio Terr.-Planning Comm.; Architect
43. Francis Solvin, 369 Santa Ana-Redv. Agency; Atty.
44. Henry Tagliaferi, 282 Silver-Port Comm.; Dentist
45. Joseph Tinney, 1 Melba Ave.-Planning Comm.; Atty.
46. Thomas Wu, 598-38th Ave.-Bd. of Permit Appeals; Dentist
47. J.C. Wellington, 2299 Sutter-Redv. Agency; Doctor

LABOR

48. Harry Bridges, 35 Kronquist-Port Comm.; Pres., ILWU
49. John Crowley, 87 Los Palmos Dr.-Bd. of Permit Appeals; Bus. Agent, Embalmers Union
50. Philip Dindia, 345 Banks-Planning Comm.; Bus. Rep., Teamsters Local 84
51. Stanley Jensen, 368 17th Ave.-Redv. Agency; Dir. Bus. Rep., Machinist Union
52. A.C. Jinkerson, 1181 Naples-Port Comm.; Sec./Treas., Retail Clerk's Union Local 648
53. James Kearney, 187-35th Ave. -Planning Comm.; Pres., ILWU Local 10
54. Alfred Lombardi, 128 Cotter-Bd. of Permit Appeals; Bus. Agent, Butchers Union Local 115
55 Joe Mosley, 680 Los Palmos-Redv. Agency; Bus. Agent, ILWU
56. Lawrence Palacious, 459 Hazelwood-Redv. Agency; Pres., Laundry Workers
57. Hector E. Rueda, 378 Crescent-Planning Comm.; Bus. Agent, Elevator Constructors Union
58. Everett Walsh, 544 Wawona-Bd. of Permit Appeals; Bus. Rep., Retail Clerk's Union 1100

OTHERS

59. Ann Alanson, 1275 Greenwich-Bd. of Permit Appeals; Housewife
60. Wilbur Hamilton, 3070 California-Redv. Agency; Sup., American President Lines.
61. Julia G. Porter, 142-27th Ave.-Planning Comm.; Housewife

EX-OFFICIO MEMBERS OF PLANNING COMMISSION

62. James K. Carr, Hillsborough (not on map); Mgr. of Utilities
63. John D. Crowley, 663 Marina Blvd.; Mgr. of Utilities
64. Thomas G. Mellon, 310 Arballo Dr.; Chief Administrative Officer

"Commissioner Mortimer Fleishhacker urged his [planning] colleagues to go on record against the [Duskin] height measure . . . because he felt it 'would destroy a monumental amount of planning'." (Chronicle 10/15/71)

Says Walter S. Newman, Cyril Magnin's son-in-law and President of the City Planning Commission: "Even if we don't live in all parts of the city, we hear what people have to say by travelling around the city for meetings with different communities. We do hear and take notice."

Members of the four commissions (Planning, Port, Redevelopment, Board of Permit Appeals) would have to do quite a bit of travelling to hear from most any communities. We studied 62 members who hac been on these commissions since 1960 and found that —

Half live in the most exclusive area of the city — the section including Pacific Heights, Nob and Russian Hills and the Marina.

, About a quarter cluster in an area including St. Francis Woods, Mt. Davidson and Diamond Heights, predominantly white neighborhoods that range from "very-nice" to quite wealthy.

The remaining quarter is scattered throughout the city in selected white, moderate-income neighborhoods including the Sunset and Richmond.

One lone member lives in a neighborhood that is racially and economically mixed (Robert Gonzales on Potrero Hill, now a Supervisor).

Not one member lives in the Fillmore/Western Addition, Hunters Point, Haight-Ashbury or Yerba Buena areas — all strategic development areas most effected by decisions of these commissions.

Other findings:

The occupational breakdown of the 62 commissioners: 52% business (mainly finance and manufacturing), 27% professional (mainly attorneys), 20% labor (up during Alioto's tenure), 1% others.

Minority breakdown: 15% from minority backgrounds: four commissioners were black, three Spanish, two Chinese.

The female breakdown: two were women: Julia Porter, a veteran planning commissioner who consistently votes with the development bloc, and Ann Alanson, 1971 Alioto appointee to the Board of Permit Appeals.

Of the present members of the four commissions, our survey showed, 75 per cent owned their own houses and 75 per cent of these lived in houses with an average market value of $70,000 as determined from assessment rolls. It's not surprising that all four commissions practice sky-is-the-limit development policies.

Note: Planning's hand-in-hand work with development interests isn't generally understood: (1) the 1967 Downtown Zoning program allowing the highest buildings in the world was originated by SPUR, then promoted by a special Downtown Advisory Committee that "helped" Peter S. Svirsky, a senior planner from New York City. The "helpers": Atty. Jake Ehrlich; Architect John Bolles of the Downtown Association; Francis V. Keesling of the Chamber; realtor Walter Shorenstein of the SF Real Estate Board; contractor John Cahill for the Building Owners and Managers; S. G. Worthington of PT&T and SPUR. (2) The program's logical 1971 successor, The Urban Design Plan, is so permissive and expansive for development (See Sletteland, p. 24) that nobody from the Ex/Chron/SPUR/Chamber/Downtown Association/Bay Area Council/labor unions bloc even bothered to find anything to quarrel about.

3. Who invests in highrise supervisors, assessors and mayors?

"What is political graft, annyhow? It ain't stealin' money out iv dhrawer. It ain't robbin' th' taxpayer direct, th' way th' gas com'ny does. All there's to it is a business man payin' less money to a pollytician thin he wud have to pay to th' city if he bought a sthreet or a dock direct."—The World of Mr. Dooley

Well, what do the businessmen get for their money? Lots of handouts like cheap land through redevelopment, city streets and air rights at a pittance, a $600,000 bridge over the River Kearny, easy access at City Hall.

More important, they get protection. Supervisors and Mayor Alioto have a) balked at doing a cost benefit study of skyscrapers; b) handed this dangerous job over to the downtown interests by letting SPUR do it (big SPUR contributors: BofA, PG&E, PT&T, Crocker, Standard Oil, Wells Fargo, Bechtel, the same old highrise gang); c) quietly approved two sleeper 1971 ballot propositions that would, first, subvert the initiative process in San Francisco (K, by doubling the amount of signatures needed to qualify for future elections) and second, subvert Duskin's 72-foot height limit initiative if it passed (by permitting Supervisors/Planning Commissioners to override it). K introduced by Pelosi, M introduced by Francois, approved unanimously.

The 244 top contributors to winning SF campaigns

Compiled by Sue Hestor.

Each person listed below made contributions to three or more of these winning campaigns: Tinney for Supervisor (1965) and Tinney for Assessor (1970), Alioto for Mayor (1967), Mendelsohn, Francois, Pelosi, Mailliard, McCarthy, Ertola for Supervisor (1967), Feinstein, Barbagelata, Boas, Tamaras, von Beroldingen for Supervisor (1969).

*Persons connected with land/development/real estate as developers, realtors, financiers, attorneys, banks and savings and loan institutions.

†Widely known contributors to conservation causes.

Key: mayor: Al is Alioto
       supervisor:
       Ba is Barbagelata (real estate man)
       Bo is Boas (Boas Pontiac)
       Er is Ertola (attorney, now Superior Court Judge)
       Fe is Feinstein (full-time Supervisor)
       Fr is Francois (attorney)
       Ma is Mailliard (Mailliard & Schmiedell food brokers; former Police Comm.)
       Mc is McCarthy (attorney, assemblyman)
       Me is Mendelsohn (consultant in urban planning
            for Lawrence Halprin landscape architects)
       Pe is Pelosi (stockbroker, Dean Witter)
       Ta is Tamaras (Tamaras Supply Co.)
       VB is von Beroldingen (attorney, with offices
            in San Rafael)
       TnS: Tinney for supervisor (1965)
       TnA: Tinney for assessor (1970)

FRANK AGNOST-Al, Fe, Ta; (Partner-Falcon Associates-Printers)
* ANN & LIONEL ALANSON-Al, Fr, Mc, Me, Pe, Bo, Fe; (Ann-Democratic Committeewoman; Alioto appointee to Bd. of Permit Appeals)

IVAN A. ANIXTER-TnS, Me, Pe, Bo, Fe, Ta; (Weinstein Investment Co.)

EDWARD BACCIOCCO-TnS, Al, Er, Bo, Ta, TnA; (Calif. Meat Co.)

* GERSON BAKAR-TnS, Al, Fr, Ma, Mc, Bo, Ta, VB, TnA; (Developer-North Pt. Shopping Center & Apts.)

* LEE BART-Al, Bo, Ta; (Bart Realty)

† ALVIN BAUM-Al, Fr, Me, Pe, Bo, Fe, Ta; (BCDC; former planning commissioner)

ALAN D. BECKER- Fr, Me, Pe, Bo, Fe; (Pres.-J&B Shoes; Pres.-No. Calif. ADA)

JOSEPH BELARDI-Al, Fr, Ta; (Pres.-Cooks' Union, Local 44)

A. BROOKS BERLIN-Al, Fr, Ta; (Atty.)

* MORRIS BERNSTEIN-TnS, Al, Fr, Me, Ta, VB; (Alioto appointee to Fire Commission; liquor dealer; Democratic fund raiser)

MARJORIE & PAUL BISSINGER, SR.-TnS, Ma, Bo, Ta; (Paul-former head of Chamber; deceased)

* ARNOLD BLUM-Bo, Ta, VB; (A. Blum Construction Co.)

* BENJAMIN BLUMENTHAL-TnS, Al, Fr, Mc, Bo, Ta, VB; (Real estate interests-owns St. James Hotel; plans So. of Market office building)

* JOHN S. BOLLES-Al, Er, Bo; (Architect; represented Downtown Advisory Bd. on Downtown Zoning Study; Candlestick Park architect)

PHILIP S. BOONE-Er, Pe, Bo; (VP-Dancer Fitzgerald Sample; War Memorial Trustee; Pres.-Symphony Assoc.)

* PETER BOUDOURES-Al, Bo, Ta, VB, TnA; (Pres.-Olympic Federal Savings & Loan; Bd. of Permit Appeals)

JOSEPH BRANSTEN-Al, Bo, Fe, Ta; (Bd. Chmn.-MJB Coffee; Legion of Honor Trustee)

ROBERT BRANSTEN-Fr, Pe, Bo, TnA; (VP-Western Can Co.)

† WM. BRINTON-Al, Pe, VB; (Corporate atty.; former planning commissioner)

GEORGE L. BURGER-TnS, Al, Er, Me, Bo, Fe, Ta, VB; (G.L. Burger Wholesale Produce)

* JOHN R. CAHILL-Er, Ma, Ba, Ta, VB; (Cahill Construction)

ALEXANDER D. CALHOUN-Fr, Mc, Me, Pe, Bo

FRED CAMPAGNOLI-TnS, Al, Mc, Pe, Bo, Ta, VB; (Atty.; Pres.-Italian American Chamb. of Comm. Pac. Coast; War Memorial Trustee)

J. PAUL CANNIZZARO-Al, Fr, Me, Bo, Fe, Ta

JAMES J. CANNIZZARO-Al, Er, Mc, Me, Bo, Fe, Ta

* ERCOLE M. CAROSELLI-Fr, Mc, Me, Bo; (Exec. rep.-PG&E)

* ALLAN R. CARPENTER, JR.-TnS, Al, Fr, Pe, Ba, Bo, Ta, VB; (Former exec. director-Golden Gateway Center)

TOMASO CASTAGNOLA-Al, Er, Mc, Me, Bo, Fe, Ta; (Partner-Castagnola Restaurant)

GEORGE CERASE-Al, Er, Bo

JOSEPH C. CERVETTO-Al, Er, Mc, Pe; (Pres.-Cervetto Building Maintenance)

* ALLAN E. CHARLES-TnS, Bo, Fe; (Atty.-firm represents Dillingham, Hale Bros.)

H. STEPHEN CHASE-TnS, Bo, Ta, VB

JOHN YEHALL CHIN-TnS, Al, Mc, VB, TnA; (J. Chin Hearing Aid Center)

* J.K. CHOY-TnS, Fr, Ma, Mc, Me, Bo, VB; (VP & Mgr.-SF Federal Savings & Loan; SPUR; mover behind Chinese Cultural Center)

* KENNETH C. CHRISTENSEN-Ma, Ba, Bo, Ta, VB; (Sr. VP-PG&E)

* MARIO J. CIAMPI-TnS, Al, Mc, Bo, Fe, Ta, VB, TnA; (Architect; does studies for SF city contracts)

* ALFRED J. CLEARY-TnS, Ma, Ba, TnA; (Clementina Ltd.-Construction equipment)

WM. CLECAK-TnS, Al, Ta, VB; (Atty.; former Police Commissioner)

* WM. K. & JEAN COBLENTZ-Al, Fr, Me, Pe, Bo, Ta; (Wm.-UC regent; atty.; represented Ford and Tishman projects; Airport Commission, SPUR; Jean-Art Commission)

73

ARTHUR H. COLEMAN, MD-Fr, Bo, Fe, Ta; (SPUR)

GENE CONNELL-Al, Mc, Pe; (Pres.-F.E. Connell & Son, Inc.-plastering contractors)

* HUNT & MARION CONRAD-Fr, Ma, Pe, Bo, Fe; (Marion-Publicist for Ferry Port, North Waterfront projects; Hunt-Sacramento lobbyist)

* BRUCE & RUTH COWAN-Fr, Ma, Mc, Bo, Ta, TnA; (Corporate atty.)

E. MORRIS COX-Me, Bo, VB; (Pres.-Dodge & Cox-investment mgrs.)

PETER CRESCI-Al, Er, Mc; (Owner-Cresci Electric)

THOS. B. CROWLEY-TnS, Al, Bo; (Pres.-United Towing Co.; Pres.-Crowley Launch & Tugboat; VP.-Shipowner & Merchants; Pres. own oil terminals)

† RALPH K. DAVIES-TnS, Ba, Bo, VB, TnA; (Bd. Chmn.-Natomas Co.; American President Lines; deceased)

HENRY F. DAVIS-Fr, Me, Ta

† CHRISTIAN DE GUIGNE III-Ma, VB, TnA; (Stauffer Chemical; DeYoung Trustee; director of Bank of California)

JOHN F. DELURY-Fr, Mc, Fe; (Exec. Secy.-Common Social Justice)

JOHN DIGARDI-TnS, Al, Er, TnA; (Atty.)

* F. MARION DONAHOE-TnS, Pe, Ba, TnA; (Pres.-Citizens Federal Savings & Loan)

JACK K. DOOLING-Al, Fr, Ba, Bo, Ta; (Atty.)

J.C. DOUGHERTY-Al, Bo, VB

DONALD K. DOYLE-Mc, Bo, VB, TnA

* J.W. EHRLICH-TnS, Al, Er, Fr, Ta, VB; (Atty.; former Counsel for Police Officers Assoc.)

* PHILIP S. EHRLICH-TnS, Al, Er, Fr, Bo, Fe, Ta, TnA; (Corporate Atty. for Hilton Hotel)

ALBERT D. ELLEDGE-TnS, Al, Bo, Fe, Ta, VB; (Pres.-Harbor Tug & Barge; Harbor Tours; Bay Cruise; Golden Gate Scenic SS)

* BURNHAM ENERSEN-Ma, VB, TnA; (Atty.-represents outstate land interests)

† MORSE & DOROTHY ERSKINE-TnS, Al, Mc, Me, Pe, Bo, Fe, VB; (Dorothy-former BCDC Comm.; conservationist; SPUR; Morse-atty., deceased)

CHARLES W. FAY-Ma, Bo, TnA; (Prescott Merrill Turben investments)

HELEN E. FAY-Bo, Ta, VB

THOMAS E. FEENEY-Al, Bo, Ta, VB; (Atty.)

* JESSE FELDMAN-TnS, Mc, Pe, Bo, TnA; (Corporate atty.)

* WM. L. FERDON-Fr, Pe, Bo, Ta; (Atty.-Chickering & Gregory; brother of DA)

JOSEPH FINOCCHIO-TnS, Al, Bo; (Owner-Finocchio Club)

* DONALD G. FISHER-Ba, Bo, VB; (Pres.-Fisher Property Investment)

E.H. FISHER-Al, Mc, Fe

JOHN F. FIXA-Al, Pe, Ta, TnA; (Former SF Postmaster)

* MORTIMER FLEISHHACKER, SR. & JR.-TnS, Fr, Ma, Mc, Bo, Ta, VB, TnA; (Natomas Co.; American President Lines; Crocker Bank; SPUR; Planning Commission; KQED board)

* THOMAS E. FLOWERS-TnS, Al, Fr, Mc, Bo; (Pres.-Western Urban Redevelopment Investment)

J.A. FOLGER-Ma, VB, TnA; (Folger Coffee)

JAYKEE FORD, SR.-TnS, Fr, Ta; (Serv. Mgr.-City & County voting machines)

RICHARD L. FRANK-Al, Me, Bo; (Business consultant)

† JAMES & LOUISE FRANKEL-Fr, Mc, Me, Pe, Bo, Fe; (Corporate atty.; SPUR, former head of Charter Revision)

* THOMAS L. FRANKEL.-Fr, Mc, Me, Bo; (Property management)

NATHAN J. FRIEDMAN-Al, Me, Bo, Fe; (Accountant)

STANLEY M. FRIEDMAN-Ma, Bo, Ta; (Owner-Ambassador Health Club; Auctioneer)

* BEN & EUGENE FRIEND-TnS, Al, Fr, Mc, Me, Bo, Fe, Ta, VB; (Howard's
   Clothes; Eugene-former Parking Authority & now Rec. & Park; Dir. of
   Market St. Development Project)
   ALFRED FROMM-Al, Bo, Fe, Ta; (Pres.-Fromm & Sichel, distributors for Chris-
   tian Bros. Winery)
* FRANK J. GALLAGHER-Mc, Ta, VB; (Frank J. Gallagher Realty)
   LOUIS GARCIA-Al, Fr, Mc; (Human Rights Commission)
   ALFRED GEE-Al, Mc, Me, Ta
* CARL GELLERT-Al, Me, TnA; (Gellert Bros. developers-tract homes)
† FRANK & MARTHA GERBODE-Bo, Fe, Ta; (Medical doctor/Philanthropist)
   RICHARD GOLDMAN-Ma, Bo, Fe, Me, Pe; (Insurance; former PUC director;
   Haas son-in-law; Sponsor of Livingston/Blayney Waterfront Plan)
   HENRY GOLDSTEIN-Fr, Bo, VB; (Hyams & Mayers Inc.-Insurance brokers)
   ROBERT GORDON-Er, Bo, Ta, Al; (Interface Agency-executive recruitment
   & employment)
* WALTER GORDON-Al, Ba, TnA; (Gordon Realty)
   MRS. HENRY GRADY-Al, Ta, VB; (former national Democratic committee-
   woman)
* TOM GRAY-TnS, Bo, Ta;   (Shaw, Hooker Investments; former Candlestick Park
   publicist; former head of Downtown Assoc.)
   ᶜRANCIS D. GREEN-Fr, Me, Bo
   CHARLES F. GREGG-Al, Ba, Ta; (Dir.-Public Affairs for West Coast-Pan Am
   Airways)
* EVERETT GRIFFIN-TnS, Ma, VB; (Chem.developer; Merchants Exchange Bldg;
   former Redevelopment Agency Commissioner)
* PETER E. HAAS-TnS, Fr, Ta, VB, TnA; (Levi Strauss; Dir.-Crocker-Citizens
   Bank)
* WALTER A. HAAS-TnS, Bo, Fe, Ta, VB, TnA; (Bd. Chmn.-Levi Strauss; Dir.-
   PG&E)
* WALTER A. HAAS, JR.-TnS, Me, Bo, Ta; (Pres.-Levi Strauss; Dir.-BofA)
   E.E. HALL, JR.-Bo, Ta, VB
   TOMMY HARRIS-Fr, Bo, Ta; (Tommy's Joynt)
* JAMES W. HARVEY-TnS, Bo, Ta, TnA; (Atty.; Bd. of Permit Appeals)
   JOSEPH C. HAUGHEY-TnS, Ma, Ta; (Atty.)
   PATRICIA HAYES-Bo, Ta, VB
* ALVIN HAYMAN-Bo, Fe, Ta; (Hayman Companies-real estate developer)
* ROBERT M. HAYNIE-Al, Fr, Me, Bo; (Haas & Haynie Construction)
† CLARENCE HELLER-Me, Pe, Bo; (Heller Estate)
* M. JUSTIN HERMAN-Bo, Fe, Ta; (Late exec. director of Redevelopment
   Agency; deceased)
* WAYNE S. HERTZKA-Er, Bo, Ta; (Hertzka & Knowles architects)
   F.J. HERZ, DDS-TnS, Er, Ta
   EDGAR A. HILLS-TnS, Ma, Ta, TnA; (Hills of California-transportation
   consultants)
* H.H. HILP-TnS, Me, Pe, Bo, Fe, Ta, TnA; (H.H. Hilp ᴾrospect Farms-real estate)
† FRANK HINMAN MD-TnS, Fr, Pe, Bo; (Pres.-Russian Hill Improvement Assn.;
   SPUR)
† JOSEPH C. HOUGHTELING-Fr, Mc, Me, Fe; (Publisher of weeklies)
* THOMAS HSIEH-Al, Er, Bo, Ta, VB; (Architect; Art Commission)
   J.W. Hull-Al, Me, VB; (VP-PT&T; Dir.-Crocker-Citizens)
   TEVIS & JEAN JACOBS-Fr, Bo, Fe, TnA; (Tevis-Corporate atty.; Jean-Family
   Service Agency Director)
   AGAR JAICKS-Fr, Bo, Fe; (Democratic County Committee head; KGO radio)
   GEORGE F. JEWETT, JR.-Bo, Ta, VB; (VP-Potlatch Forests Inc.)

WALTER S. JOHNSON-TnS, Al, Ma, Ta, VB; (Retired Bd. Chmn.-American Forest Products Corp.)

CHRIS K. KATON-Mc, Me, Ta; (Retired exec.-Spreckles Dairy)

ANDREW KATTEN-Al, Fr, Mc, Bo

MARION M. KAUFMAN-Fr, Fe, Ta

* VERNON KAUFMAN-TnS, Al, Fr, Me, Fe, VB, TnA; (Pres.-Safe Cut Inc.; V. Kaufman Co.-Comm. real estate; Advisory Bd.-SF State; City's official greeter)

FRANCIS KEESLING, JR.-TnS, Mc, Me, TnA; (Bd. Chmn.-West Coast Life Ins. Co.)

JOSEPH I. KELLY-Fr, Fe, Ta; (Atty.; ex-Gov. Brown's son-in-law)

NOEL KELLY-Ba, Bo, Ta

CHARLES KENDRICK-TnS, Ma, Bo, VB, TnA; (Bd. Chmn.-Schlage Lock Co.; deceased)

DONALD B. KING-Al, Er, Mc, Pe, Bo, Fe, Ta, TnA; (Atty.)

*† DANIEL E. KOSHLAND-TnS, Fr, Bo, Fe, TnA; (Levi Strauss; Dir.-Wells Fargo)

WM. B. KUDER-Al, Fr, Bo

SAMUEL A. LADAR-VB, Fr, TnA; (Atty.)

* ROGER LAPHAM-TnS, Ba, Ma, Me; (Insurance exec.; North Waterfront principal; influential BART principal)

IVER C. LARSON-Bo, Fr, Ta; (Exec. VP -Natl. Safety Council)

WM. LAZAR-Mc, Bo, Ta; (Pres.-Luxor Cabs)

MEL LEE-Mc, Me, Ta

BEN K. LERER-Bo, Fe, Fr, Me, Ta; (Partner-Joseph Lerer & Sons atty.)

BEN LEVIN-VB, Fr, Ta; (Owner-General Theatrical Co.; Pres.-Empire Theater)

ERNEST LILIENTHAL-Al, Bo, Ma, Me; (Pres.-Haas Bros.-wholesale liquors)

* ROBERT P. LILIENTHAL-TnA, Bo, Fe, Me, Mc, Al, Fr ; (Pres.-Presidio Heights Assn. of Neighbors; former planning commissioner; Chmn.-Citizens Advisory Commission SF Renewal Progress; owns extensive SF property)

† MRS. SALLY HELLYER LILIENTHAL-Fr, Me, Bo, Fe; (Contributor to liberal/ conservation causes)

PUTNAM LIVERMORE-Ba, Ma, TnA, TnS; (Atty.-Chickering & Gregory; State Republican Chairman)

SINCLAIR LOUIE-Al, Ta, TnA; (Owner-Mgr.-Empress Fine Arts; Canton Bazaar; Pay Less Imports; Bargain Bazaar; China Bazaar; Cathay Bazaar)

* WM. LOWENBERG-Al, Bo, Fr, Me; (Lowenberg Realty Co.)

FRANCIS L. LUCCHETTI DDS-Me, Bo, Fe

LLOYD D. LUCKMANN-TnS, Mc, Bo, Ta, VB; (USF-Dean of Arts & Sciences)

JAMES J. LUDWIG-Al, Bo, Ta, TnA, TnS; (Gen. Mgr.-Saks Fifth Ave.; Bd. Chmn.- S.F. Ballet)

* LOUIS R. LURIE-VB, Bo, Fe, Ma, Ta, TnA; (Mark Hopkins Hotel; Curran Theatre; Lurie Associates-Major downtown property holdings)

THOMAS LYNCH-Bo, Fr, Me; (Former State Atty. General)

* RICHARD M. MACFARLANE-VB, Bo, Ta; (VP-Castle & Cook; Mgr.-Oceanic Properties)

STEVEN D. MAFFINI-Al, Er, Pe; (Atty.)

* CYRIL MAGNIN-VB, Al, Bo, Fr, Ta, TnA, TnS, Mc; (J. Magnin; Port Commissioner; ex-Chamber president)

* DONALD MAGNIN-Al, Bo, Ta, VB; (VP -J. Magnin; Cyril's son: Parking Authority)

JOHN WARD MAILLIARD- VB, Al, Ba (Dir.-Wells Fargo; Chmn.-Mailliard & Schmiedell food brokers & importers; former Police Commissioner)

* ALEXANDER MAISIN-Er, Fr, Ta, TnA; (Industrial Properties; Maisin-Taylor Assoc.-general contractors)

WM. M. MALONE-VB, Al, Me, Ta, TnS, Er; (Long time Democratic leader)

EDWARD T. MANCUSO-Bo, Fr, Ta; (Public defender)

GERALD D. MARCUS-Fr, Mc, Bo; (Atty.)

* VICTOR L. MARCUS-Bo, Me, Ta; (Exec. VP.-Milton Meyer & Co.)

* ALAN S. MAREMONT-Fr, Me, Bo, Ta; (Mgr.-Kate Maremont Foundation/ Philanthropist)

* MELVILLE MARX-TnS, Me, Pe, Bo, Fe; (Co-owner-H.H. Hilp Prospect Farms- real estate)

* WM. MCDONNELL-Al,Ba,Bo,Me; (Pres.Tarantino's Restaurant; Former Pres.- City PUC; head of the Airport Commisssion)

* GARRETT MC ENERNEY-VB, Al, Bo, Ta, TnA, TnS; (Examiner atty.; BofA; Dir.-PT&T; DeYoung Trustee)

* RALPH MCGILL-Al, Bo, Me, TnA; (Realty & insurance)

* JOHN MERRILL-Bo, Ma, Me, TnS; (Skidmore, Owings and Merrill architects; SPUR; Chamber; Bay Area Council director)

A.H. MEYER-Fe, Ma, TnA

FRED J. MEYER-Bo, Fe, TnA

OTTO E. MEYER-Bo, Me, Ta; (Pres.-P. Masson Vineyards)

WILSON MEYER-VB, Bo, Fr, Ma, Pe, Ta, TnS, Tna; (Wilson & George Meyer Co.-distributors of chemcials, fertilizers & plastics; Dir. Wells Fargo; War Memorial trustee)

RICHARD K. MILLER-Er, Bo, Ta; (Police commissioner)

ROBERT WATTS MILLER-Er, Mc, VB; (Bd. Chmn.-Pacific Lighting; Dir.-Wells Fargo, Fibreboard, Standard Oil of Calif.; Bd.-Symphony & Opera; deceased)

FRANK MINAHAN-VB, Al, Bo, Fr, Ta; (Pres.-S.F. Firefighters)

HENRY R. MORRIS-Bo, Fr, Ma, Me, Ta, Mc; (Pres.-Salesian Boys Club)

BENJAMIN MORTARA-Al, Er, Ta

WM. F. MORTON-VB, Bo, Ta; (Former VP & Gen. Mgr.-Crocker Land Co.; retired)

JOHN P. MOSCONE-Bo, Ma, Me, Ta, TnA; (Pres.-Golden Gate Disp. Co.)

ETSUKO MURAYAMA-Bo, Me, Ta

DONALD K. NEGI-Bo, Fr, Me, Ta, Er; (Deputy city attorney)

CHARLES L. O'CONNOR-Al, Bo, Fr, Ta, Mc; (VP-Yellow Cab Co.)

* S.E. ONORATO-Al, Bo, TnA, TnS; (Owner-Flood Garage; Exchange Center Garage; Dir.-Portsmouth Sq. Garage; Downtown Assn. director)

WM. ORRICK JR.-Al, Bo, Ma; (Atty.-his law firm passes on all municipal bonds; former US anti-trust atty. under Kennedy; SF Foundation director)

JACK H. OLIVE-VB, Fr, Pe, Mc; (Atty.)

FRANK L. PAGGANNINI-Me, Bo, VB

J.A. PARDINI-TnS, Al, Pe; (Atty.)

* PIERO PATRI-Fr, Me, Fe; (Architect)

E.R. PETERS-Al, Bo, Fe; (Public relations)

* LOUIS PETRI-Al, Bo, Ta, Er, TnS; (Bd. Chmn.-United Vintners; Dir.-BofA; City PUC Commissioner)

WM. L. PORTER-Fe, Fr, Me; (Corporate atty.)

WM. A. PRICE MD-Fr, Ta, TnS

* THOMAS K. PROCTOR-VB, Bo, Me; (Sr. VP-Coldwell, Banker)

FRANK QUINN-Al, Fe, Fr; (Former head of Human Rights Commission)

SALVATOR REINA-VB, Bo, Fr

H.B. REYNOLDS-Bo, Fe, Ma

* QUENTIN REYNOLDS-Ba, Bo, Ta, TnA; (Pres.-Safeway; Bay Area Council director)

* J. ALFRED RIDER MD-VB, Bo, Fr, TnS

ARTHUR ROCK-Al, Bo, Me; (Investment broker; chief money-raiser for McClos- key for President)

* DAVID LEIGH RODGERS MD-Bo, Fr, Ta
  MILTON L. ROSENBERG MD-VB, Al, Fe, Fr
*† WM. MATSON ROTH-VB, Bo, Fe, Fr, TnS, TnA; (Roth properties; Ghirardelli
  Sq. developer)
* OLIVER ROUSSEAU-VB, TnS, Ta, Al, Bo, Fe; (Oliver Rousseau Homes; City
  PUC Commissioner)
* JAMES J. RUDDEN-VB, Al, Bo, Me, Ta, Er, TnS; (VP-Ray Oil Burner Co.; SF
  Port Commission)
† MADELEINE HAAS RUSSELL-Al, Bo, Fe, Fr, Pe, Ta, Mc; (Major Stockholder-
  Levi Strauss; War Memorial trustee; SPUR)
  DAVID SACHS MD-Fe, Fr, Me, Pe
  FRANKLIN A. SANCHEZ-Fr, Mc, Me
* ANGELO SANGIACOMO-Ba, Ta, Er; (Builder)
  S.M. SAROYAN-VB, Al, Fe, Pe, Ta, Er, TnS
* JOHN E. SCHAEFFER-Al, Ba, Ma; (Atty.-Cooper, White & Cooper-KRON/
  Chronicle attorneys)
* ALBERT SCHLESINGER-Bo, Fe, Me, Ta, TnA, Mc, TnS; (Yerba Buena Devel-
  oper; former Pres.-Convention & Visitors Bureau)
* ADOLPH P. SCHUMAN-Al, Bo, Fe, Me, Mc; (Pres.-Lilli Ann dresses; major
  Democratic contributor)
† E. ROBERT SCROFANI-Fe, Fr, Me; (Teacher; SF Tomorrow)
* CHARLES H. SEDAM-VB, Al, Bo, Ba, Ta; (VP-PG&E)
* PAUL H. SEDWAY-Fe, Fr, Me; (Partner-Sedway & Cooke-planning consultants)
* WALTER SHORENSTEIN-VB, Al, Bo, Fe, Fr, Me, Ta, TnS, TnA; (Milton Meyer
  real estate; former Park & Rec.)
  ALBERT SHUMATE MD-Al, Pe, Ta, TnA, Mc, TnS; (Trustee-Calif. Historical
  Society)
  SOL SILVERMAN-Al, Bo, Fe, Fr, Ta, TnS; (Atty.)
  STANLEY H. SINTON, JR.-Bo, Fe, Pe, Ta, TnA, TnS; (Pres.-DN&E Walter & Co.-
  personal holding co.; SPUR)
  DR. & MRS. ABRAHAM SIRBU-Me, Bo, Fe
  STANTON SOBEL-Al, Bo, Fr, Me, TnA, Mc, Fe, Ta; (Sobel Liquors)
  LOUIS SPADIA-Bo, Me, TnA; (SF 49ers)
  LT. COL. ROBT. SPIEGEL-Er, Me, Fe
† WALTER K. STANTON MD-Er, Mc, VB; (SF Tomorrow/Conservationist)
  HAROLD STELLING- Er, Ta, TnA
  MRS. CARL W. STERN-VB, Al, Ta; (Carl-Pres.-Lawson, Williams & Stern-invest-
  ment securities; SPUR)
  SAMUEL B. STEWART-Ba, Bo, Ta, TnS; (BofA; Chamber)
  DANIEL E. STONE-Al, Er, Fe; (Investment securities)
* BEN H. SWIG- Al, Bo, Fr, Me, TnS; (Fairmont Hotel; major downtown property
  holdings)
* MELVIN M. SWIG-VB, Al, Bo, Fe, Fr, Me, Mc, Er; (Fairmont Hotel; Ben's son)
  JOSEPH C. TARANTINO-TnS, Fr, Bo, Ta
  JAMES F. THACHER-Bo, Ma, Pe, TnS; (Atty.; SPUR)
  QUAILAND TOM-Fr, Me, Mc
  M.C. URY-Bo, Fe, Fr
  CHARLES T. VAN DEUSEN-VB, Bo, Ta
  JOHN A. VIETOR-Bo, Fe, Fr; (San Francisco Magazine publisher)
  LES VOGEL, JR.-VB, Ma, TnA; (Les Vogel Chevrolet)
  MRS. ELKAN C. VOORSANGER-Fr, Mc, Me

  JACOB VOORSANGER-Er, Pe, Bo
  YORI WADA-Al, Bo, Fe, Fr; (Exec. dir.-YMCA; Social Services Commission)
  WM. R. WALLACE-Al, Bo, Ta

```
* BROOKS WALKER-VB, Me, Pe, TnA; (Pres.-Shasta Forests Co.; VP -North Water-
    front Assoc.; Chairman of US Leasing; Dir.-Leslie Salt)
  J. WARNOCK WALSH-VB, Al, Bo, TnS; (Acct. Exec.-E.F. Hutton & Co.-invest-
    ments)
  MRS. JACKIE WALSH-Mc, TnS, Fe; (Head of Waitress Union)
  STEPHEN WALTER-VB, Al, Bo, Fr, Ta, TnA, TnS; (Exec. VP-DN&E Walter &
    Co.-personal holding co.)
* TELLER WEINMANN-Bo, Fe, Me, Ta; (VP-Downtown Assoc.; Pres.-Emporium-
    retired)
  WORLEY K. WONG-Bo, Fe, Ta; (Architec )
* J.D. WORTHINGTON-VB, Bo, Ma, Ta; (VP Eng.-PG&E)
* HAROLD L. ZELLERBACH-VB, Bo, Fe, Fr, Ta, TnA, Mc, TnS; (Crown Zeller-
    bach; head of Art Commission; Legion of Honor trustee)
```

Here are other major links in the relationship between the officials, their highrise voting record and their land-connected campaign contributors.

1. Sue Hestor's list of major contributors (to three or more winning candidates) showed a substantial number of land-connected
contributors.

2. Some big land/development-connected companies put in lots
of money in many campaigns through their directors and their
highly paid corporate officers. For example, at least 24 PG&E executives contributed to 12 of the 14 campaigns studied by Sue Hestor.

This is corporate investment on a large and calculated scale
from a private utility that not only profits enormously from high-
rise/high density policies (see Petrakis, p. 87), but puts enormous
political influence behind these policies in San Francisco (see

*PG&E's campaign contributions: John F. Bonner (Ba), executive VP of PG&E;
Donald Bell (F, Ba), VP of finance; Howard B. Brown (Ma, Ba), VP of electric opera-
tions; F.A. Peter (Al), VP and controller; C.E. Ginochio (Ba), senior VP; E.H. Fisher
(Al, Me, Fe), VP of gas operations; R.H. Petersen (Mc), executive VP; J.F. Roberts,
Jr. (Ba, Fe), VP for rates and valuations; F.T. Searle (Al), VP and general counsel;
C.H. Sedam (Al, Ba, Bo, Ta), VP for general construction.

J.D. Worthington (Ma, Bo, Ta, VB), VP for engineering; J.F. Taylor (Ba, Ta),
secretary; R.B. Dewey (Al, Ta), assistant to the president; J.C. Morrissey (Al, Er),
associate general counsel; W.E. Johns (VB), assistant general counsel; M.A. MacKillop
(Al), assistant general counsel; C.T. Van Deusen (Bo, Ta, VB), assistant general counsel; K.C. Christensen (Ma, Ba, Bo, Ta, VB), senior VP, resigned in July, 1970, to become director of B of A's real estate investment trust.

Ransom M. Cook (Bo), director of PG&E, Wells Fargo; Walter A. Haas (Bo, Fe,
TnS), director of PG&E; Porter Sesnon (Ta, VB, Ma, TnA), director; Emmet G. Solomon (Ba), director of PG&E and PT&T; Carl F. Wente (VB), director of PG&E and
former president of B of A.

PT&T's campaign contributions: Robert M. Cunningham (VB), VP of PT&T and
president of the California Taxpayers Assn., powerful lobbying group in Sacramento
for utilities, banks and oil companies; John A. Sutro (Al, Ba), general attorney; J.S.
Dills (TnS), VP and general manager; Walter A. Haas, Jr. (Me, Bo, Ta, TnS), director
and head of Levi Strauss; Jerome A. Hull (Al, Me, VB), director and president; Emmet G. Solomon (Ba), director of PT&T and PG&E.

If you raise the money, you get the votes

	Votes	Total Campaign Expenditures
1967 Mayoralty Campaign		
ALIOTO	110,405	$395,975
DOBBS	94,504	289,742
MORRISON	40,436	45,293
1969 Supervisor Campaign		
FEINSTEIN	93,519	81,368
TAMARAS	92,251	74,142
BOAS	91,135	85,277
BARBAGELATA	82,331	33,329
VON BEROLDINGEN	80,996	59,320
BLAKE	80,566	54,629
MORRISON	73,094	65,926
CHINN	70,513	36,256
LAU	55,927	14,000
ROURKE	41,872	12,170
1967 Supervisor Campaign		
ERTOLA	130,038	46,732*
FRANCOIS	112,157	35,944*
MCCARTHY	110,279	30,116
MENDELSOHN	101,776	38,272
PELOSI	99,033	33,380
MAILLIARD	92,183	33,776

Source: SF Registrar of Voters
*Reported income, not expenses

Above, the campaign spending and total votes of all leading candidates in recent elections. With a couple of explicable exceptions, the amount of money a candidate spent was in direct proportion to how many votes he or she got.

1967 Mayor: One, two, three. Dobbs might be mayor if he spent more money. Alioto's charisma raises big money fast, $100,000 at a crack at a Swig fund-raiser.

1969 Sup: Dianne Feinstein's "miracle" victory was less a miracle than it was a testament to her ability to raise money. She spent the second amount. Von Beroldingen spent the fifth amount of money and came in fifth. Blake spent the sixth amount and came in sixth.

There were two real exceptions: Morrison, who incurred the wrath of downtown forces because of his 10-1 anti-highrise votes and ran behind his spending. Barbagelata (who enjoyed a big bullet, vote-just-for-me-vote), who ran ahead of his spending.

1967 Sup: The only real exception in the top six was Mendelsohn (who ran behind his spending probably because this was his first time out) and William Newsom (who came in 8th after spending the fourth amount of money). However, Beeman and O'Shea helped nail down the rule of thumb: both were incumbents, but they lost because they could only spend $22,000 and $27,000 respectively. Beeman ran 9th and spent the 9th amount of money, O'Shea ran 7th and spent the 7th amount of money.

3. Many important land/development contributors gave to less than three campaigns.[1]

4. At least 25 land/development-connected contributors put money ($18,531 reported) into the 1970 assessor's campaign for Joseph Tinney, the incumbent, who smothered one weak candidate 159,609 to 45,797.[2]

5. At least 13 hotels and six realty firms put money into the $17,070 campaign for George Reilly, running for reelection in 1969 for the State Board of Equlization from San Francisco.

6. Only Morrison and von Beroldingen of the major candidates listed amounts given by each contributor (the rest merely listed names), but it was obvious much of the candidates' support came from land/development interests. For example, John Barbagelata of Barbagelata Realty, who reported expenses of 33,329, collected contributions from 11 developers/realtors.[3]

[1]Prentis Cobb Hale of Broadway Hale (TnA); Donald Pritzger of the Hyatt House (Bo); Architect John Portman of the Embarcadero Center (Al, Ta); John Ritchie of the Planning Commission and Ritchie & Ritchie real estate (Me); Stephen D. Bechtel (VB, Ma) and Kenneth Bechtel (VB) of Bechtel Construction; Fred Merrill of Fireman's Fund (Ba, Ma); R.P. Cooley of Wells Fargo (Bo, Fr); Walter Newman, Cyril Magnin's son-in-law and Chairman of the Planning Commission (Al); Emmet G. Solomon of Crocker Bank (Al, Ba) the late Carl Wente of the Bank of America (VB), etc.

[2]Among Tinney's land/development connected contributors in the "no contest" race: Gerson Bakar, Bruce Cowan, F. Everett Cahill, F. Marion Donohue, Philip S. Ehrlich, Jr., Mortimer Fleishhacker, Jr., Carl and Fred Gellert, Walter Haas, Peter Haas, Prentis Cobb Hale Vernon Kaufman, Louis Lurie, Cyril Magnin, Garrett McEnerney II, John Moscone, S.E. Onorato, William Roth, Walter Shorenstein, Albert E. Schlesinger, Harold Zellerbach (identification in the contributor list). Tinney also listed 49 business contributors and attorneys (Les Vogel Chevrolet, Hale Bros., Redlicks, Ghirardelli Square, Chickering & Gregory Attys., Heller Ehrman, White & McAuliffe Attys. and Jacobs, Sills & Coblentz).

[3]Roger Boas collected contributions from such sources as 44 labor unions and 2 law firms.

Ertola: 3 buildings/garages, 11 real estate/construction firms (including Buckbee Thorne); 3 unions; 4 law firms (including Chickering & Gregory).

Francois: 22 labor unions, Eureka Fed. Savings & Loan, 1 building firm, 1 contractor, 22 unions. (Francois' fund-raising dinners for his 1971 judge and supervisor's race indicate heavy development-connected support.)

Mendelsohn: United California Bank, Coldwell Banker & Co., 8 unions.

Tamaras: 5 banks (Wells Fargo, Crocker), 26 buildings/hotels/garages (Mark Hopkins, Sheraton Palace, Cannery, St. Francis, Ghirardelli Square, Hilton, San Francisco), 25 real estate/construction firms (Hertzka & Knowles architects, Cahill Construction, Allied Properties), 35 labor unions, 5 law firms (Tobin & Tobin, Chickering & Gregory).

Von Beroldingen: 5 buildings/hotels (Ghirardelli Square, Wharfside, Russ Building), 12 real estate/construction firms (Bechtel, Buckbee Thorne, Hertzka & Knowles), 19 labor unions, 6 law firms (including $100 from Cooper, White and Cooper Attys., perhaps in appreciation for VB's valiant fight, as head of the board's finance committee, to exempt the Examiner/Chronicle as "failing newspapers" from the city's gross receipts tax. CWC represents the Chronicle and Chronicle owners.

Feinstein, McCarthy, Pelosi and Alioto reported no contributions from labor or business. Note: individual contributions listed on p.72

Why are there more muckmakers than there are muckrakers?

STOP THE PRESSES: In Alvin Duskin's full page advertisement on campaign contributions, the Chronicle attorneys censored out a reference to Transamerica and how it had whisked its Pyramid Building plans through all inspection points in City Hall (many of them in one day) in a fraction of the time it would take an ordinary citizen.

This Transamerica reference would "defame a corporation," explained the man from Cooper, White and Cooper/Chron/KRON/Western Communication/Allied Properties/Pacific Lighting/Ortega/Hacienda/ Parrott Investment Companies.

The media in San Francisco has consistently underplayed and underreported the anti-highrise movement while, at the same time, giving virtually every news and editorial break to the Chamber's pro-development forces.

There are good non-editorial reasons for this, notably the fact that much of the media in San Francisco is owned and controlled by owners involved in land/development and almost all media management is directly tied in as members and directors of the Chamber/Bay Area Council/Downtown Association bloc promoting highrise/high density development.

● KPIX, for example, has broadcast several Lou Simon/Bill Osterhaus editorials supporting the Chamber and criticizing Duskin. Note: Westinghouse owns KPIX and Westinghouse is a major local developer

(half owner of the huge Westinghouse/Deane & Deane development project in Half Moon Bay) and a major supplier of BART. More: Simon himself is a director of the Chamber, sits on the Chamber's key economic development committee with Ben Swig (Fairmont), John Bonner (PG&E), Edmund Hartsook (Standard Oil) and Johnson S. Bogart (Coldwell, Banker realty), is a Bay Area Council governor, is the 1971 president of the San Francisco Visitors and Convention Bureau.

● ABC/KGO owns Marine World, a marshland fill project in Leslie Salt's Redwood Shores development off Belmont. KRON/Chron/Ex have extensive real estate holdings. Kaiser owns KBHK and KFOG. Signal Oil owns 49% of KSFO.

● Almost all station managers are members of the Chamber and/or Downtown Association. All television and radio stations with major news operations (KTVU, KRON, KPIX, KGO, KCBS, KABL) are represented on the Chamber's "communications committee."*

● It's hard for broadcasters to talk critically about highrise with their 981 foot television tower (KRON, KTVU, KGO, KPIX) in the middle of residential San Francisco from Mt. Sutro. The broadcasters agreed to say nothing publicly about the tower. The Chronicle's law firm, Cooper,

*The hard-hitting committee: Ivan Ladizinsky (chairman), KTVU promotion director; Roy Heatly, KRON news manager; Robert Vainowski, who writes radio editorials 32 stories up in KCBS's new 1 Embarcadero Center suite; Jerry Minnucci, KGO-TV promotion director; Knowles Hall, KABL general manager, and Len Schlosser, KPIX-TV director of public affairs.

The pitch: to "get across to the public through the media," said Ladizinsky, "that the Chamber of Commerce is an involved body and not simply interested in the business establishment." Added the Chamber's Scot Stewart, the committee is not "trying to push the Chamber of Commerce but rather attempting to tell the public that the Chamber is known for other things besides big buildings and high taxes." Is this to "change" the Chamber's image, we asked? No, to "improve" the Chamber's image, Stewart replied. Note: the committee was started last winter as the anti-highrise movement gained momentum and the Chamber was promptly tagged as the biggest heavy on the boards.

The method: 30 second color spots as Chamber public service announcements, worked up free by the committee, produced free by KTVU, distributed free by KRON, run free for the Chamber by stations as PSA announcements. (Equal time, anyone? Complaints to the FCC for using PSAs for image-improving, political purposes for the Chamber? The point: two University of California journalism students produced a documentary on the San Francisco highrise, but it was rejected by KRON/Chron and KPIX/Westinghouse on equal-time grounds.)

Project No. 1: a campaign to "remind the public" that the Chamber was influential in rerouting traffic downtown through one-way streets and thereby lowering congestion, Ladizinsky said. (Question: Is it the lack of one-way streets that's been causing congestion downtown? We thought it had to do with such Chamber-promoted things as highrise, BART and more freeways.)

The next big committee project: to compile a list of Chamber members who are expert in their business fields and ready to talk to the press "on any issues that should arise on a 24-hour basis," Ladizinsky said. Added he, "When the media needs to consult an expert, the Chamber will be ready to help."

Results: the PSAs are "getting good play, you can be sure of it," said Ladizinsky. Added Stewart: the committee has been so successful it will be expanded to include every broadcaster "of any note." Chamber membership, he explained, "is a must for media bios."

White and Cooper, handles the legal work for the four station combine, and routinely refers all tower questions to Clifford Kirtland, Jr. of Cox Broadcasting in Atlanta, Ga., owner of KTVU. Kirtland, chairman of Sutro Tower, Inc., didn't answer or reply to our phone queries about the tower.

● Chron/KRON/Ex are owners extensively involved in land and development in San Francisco and in the state.*(The Ex/Chron is locked in a joint agency monopoly by a special act of Congress which allows them, as "failing newspapers," to fix prices, divide profits and allocate markets.) Both have South of Market holdings that were gerrymandered out of the Yerba Buena Redevelopment project (See Redevelopment, p.202). Hearst owns 140,000 acres of land in the state, mostly in Kern, San Bernardino and Fresno Counties.

Trust me.

*Examiner publisher Charles Gould and Chronicle publisher Charles deYoung Thieriot are governors of the Bay Area Council. The Chronicle family DeYoung and heirs largely own and control the Parrott Investment Co., which got $680,994 in 1970 rental income from land it owns benath the Emporium on Market St. In 1970, Parrott received over $53,000 from the sale of natural gas to PG&E. Parrott's secretary-treasurer, George F. Newman, is an influential member of the Downtown Association. The Joseph Tobin wing of the Chronicle clan controls the Hibernia Bank. The major Chronicle officer and stockholder is Joseph Tobin, son-in-law of M.H. DeYoung and an uncle of Thieriot and of Sheldon Cooper, senior partner in Chronicle law firm.

The Chronicle heirs are heavily invested in Pacific Lighting Corp. (which sells natural gas to much of Southern California) and in Allied Properties (which owns or controls $35 million in real estate and wheels and deals with big downtown properties: Clift Hotel, 111 Sutter, 600-640 Battery, 79 New Montgomery, Geary and Mason St. Building). Cooper sits on Allied's board of directors (which interlocks Fireman's Fund, Pacific Far East Lines/Natomas, Bank of America, Wells Fargo, Bank of California, PT&T) and on PLC's board (which interlocks with Fireman's Fund, PT&T, Foremost McKesson, Bank of America, Wells Fargo). Chronicle family also owns 60,000 acres of California land through subsidiaries. Its Hacienda Invest. Co. subsidiary receives payments for as much as $50,000/month from Getty Oil Co. leases).

The Chronicle owners also have substantial investments in several big S.F. corporations; for example, the $16 million estate of Helen DeYoung Cameron, a Chronicle owner who died in 1968, showed investments of $2,499,325.88 in these SF/Chamber-connected corporations: 8,600 shares of Allied Properties/State Guaranty Aux. ($540,350.00); 7,731 shares of Crocker Bank ($360,485.44); 735 shares of Del Monte Corp. ($20,543.06); 1,080 shares of Fibreboard Corp. ($29,497.50); 5,775 shares of PG&E ($208,621.88); 11,320 shares of Pacific Lighting ($307,762.50); 6,601 shares of Pacific Telephone ($138,208.44); 1,000 shares of Safeway Stores ($26,000.00); 3,059 shares of Standard Oil (Cal.) ($250,245.56); 702 shares of Wells Fargo Bank ($35,626.50); 500 shares of Westinghouse/KPIX ($28,812.50).

What is the Corporate Power Behind Highrise?

1. The political/economic power behind highrise starts with the concentration of power in SF's biggest landowners and property taxpayers. Almost all are involved in highrise construction/development.

The top 9 landowners: (1) Southern Pacific - 335 acres; (2) Olympic Club - 156; (3) Metropolitan Life - 146; (4) SF Golf & Country Club - 144; (5) PG&E - 100; (6) Sunset Scavenger - 84; (7) Stoneson Development - 66; (8) Bethlehem Steel - 33; (9) PT&T - 25.

TOTAL: 1,089 acres. Thus, these nine largest private landowners own 7.3% of the city's total acreage, about 35% of the city's choice acreage. (Assessor survey from 1970-71 rolls.)

The top 10 property taxpayers: (1) PT&T - $7,784,819 in property taxes; (2) PG&E - $7,046,032; (3) Bank of America - $3,254,458; (4) Metropolitan Life - $1,859,082; (5) Southern Pacific - $1,598,360; (6) Stoneson - $1,057,992; (7) Golden Gateway - $1,042,378; (8) Hilton Hotels - $1,012,780; (9) Wells Fargo - $929,450; (10) Fairmont Hotel - $783,747.

TOTAL: $26,378,098 in property taxes. Total property taxes paid city-wide: $161,800,000. Thus, these 10 largest taxpayers pay 16.3% of all property taxes collected by the City of San Francisco. (Assessor survey from 1970-1971 rolls.)

2. This chart shows the interconnection of major corporate powers in the Chamber (through interlocking directors) and how they interconnect with four major highrise groups—the Chamber (fighting the big public highrise battles), the Bay Area Council (a super chamber pushing BART, regional freeways, the Southern Crossing, development-dominated regional government), the Downtown Association and SPUR. Also: their corporate and individual director/executive contributions to local political campaigns. (See Guardian newspapers for more extensive power structure analysis.)

KEY TO INTERLOCKING DIRECTORATES OF MAJOR

CHAMBER OF COMMERCE CORPORATIONS

(1) Interlocks with other companies on Chamber Board of Directors

(2) Interlocks with big, local companies not on Chamber Board

(3) Interlocks with the four big banks

SYMBOLS:

Has directors on Chamber of Commerce (C), SPUR (S), Bay Area Council (BAC), Downtown Association (DA).

*BofA: (world's largest; 3rd largest SF prop. taxpayer): (1) interlocks with FF--2; Emp.-Cap.--2; PG&E--2; PT&T--4; Foremost--2; Standard. (2) DiGiorgio; Kaiser Indus., Steel, Cement, Alum.; Litton; Calif. Canners & Growers; Producers; Cot. Oil; Calif. Pacif. Util.; Bekins; Sears; Dillingham; Getty Oil; Pacif. Mutual; L. Strauss; Times-Mirror; United Vintners; Leslie Salt; Pacif. Light.; Pacif. Veg. Oil. (C,S,BAC,DA)

*BofC: (23rd largest in US): (1) interlocks with PG&E--2; PT&T; SP; DM--4; Standard; Fibreboard. (2) Safeway--2; Shell; West. Union; Cahill Construction; Potlatch Forests; West. Pacif. RR.; Stauffer Chem.; Hyster; Pacif. Lumber; Coldwell Banker. (C,BAC)

+*CROCKER: (12th largest in US): (1) interlocks with FF--2; Bechtel; PG&E--2; PT&T--2; SP; DM--2; Natomas; Fibreboard. (2) Crown Z.; Berry Oil; Max Factor; Moore Drydock; FMC; Allied Prop.; Marcona; Pacif. Nat. Life. (S,BAC)

*DEL MONTE (DM): (1) interlocks with FF--2; Standard; PG&E;PT&T; Emp.-Cap.; Transam. (2) Allied Prop. (3) Wells Fargo--2; Crocker--2; BofC--4. (C,BAC)

*EMPORIUM-CAPWELL: (owns 28 dept. stores thru Broadway-Hale merger) (1) interlocks with PT&T; Foremost; DM. (2) DiGiorgio; Pacif. Veg. Oil; Leslie Salt; Consol. Freight. (3) BofA--2. (C,DA,BAC)

*FIREMAN'S FUND: (owned by Amer. Express): (1) interlocks with PG&E--2; DM--2; Pacific Far East; Dillingham. (2) Allied Prop.; Kaiser Steel, Alum., Cement Indus.; Pacific Light. (3) BofA, Crocker. (C,BAC)

*NATOMAS/PACIF. FAR EAST/AMER. PRES. LINES: (1) PFEL interlocks with FF. (2) both with Allied Prop.; Transam. (3) Natomas with Crocker, BofC. (C,BAC)

*PG&E: (5th largest SF landowner; largest private util. in US): (1) interlocks with FF--2; PT&T; Foremost; DM. (2) DiGiorgio; Safeway; L. Strauss; PIE; Hewlett-Packard. (C,S,DA,BAC)

*PT&T: (9th largest SF landowner; owned by AT&T--world's largest corp.): (1) interlocks with PG&E--2; DM; Emp.-Cap.; Fibreboard. (2) L. Strauss; Pac. Light.; Pacif. Veg. Oil; DiGiorgio. (3) BofA--4, Crocker--2, Wells Fargo; (C,S,DA, BAC)

+*SOUTHERN PACIF. RR (SP): (largest US RR; largest SF landowner) (1) interlocks with Bechtel--2; Fibreboard. (2) Safeway. (3) Crocker, BofC. (C,BAC)

+*WELLS FARGO: (11th largest in US; 9th largest SF prop. taxpayer): (1) interlocks with Bechtel; PG&E--2; PT&T;DM--2; Transam. (2) Aetna Life; Castle & Cooke; Safeway; Hewlett-Packard; Utah Construction; Firestone; Folger; Northrup; Mailliard & Schmeidell; Stanford U.; Pacif. Light.; Ampex.; C&H; Homestake Mining; Tenneco; Allied Prop. (C,S,DA,BAC)

+Direct campaign contributions from corporation
*Campaign contributions through corporate officers

3. Conclusion: The extent of tight interlock between the land/development forces, together with their economic/political concentration of power and their Chamber/BAC/DA/SPUR front, constitutes the formidable and highly organized bloc of power behind San Francisco development. That's why Duskin titled his full page ad just three weeks before the 1971 election, "Hold the confetti even if 'T' wins— the builders still run the city."

4. Who profits from highrise?

PG&E and PT&T, among other big firms. This is a mini-study of two firms with immense political muscle in San Francisco (deriving from their monopoly utility status and from their largest in the city landholdings) and how they profit enormously from the highrise/high density development they so effectively promote (through their vast pr/advertising/lobbying budgets, their campaign contributions and their major influence in the Bay Area Council/ Chamber/SPUR/Downtown Association).

By Peter Petrakis

During the past ten years, San Francisco has lost 25,000 people, thousands of families with children and 5,900 small businesses. Yet, Pacific Gas and Electric Company and Pacific Telephone and Telegraph Company are selling more power and telephone service and making more money than ever in San Francisco.

How can both things be going on at once? The PG&E/PT&T line is that we are individually using more power and telephone service, and that our increased per capita consumption is more than enough to offset the city's population loss.

That's only part of the story, however. The other part PG&E and PT&T don't talk about very loudly — that changes in the demographic characteristics of San Francisco, as the city shifts from a balanced residential-commercial-industrial community to a corporate headquarters city, are providing enormous financial benefits to these two utility companies, by reducing their operating expenses and increasing their rate of return on local investment.

Data provided by PG&E and PT&T in their reports to the state PUC, taken together with figures from the U.S. Census, make a strong case that the more Manhattan-like San Francisco becomes, the more profit these companies make and the better they like it. Both companies are actively promoting Manhattanization through their ad and promotional policies, through their interlocking directorates with the four big banks in San Francisco and through their influence and representatives on the Chamber of Commerce, the Downtown Association, Bay Area Council and SPUR.

Here are several pieces of evidence that provide background for the conclusion that PG&E and PT&T are thriving on demographic trends that are disastrous for San Francisco:

1) Even though San Francisco's population dropped by 25,000 in the past ten years, the number of San Francisco households served by PG&E increased by 20,000 in the same period. This can only mean that the average San Francisco household is smaller than it was in 1960.

2) The 1970 census shows 24,473 children under the age of 15

moved out of the city with their parents between 1960 and 1970, a fact that is consistent with smaller "PG&E households." It proves that smaller households are not entirely caused by a drop in the birthrate.

3) Despite the loss of 25,000 population and an increase of 20,000 in the number of households, the vacancy rate for living quarters dropped from 6.6% in 1960 to 1.2% in 1970. This means that when families with children moved out, they were promptly replaced by childless people, and that the immigration of childless residents more than compensated for the loss of families.

4) The only age groups that showed an increase in population in San Francisco between 1960 and 1970 were the 15—24 age group (up 37%) and the over-65 group (up 6.5%). All other age groups declined greatly. The 15—24 group's increase is probably due mainly to the influx of young adults 18 to 24, since that is the only subgroup between ages 15 and 24 that could have contributed substantially to the reduction in the housing vacancy rate that occurred in the same 10-year period. (People 15 to 17 years old don't buy or rent property.)

From this data, the following picture emerges: Families with children are being replaced largely by 1) single adults, 2) childless couples and 3) elderly parents whose children have married and moved away, presumably to the suburbs to raise their families and become commuters.

The social and political implications of these trends are disturbing. Suburban commuters don't have much of a stake in the future of San Francisco as a place to live in and grow up in; to them, it's a place to find work and use public services they do not pay for. Likewise, young single adults make the scene here, in the interlude between school and more mature responsibilities, but they don't always have much of a stake in San Francisco either. And, of course, an increase in the number of retired people has the potential of increasing resistance to needed change.

Perhaps these factors partly explain the social and political apathy and paralysis that grips San Francisco in the face of the city's most difficult urban problems in history.

Despite the social and political deterioration of San Francisco (to say nothing of its visual deterioration), the cash registers jingle merrily at PG&E and PT&T and their San Francisco profits mount steadily.

Part of the reason is those 20,000 additional households. One thing is clear: you can't add 20,000 households to San Francisco without stacking a lot of them vertically in the form of apartment houses (for childless people, naturally). It is a fact power and telephone service is inherently more profitable if delivered in big quantities to multiple-occupancy buildings than if delivered to numerous small consumers spread out over a wide area. The principle is called "economy of scale."

Thus, the 20,000 new households, which are mostly apartments (since there is no vacant land left for single family dwellings or duplexes), are a profit windfall for PG&E and PT&T because they reduce operating expenses by concentrating people.

PG&E residential revenues from power in San Francisco rose from $13 million in 1960 to $18 million in 1970. It is highly probable that the cost to deliver power to city residents did not increase at the same rate.

The concentration of population in apartment houses, which don't want families with young children, also has its counterpart in concentration of business, which means fewer small businesses in town. PG&E power sales to commercial and industrial customers in San Francisco increased 64% between 1960 and 1970. Yet, PG&E records show there are 5,900 fewer commercial and industrial customers here than there were 10 years ago, a 15% decline. With 15% fewer businesses in San Francisco, PG&E revenues from power sales to businesses nevertheless rose in 10 years from $26.7 to $36.6 million.

Two PG&E officials, Herbert Blasdale of the statistics section and Loren Wolf of the San Francisco division, explained the concentration of business in this way: a significant cause of the drastic decline in the number of business firms in San Francisco is the fact that, when a highrise apartment house or office building goes up, or when an area is cleared for other forms of redevelopment, numerous small businesses are torn down.

Wolf said that, because many are "marginal operations," small and presumably family-owned, the mortality rate from the blow is high. Many have no place to go because commercial property is becoming too expensive. Although Wolf didn't say it, this is probably because big highrise builders have "bid up" the cost of good commercial property in San Francisco.

Direct removal caused by highrise construction could not account for all 5,900 businesses, of course, and it is likely that many firms went out of business because the population shifts that accompany Manhattanization caused their natural clientele to dwindle or move away.

At the same time 5,900 business firms were disappearing, U.S. Census figures show that 14,000 blue collar jobs, many of them union jobs, also disappeared from San Francisco. These statistics can't be separated; many lost jobs were provided by the lost business customers of PG&E. Thus, to loss of diversity in the population, and to loss of diversity in the business activity, we must add loss of diversity in the work force. San Francisco is becoming an office town.

Wolf explicitly cited highrises as a cause of PG&E's increased sales of power to the business sector, despite a 15% loss in the number of firms. Highrise buildings, he said, require powerful air conditioning systems, elevators and escalators. Their thousands of windowless inner offices require artificial lighting all day long. Many leave their lights on all night (for "security," they say, but also to show off). All of this consumes hundreds of millions of extra kilowatt hours a year. In the simplest possible terms, then, PG&E sees highrises as "better" power customers.

I challenged Wolf with this point: that Manhattanization of San Francisco — highrises, high density, concentration of power load — means bigger profits to PG&E because of lower operating costs per unit of power sold. He conceded the point, but added PG&E wouldn't like to lose small consumers like residential customers because, as he put it, it likes "to stay close to the public to stay in business," that is, to avoid public takeover.

Despite Wolf's sentimentalizing over the little man, the reality is that the rate structures established by the state PUC make commercial accounts inherently much more profitable for private utilities. For example, PG&E's authorized rate of return on investment is 9.49% on commercial electric facilities, 4.78% on residential. That means, in effect, that every step toward total commercialization of San Francisco results automatically in an increased rate of return on PG&E's total capital investment in San Francisco — plus the added benefits of lower operating costs resulting from high density when large businesses replace small ones.

Detailed rate of return figures are not readily available from PT&T, but Bill Kern of PT&T's public affairs department put it this way: "Commercial phones subsidize residential phones," which is another way of saying that commercial service is also more profitable for PT&T than residential service. He gave an example: the basic monthly rental for a phone in, say, the Bank of America highrise is $10; for a home phone, $5.65. And, of course, hundreds of telephones in the Bank of America provide much more traffic and therefore much more PT&T profit than would fewer phones in a smaller building on the same site.

Just as the exodus of San Francisco families has unpleasant social and political consequences, so do these dislocations in the city's business community. Independence and economic diversity are diminished. Competition decreases, since big corporations to a great extent are able to administer prices and pass many wasteful expenditures on to the consumers. Land/property ownership and political influence at City Hall becomes concentrated in progressively fewer, and progressively richer, hands. The city becomes even less tolerant and democratic.

Big money has already seriously damaged popular government in San Francisco. Even anti-corruption measures written into the city charter, such as public ownership of all public utilities (intended to help the small businessman as much as anyone) and prohibition of conflict of interest, are laughed at by Mayor Alioto and his wealthy corporate appointees.

Best example: Marvin Cardoza and Louis Petri, vice-president and board member respectively of the Bank of America, who were appointed to the San Francisco Public Utilities Commission. Cardoza/Petri/B of A have, since their appointment, acted as sword and shield for PG&E and its lucrative private power monopoly in San Francisco and have actively opposed all moves leading to the acquisition of PG&E as required by the city charter, federal law and the U.S. Supreme Court.

From the PG&E/PT&T point of view, then, the ultimate in profitability would be a city of skyscrapers, consisting of highrises for commerce and highrises for residence. In other words, Manhattan, which is where the PT&T/PG&E/development combine is taking us.

For PG&E, the frosting on the highrise cake is BART, which will use 430 million kilowatt hours of electricity a year at the outset — enough to supply a city of 25,000 people. It will bring in tens of thousands of commuters to work in the highrises and consume the billions of kilowatt hours of commercial power so profitable to PG&E.

In view of all this, it came as no surprise that both PG&E and PT&T vigorously opposed Duskin's highrise control charter amendment on the November San Francisco ballot.

Kern of PT&T explained to me in September: "We are members of the Chamber of Commerce. They represent us. I suspect that we will contribute [to the campaign to fight highrise control] if the Chamber asks us to."

The Chamber surely asked. A PT&T board member, E. Hornsby Wasson, was the chief fundraiser for the Chamber of Commerce front group, "Citizens for San Francisco," which fought the charter amendment.

And PT&T surely contributed big. Kern told me PT&T wanted to build its own highrise building to handle greatly increased demands placed on its system by other highrises — a good example of how highrises generate more highrises. This will be reflected in your phone bill, of course, because that's the way the state PUC has set things up.

A.R. Todd of PG&E's governmental and public affairs department said pretty much the same thing: "Our annual report will probably show our contribution to oppose the highrise amendment, as we would oppose any measure that threatens the economic life of the city." PG&E already has its new highrise, a big view-blocker on lower Mission, "justified," of course, by the big local power demands that PG&E itself has promoted — by such devices as full page ads in eastern newspapers to entice more big power consumers to move to the Bay Area. These costs, too, appear in your utility bill.

Whose economic life, and whose city, is being threatened? PG&E, PT&T and U.S. Census figures provide the answer: the threat is to the people of San Francisco, and it's coming from the big private utilities and their big corporate customers. With their monopoly position, and the grand prizes that await them in the highrise sweepstakes, all PG&E/PT&T statements really mean is, "We will spend as much of ratepayers' money as we have to to defeat this measure that threatens to curb our profits."

4.

On the Waterfront:
The Great Wall of Magnin

By Richard Reinhardt

For more than two decades, San Francisco's downhill slide into the disaster of urban development has gained momentum, urged along by well-meaning civic organizations, ambitious officials, job-conscious unions and profit-seeking corporations. Almost every pressure group in the city has joined in the push. Liberals and conservatives, black and white — San Franciscans of every class and occupation have given their support to "development" in the belief that new structure was an ornament to their beloved city, a source of pride, of wealth and tax revenues.

Now and then, an individual or a neighborhood has challenged a project that would block a favorite view or compete with an existing enterprise. But, in the main, San Francisco has been "development-minded." Local boosters glowed with pleasure a few years ago when an Eastern real estate man wrote admiringly: "San Francisco could be the New York of this generation."

In the late 1960's, however, the prospect of becoming a Pacific Coast Manhattan began to lose its charm and to sound more and more like a civic calamity. New York's social and economic problems alarmed the entire nation, and many of the same problems had begun to plague the blithe little city by the Golden Gate. San Franciscans who had previously seen the skyscraper boom as an undiluted blessing began to question the value of monster buildings. With each new evidence of the destructive effects of high-density development, these questions grew sharper and more persistent until the whole concept of development-for-development's-sake came under vehement attack. Every large-scale project was greeted by a pertinacious, "Why?"

The most important impetus in changing this attitude was a development scheme sponsored by the San Francisco Port Commission with the enthusiastic support of Mayor Joseph Alioto, Port Commissioner Cyril Magnin and realtor Walter Shorenstein. This scheme, in brief, was to extract non-maritime revenues from the city's waterfront and use these revenues to modernize the cargo handling facilities of the port.

Toward this end, the Commission invited corporate land developers (notably the U.S. Steel Corporation and the Oceanic Properties division of Castle & Cooke) to the Bay Area, urged them to construct huge buildings at the water's edge and then tried to persuade the public to accept this program against the advice of many professional planners and economic consultants.

The Port Commission's grand design was thwarted, at least temporarily, by various legal obstacles. But the economic and political forces behind the scheme are still very much alive. As soon as the present furor dies down, the real estate entrepreneurs, labor chiefs and business executives who tried to foist these waterfront monstrosities upon the city will spring into action again. For highrise disease is based on fast-buck economics—and the thirst for quick profits is stronger than all arguments that have been raised against the "Manhattanization" of San Francisco. Only by understanding the factors that led to the waterfront crisis can San Franciscans hope to save their city from ruin at the hands of highrise maniacs.

1. The Port's Plans and How They Began

The San Francisco Port Commission is a city agency. Its role is to build, maintain and lease out the facilities of the city's "working waterfront" — six miles or so of sheltered, deep water coast on San Francisco Bay, one of the world's finest natural harbors. The Port is a big operation, grossing around $12 million a year, and its activities are said to provide between 11 and 14 per cent of all jobs in San Francisco.

For more than a century, from the early 1860's until 1969, San Francisco's harbor was administered by a quasi-independent agency of the state government — the Board of Harbor Commissioners, or San Francisco Port Authority. Members of the Authority were appointed by the governor of California, drew their funds from state sources and went about their work in a dense fog of public indifference. Their meetings seldom were reported in the press, as were those of other local boards and commissions. Nobody outside the maritime industry seemed to know or care who ran the port so long as ships steamed in and out on schedule.

State operation probably would have continued to everyone's satisfaction had it not been for the disturbing impact of new technology on the long-established harbor. There have been many changes in cargo handling and transportation during the years since San Francisco was a gold rush village with rows of scuttled brigantines standing duty as piers along the muddy shores of Yerba Buena Cove.

But many of these changes have been gradual or diffused in their impact — for example, the transition from sails to steam, from coal to diesel, the growth of motor trucking, the construction of vehicle bridges across the bay, dispersal of industry into suburban and rural areas, and the long decline of warehousing and manufacturing below the cliffs of Telegraph Hill. Equally important have been recent innovations in ocean shipping: immense "bulk ships" that carry such cargoes as petroleum, grain, wood chips and metal ores in liquid suspension; enormous LASH ("Lighter Aboard Ship") vessels that engulf whole barges loaded with cargo, ferry them to their destination and disgorge them like navy landing craft; and, above all, containerization — the use of large, pre-packed containers, loaded and unloaded by shoreside cranes.

Like most institutions, the Port acquired a certain inertia. Building a harbor is an expensive, long-range activity. It took more than half a century for the State Board of Harbor Commissioners to construct the great seawall that now forms the basic outline of the Embarcadero; and it was only in this century (just before World War I and again in the 1920's) that the Port mustered funds and enthusiasm to build most of the sheds and finger piers that are now so intimately and sentimentally associated with the San Francisco waterfront. Improvements to the Port have almost always lagged behind the demands of the maritime industry.

In recent years, however, the gap between new shipping technology and the Port's facilities began to widen. The reasons were numerous and complex: economic depression, labor strife, inept management, civic indecision, war.

San Francisco began to lose business to rival ports. The decline was relative, not absolute, and it was masked in the annual balance sheet by increased income from non-maritime sources — restaurants, offices, parking spaces, car washing concessions and other privately run facilities on Port-owned land. The ships continued to come and go, white-capped stevedores smoked their pipes in the midday sun and the Port remained, so to speak, in the black. But the dependence on non-maritime revenues grew relentlessly. Before long, more than 50 per cent of the Port's income was derived from non-maritime sources.

In the 1950's, despite this shift in function, it became obvious, even to outsiders, that San Francisco was losing its position as the major port of the Pacific Coast. Existing facilities were not suitable to handle pre-packed containers, and the rush to containerization was underway. Some authorities predicted that half of all ocean-borne general cargo would be containerized by 1975 and perhaps 80 to 90 per cent by the end of the century.

U.S. flag carriers, in particular, were adopting containers. Unless San Francisco could create facilities for handling these enormous new crates, it would not only lose its position on the Coast but even its dominance in the Bay Area. Oakland, with a vast reserve of flat industrial land, was grabbing the lead in containerization.

While the technological problems of the Port were obvious, the solution

was not so clear. San Francisco, with its shortage of industrial land and its dense concentration of "service" businesses, was not an ideal location to handle container cargoes, which require acres of open storage space. An objective study of all port facilities within the "San Francisco Gateway" (that is, the bay and its tributaries) might have disclosed that the city is better suited to the sort of "break bulk" cargo that can be accommodated at the historic finger piers of the northern waterfront.

But policy decisions in the field of harbor construction, like policy decisions in air transportation, seldom are made by rational processes. They are boiled out in political crucibles, heated by local, short-range economic interests.

Thus it was that the Port of San Francisco, without giving any formal consideration to regional alternatives, decided to build a series of massive container terminals in competition with other Pacific Coast ports and other harbors in the San Francisco Gateway. By the late 1950's, the Port was more or less committed to this policy — an unwritten, unilateral policy that would have a resounding impact upon the city a decade later.

To carry out its modernization plan, the Port had to overcome certain unfavorable political factors. The Board of Commissioners, as a state agency, was required to ask the voters of the entire state for permission to issue improvement bonds — and the voters of Los Angeles, Long Beach, San Diego, Stockton, Sacramento, Richmond and Oakland all had ambitious harbor programs of their own. But the management of the Port saw a way out of the dilemma. By vastly increasing the size and number of non-maritime concessions, the Port would raise a surplus to pay for its new maritime facilities. It would get all the cargo handling space it wanted, and more besides.

In 1959 Cyril Magnin, chairman of the Board of Commissioners, unveiled a grandiose and visionary plan for a new "Embarcadero City," a totally non-maritime redevelopment of the northern waterfront into commercial and residential structures stretching from Fisherman's Wharf to the Ferry Building.

This cordon of buildings — offices, hotels, sports arenas, boat harbors, theaters and convention halls — would not only pay for new port facilities to the south, it would also, in Magnin's opinion, make San Francisco "the most beautiful city in the world."

As sketched by Magnin's consulting architects, John S. Bolles and Ernest Born, Embarcadero City was to be a relatively low-rise development — small buildings, wide-open spaces, esplanades and walkways jutting into the sparkling bay. All the shipping facilities displaced from the northern waterfront would be accommodated in a new terminal at the foot of Army Street, and the terminal would be financed by the 1958 State Harbor Bond issue of $50 million. Easy as pie, the northern waterfront would fall vacant of commercial shipping and the whole magnificent 80 block area would ascend to the heavenly condition that planners and real estate men call "the highest and best use."

"The Port Authority took the ermine wraps off 'Embarcadero City' yesterday, then sat back with broad grins to hear the oohs and aahs," The Chronicle reported. Magnin was justifiably delighted.

The news that the northern waterfront was destined for major rebuilding did not seem to horrify any significant number of San Franciscans. To the contrary, it pleased and excited most of the City Beautiful fraternity of architects and planners, who reap immediate benefit from tearing down old neighborhoods and replacing them with glistening renewal projects, resembling as closely as possible scale models, complete with trafficless streets, tiny Henry Moore figures, balsa wood skyscrapers and neat little trees made of sponge rubber, painted green.

The notion of reshaping the northern waterfront into an alabaster water-city became a sort of holy crusade for such organizations as SPUR (the San Francisco Planning and Urban Renewal Association) and such architect-planners as Thomas Creighton, erstwhile architectural writer of San Francisco Magazine.

In a prescient essay in 1964, Creighton enthused over the wonderful possibilities of the old Embarcadero. He saw much of the land converted into waterside recreation space — parks, playgrounds, marinas, maritime museums. Along with the public areas, there would be "light, specialized commercial use — somewhat as Fisherman's Wharf has developed, with restaurants, some specialty shops, paid admission amusement facilities ... fishing piers ... hotel space." There might also be residential developments — "low density, openly planned, view-and-water-use oriented."

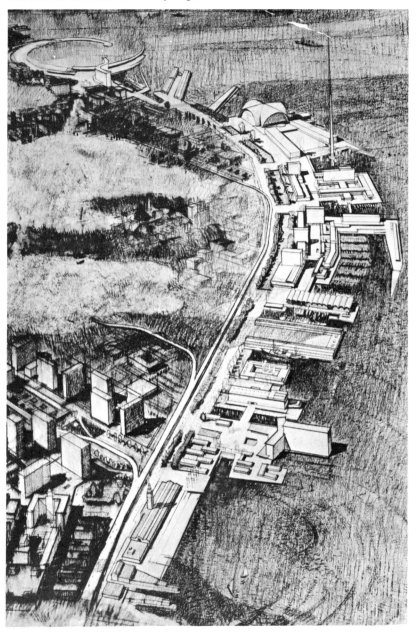

Even the Port Authority's own heavily doctored drawing shows how dramatic
will be the impact of its plan to do away with the famous finger piers and
turn the waterfront over to U.S. Steel/Ford Motor/Oceanic Properties.

Of course, there would be pedestrian walks, trafficways — one might even consider a university campus or a hospital complex on the waterfront — and, withal, the continued comings and goings of the sort of small passenger and merchant ships that could be accommodated at conventional finger piers without acres of "backup" facilities.

Nothing in Creighton's pretty daydreams, Bolles and Born's sketches, nor Magnin's lyric description ever suggested the nightmarish possibility that the Port would decide to ornament the waterfront with corporate office towers taller than the pylons of the Bay Bridge, 2,500-car underground garages or so-called "gallerias" on the scale of the Moffett Field dirigible hangar.

Lulled — or gulled — by assurances that Embarcadero City would conform to the scale and character of the city, San Franciscans cheerfully accepted the idea that the old gray piers north of the Ferry Building were doomed and in their passing would bequeath to the city a waterfront that would enrich the environment — not a cohort of real estate speculators and their political cronies.

2. The Port Commissioners Sharpen Their Pencils

Magnin's Embarcadero City, as drawn by Bolles and Born, was a relatively unsophisticated proposal, a grand design rather than a detailed plan of action. It suggested removing all shipping (except pleasure craft and tour boats) from the northern waterfront, but it did not attempt to assess the economic consequences of this move. To bolster the concept — and to give substance to the policy to pay for maritime facilities with non-maritime real estate developments — the Port needed facts and figures.

To this end, the Commissioners hired Arthur D. Little, Inc., a firm of economic consultants, in mid-1964 to appraise the Port's present and future operations. The study took 18 months to complete, cost about $75,000 and was published in September, 1966. It was directed by Claude Gruen, who later founded his own consulting firm and is today doing anti-Duskin studies for the Chamber of Commerce.

To nobody's great surprise, the report amounted to a general confirmation of the Port's existing policies. But it departed in several significant respects from Magnin's ideas for Embarcadero City.

In the first place, the consultants felt the Port of San Francisco, far from a dying institution, was still the city's most important single industry and would continue to be of major importance if the Port could succeed in maintaining its position in the face of technological change.

The consultants agreed that the Port needed new cargo facilities and that these should be constructed, generally, to the south of the Bay Bridge where there was ample space to handle containerized cargo, trucks and trains could serve the piers without having to pass through the central business district and there were no conflicting developments such as the Golden Gateway and the financial district.

Finally, the consultants found only two areas of the northern waterfront that were subject to major change: (a.) the section between Pier 35 and Fisherman's Wharf, which would be redeveloped for residential and tourist use, and (b.) the section around and immediately south of the Ferry Building (Piers 1 through 24) which would gradually be rebuilt into a neighborhood of parks, open spaces and "a small, mixed use office-parking complex." The consultants suggested the Port Authority build this complex and lease it to tenants.

In short, the Little report accepted the view that there would be *some* non-maritime development on port properties north of the Bay Bridge but by no means endorsed the idea of turning the whole Embarcadero into a sub-city. Although a few old-timers in the shipping business felt that A.D. Little had capitulated to the odious myth of the "dying port," the consultants actually upheld the principle that break bulk cargo handling — not hotels and office towers — should continue to dominate the northern waterfront.

The Little Report ran counter to the Port's unofficial development policy in still another way, for the consultants neither stated nor implied that it was essential to extract maximum non-maritime revenues from the northern waterfront to finance necessary improvements in the Port. Instead, the consultants suggested the Port management build relatively small office structures, parking garages and other buildings in the area near the Bay Bridge, presumably financing these projects with revenue bonds. Rents from the new buildings apparently would be more than sufficient to pay back these revenues bonds. Any surpluses could go toward the costly maritime developments on the southern waterfront.

Rereading the 1966 Little Report with the wisdom of hindsight, one is struck by the lack of specific suggestions on how the Port should finance new maritime facilities. But the consultants made no such recommendations, nor did they comment on the administrative problems that were bound to develop as the Port got deeper into such fields as tourism, land planning, recreation facilities and building management.

But there were even more important shortcomings in this study, which was to become a basic document of city policy, guiding the redevelopment of San Francisco's entire bay waterfront. No one had bothered to figure out how large or tall the office structures in the Ferry Building area might have to be to pay for themselves and also produce surplus revenues for maritime projects. Still worse, no one had studied the Port of San Francisco in relation to other ports nor contemplated the possibility of making this Port a working unit in a larger, regional port authority.

Given these blind spots, the conclusions of the Little Report were almost inevitable. The consultants did not comment on the functional disorders of the Port, its overlaps and conflicts with other local agencies; they did not even mention the possibility of a regional port authority. Within a year after the report was published, San Francisco began a campaign to bring the Port under city control. By then, the political policies and economic assumptions that would shape the future of the waterfront had been frozen into unshakable dogma.

3. San Francisco Plays "Capture the Port "

In the minds of the Harbor Commissioners — and of a good many shippers and shipping executives — state management presented an almost insurmountable obstacle to renewal of the San Francisco waterfront. The state, after all, had allowed San Francisco to slip behind its rivals. Would the state now be likely to allow her to catch up and surpass them? Feverish with competitive zeal, San Francisco's Port boosters gazed with envy at the local agencies managing the ports of Oakland, Long Beach and Stockton.

Many downtown leaders, including R.G. Follis, then chairman of the board of Standard Oil of California, and John Hirten, then director of SPUR, lent their names and energies to a legislative campaign to transfer Port ownership to the city. Assemblyman John Burton, a liberal Democrat from a district abutting the bay, agreed to author a transfer bill. His motives were simple: "We thought the Port would make money for the city. Someone pointed out how much money Richmond was making (from its port). I sincerely believe that no one knew the troubles the Burton Act would cause, or how the Port Commission would use it. God knows, I didn't."

Mayor Alioto, newly elected and glowing with political luster, made several trips to the state capitol in behalf of the transfer bill. (His efforts included an unsuccessful attempt to get someone else to author the bill, since Burton's doctrinaire liberalism was a political handicap in the relatively conservative legislature.)

After a series of hearings, the Legislature agreed to relinquish state control of the Port if the voters of San Francisco would accept all debts on the harbor, pledge themselves to a large improvement program and give the state a heavy share of any future operating profits. By the time Gov. Ronald Reagan had signed the Transfer Act, the Port boosters were already making plans for the election campaign.

Chairman Magnin, who had remained discreetly aloof from the legislative debate, endorsed the transfer proposal and joined in rounding up a "citizens' committee" to raise money for the ballot campaign. The widely known political public relations firm of Whitaker & Baxter hired on as consultants and began a campaign of enticement: "The Port means money in our pockets

... Opportunity knocks ... The Greatest Bargain of the Century."

The transfer agreement came to the voters in the form of two propositions, designated "B" and "C" on the November, 1968, ballot. Proposition B sketched the financial arrangements:

"Transfer of the Harbor of San Francisco and Assumption of Indebtedness and Liabilities: Shall the harbor of San Francisco be transferred from the State of California to the City and County of San Francisco under the terms and conditions specified in California Statutes 1968, Chapter 1333, and the City and County of San Francisco assume the bonded indebtedness of the State of California incurred for San Francisco harbor improvements and the liabilities, obligations and duties of the San Francisco Port Authority estimated in the aggregate to be not less than $60,939,000 and perform all of the terms and conditions set forth in said act?"

Proposition C, the companion measure, was an amendment to the city charter, setting up a local Port Commission, with almost autonomous powers, to run the harbor. The Board of Supervisors, in endorsing and presenting this charter amendment, had voted 10 to 1 to deny themselves any review of Port Commission contracts, commercial agreements or development plans. All members of the Board except Leo McCarthy apparently accepted Magnin's view that "the Port is a business and ... can't be expected to run to the Supervisors with every contract."

(The Examiner, in a flash of creative typography, reported later: "With a strong Commission that could function with a free hand from the Board of Supervisors, (the Port Director) could do a great gob with the Port.")

In any case, voters accepted the word of the "citizens' committee," as transmitted by Whitaker & Baxter, that the Port transfer would make them rich and joyful. They voted that November to accept the deal, including some $55 million in port debts and a civic obligation to spend at least $100 million for harbor improvements during the next 25 years.

Apparently, the terms did not strike many voters as onerous, for there was relatively little opposition to the transfer. The $55 million debt seemed a small burden to accept in return for the presumed benefits of owning one's own Port, which obviously was worth far more than that. As for spending another $100 million to modernize and expand maritime facilities, that, too, sounded like a good investment — especially if the Port could hold to its historic policy of paying off its debts out of its own revenues. Modern cargo facilities would mean blue-collar jobs, wharfage receipts, commercial vitality for the city. San Francisco voters could be counted on to approve the necessary expenditures.

In the several years since the approval of the Transfer Act, however, the

"Greatest Bargain of the Century" has turned out to be a pig in a poke. Even the author, Assemblyman Burton, has come to believe that the terms were unfavorable to the city, and he has suggested that the $100 million obligation be lowered or eliminated. The figure is arbitrary, at best, and it seems to have been conceived in haste and carelessness, not to say irresponsibility. Where did it come from?

"I remember Tom Mellon (San Francisco's chief administrative officer) told me he put in the $100 million figure when he appeared before a Senate committee and someone asked him what the city was going to do with the Port," Burton recalls. But John Jacobs, executive director of SPUR, thinks the figure was suggested by Donald W. Cleary, the late legislative lobbyist for San Francisco.

"I know who it was," says Rae Watts, former Port Director. "It was Ralph Davies (of American President Lines) who was on the Mayor's Committee, who stuck that figure in." But Gwin Follis, who headed up the lobbying effort for the Burton Act, declares: "It was not the idea of any one man. Some committee that knew about such things put in the $100 million figure in Sacramento."

This $100 million caprice may never be properly explained, for the Legislature does not make transcripts of committee hearings. In any case, it was not the *size* of the investment that brought sudden developmental pressure onto the northern waterfront; it was the method by which the newly created Port Commission now decided to carry out its dreams for a modern waterfront.

4. The Port Commission In Action

In a sense, the Port of San Francisco now was no different from any other city department. True, it had exclusive power to administer leases and franchises; but the Public Utilities Commission and the Airport Commission have equivalent powers. Like those agencies, the Port Commission would be under the indirect supervision of the mayor and the direct budgetary control of the Board of Supervisors, which acts as a city council in San Francisco's combined city-county government. Like other public and private enterprises, the Port would have to submit its development projects to the scrutiny of the city planning department; and if its plans became pernicious or outlandish, they supposedly would be restrained by the city's master plan.

But, technically and psychologically, the Port Commission was as distinct from the rest of San Francisco's local government as it had been under state operation. The men and women who ran the harbor tended to think of themselves as a wholly separate entity, almost an independent domain.

This sense of autonomy resulted, in part, from the Port's historic isolation, or insulation, from local interference. Whereas most city departments had to depend on other bureaus for janitorial service, accounting, utilities, and so forth, the Port could do almost everything for itself: its own police surveillance, its own maintenance, its own engineering, its own advertising, its own rental agreements. Understandably, Port officials liked to think of themselves as independent business operators rather than government servants. Watts, the former director, was fond of comparing the Port to a business in competition with other businesses — and this, despite the obvious fact that the Port is really a public utility, the purpose of which is not to make a profit but to give service to the city and its maritime industry.

In short, the Port of San Francisco came under city direction deeply infected with authority-itis, which can be defined as a pervasive sense of knowing more than the people who own you.

This condition showed up the very first time the Port tried to justify its annual budget before the finance committee of the Board of Supervisors. Several supervisors were distressed by items in the budget ($65,000 for promotion, $65,000 for advertising, $60,000 for contributions to conventions and $15,000 to entertain visitors from out-of-town — plus $107,000 for the "expert advice" of private real estate consultants), but Port Director Watts defended these and other proposed expenditures on grounds the Port was involved in a fierce competitive struggle with other harbors and should not, in any case, be bound by the budgetary restrictions imposed on other city departments. The Port, after all, was a "self-supporting agency" that did not require tax support.

In the conventional wisdom of petty officials, self-sufficiency is one of the highest virtues of a public agency, a quality that should be rewarded with carte-blanche to spend the proceeds to extend the realm of the subject agency, whether it be a toll bridge, an airport, a waterworks or a harbor. To "stay out of the tax rate" is a mark of bureaucratic achievement comparable to winning one of those "E" for efficiency flags the government used to bestow on well-run navy yards. The Port of San Francisco, during its century of state operation, had made a fetish of self-sufficiency — although, in truth, this standard of operation was forced on the Port by political necessity. In a perfectly human way, the Port management made of this necessity first a virtue, then an excuse for avoiding outside supervision and, finally, a justification to act as though it was an independent development company.

"The Port is a business and can't divulge its secrets to its competitors," Cyril Magnin once said. "The Commission can't be expected to run to the Supervisors with every contract."

To the finance committee, however, the self-sufficiency argument had a familiar sound. It quickly pointed out that, although the Port Commission ran the harbor, the Supervisors ran the budget — even for such revenue-producing departments as the airport and the water department.

But the Port was not stifled by this supervisoral damper. Later in the year, the Commission succeeded in impressing its case on the port committee of the county grand jury, which issued a superficial report urging that the Port be exempted from the tedious budget review of the city government. The grand jurors liberally seasoned their report with sayings that might have come from the mouth of Chairman Magnin, to the effect that the Port rated special treatment because of its fast-moving, competitive role — and its self-sufficiency.

It was apparent from these manifestations of authority-itis that the Port never intended to allow a real assertion of local control in the change from state to city ownership. Certainly the Port did not want to fall into the clutches of City Hall! No, the celebrated transfer, "The Greatest Bargain of the Century," was really intended to remove the Port and its immensely valuable waterfront properties from *both* state and local control.

Magnin, in his long tenure as chairman of the Port, never concealed his desire to keep the operation semi-autonomous, not "under the thumb of the Board of Supervisors." Impatient of restraint, he and his fellow commissioners resented all advice and intrusion, not only from the elected supervisors, but also from other city departments, especially those in the fields of finance and planning. Members of the Commission repeatedly said they would like the City Planning Commission to bow out and let the future of the waterfront be determined by the Port management in negotiation with private developers; for, in the eyes of the Port Commissioners, the Planning Department is only another local agency trying to impose its will on the Port. (San Francisco Chronicle, June 20, 1969.)

Authority-itis, the Port's "special agency syndrome," was a critical factor in causing the developmental crisis on the San Francisco waterfront. Freed at last from state interference, immune from intrusion at City Hall, the Port set out to be what it had always longed to be — a free-swinging, independent operation, liberated from bureaucratic powers of government and all the latitude of private enterprise.

5. Laying Plans to Lease the Waterfront

At the heart of the Burton Act was a clause empowering the Port Commission to lease harbor properties for periods up to 66 years for *any purpose that would yield a maximum profit*, if, in the opinion of the Commission, the properties were no longer needed for harbor, transportation or recreational use. The proceeds of these non-maritime leases were to be used "in furtherance of commerce and navigation."

This clause was the key that would open the way to Magnin's Embarcadero City. From the beginning, the Port Commission took it as an invitation — perhaps even a mandate — for the city to exploit the commercial possibilities of the northern waterfront to an absolute maximum. Out of the proceeds of this great real estate raffle of "surplus" port properties, the Commission would build container terminals, LASH terminals, docks and fences to dazzle the world. With a spirit of independent enterprise that would have done credit to a company of 13th Century Venetian merchants, the Port Commission decided to undertake a building program even bigger than Tom Mellon, or whoever it was had promised the state: $160 million in new facilities, all of which would be paid for by milking commercial revenues out of the Port's "own" property (that is, the *city's* property) in the vicinity of the Ferry Building.

Actually, these non-maritime revenues would not be sufficient, of themselves, to pay all the cost — only to make up the difference between the expense of these new facilities and their income. In other words, the non-maritime revenues extracted from the exploitation of the northern waterfront would be used to keep the Port "in the black." The profitable non-maritime leases would carry the unprofitable maritime developments "piggy-back." How else could the Port build $100 million in new facilities and still stay "out of the tax rate?"

In the murky logic of the Port Commission, the commercial exploitation of the northern waterfront thus became more than just a clever use of "surplus" properties (which the A.D. Little consultants had found to be far from surplus). It became an absolute necessity to fulfill the legal requirements of the transfer agreement.

Piggy-backing is a standard administrative gambit in thousands of businesses. Profitable bars support unprofitable restaurants. Profitable terminals carry unprofitable airports. Profitable lines of merchandise piggy-back unprofitable or slow-moving lines.

In business, this practice is acceptable (as long as the manager understands what he is doing.) But in government agencies it is an invitation to disaster. Piggy-backing not only obscures the true cost and benefit of publicly owned enterprises but often gives false economic justification to misbegotten projects.

For years, the Port of San Francisco has practiced a mild form of piggy-backing, or jiggery-pokery, by mixing up maritime and non-maritime revenues in the annual financial report. By this more or less innocuous bookkeeping trick, the Port has been able to show a slight running surplus and to avoid asking for a tax subsidy.

(Actually, the Port has been receiving certain concealed subsidies for years. In adding up its "receipts," which totalled something over $12 million in 1970, the Port is permitted to retain some $100,000 a year collected from parking meters on "port property" and to call these "operating revenues," although parking meter charges are, by legal definition, regulatory fees and not rents. The Port also collects and keeps bank interest on surplus funds accumulated in years past; and, unlike most other city departments, the Port bills its own tenants for various managerial services and credits these payments to the revenue side of its ledger.

(The black ink side of the Port's ledger accordingly is bolstered by revenues from a number of sources that are quite unrelated to the basic operations of the Port. They are, in other words, *city* revenues that the Port is allowed to use.)

It is difficult if not impossible to learn whether the Port makes or loses money on its services to the maritime industry. The Port's yearly financial report makes no distinction between income from maritime and non-maritime functions. One cannot tell whether non-maritime functions such as the restaurants at Fisherman's Wharf contribute more or less than their fair share of the cost of running the harbor. It is known, however, that non-maritime revenues are about half the Port's total income, and this proportion is expected to rise.

As for the expensive new cargo handling facilities in the Port's expansion program, it is a safe bet that these will not show a margin of profit for many years. If the new LASH terminal, now under construction at India Basin, is an example, the modernized cargo terminals on the southern waterfront will barely break even. The LASH terminal, a $21 million project, will be paid for by 30-year revenue bonds bearing 7¼ per cent interest. The annual return from the terminal is expected to be about $2 million — barely enough to pay back the principal and interest on the borrowed money. The terminal will contribute nothing toward the administrative and supervisory and promotional costs of the Port.

All this is not to say that the LASH terminal and other new cargo handling facilities are of no value to the city — only that they are, in effect, subsidized allurements to keep maritime activity in San Francisco. The subsidy comes from other operations of the Port.

Subsidy is a horrible word in the harbor business, because direct, overt subsidies to Port tenants are illegal. The Federal Maritime Commission, in an effort to minimize cutthroat competition among American ports, insists that maritime leases be set at terms that are "compensatory" to the port.*

Be this as it may, the Port Commission's policy of extracting maximum revenue from the northern waterfront to finance port expansion constitutes *indirect* subsidy — i.e., piggy-backing — on a Brobdingnagian scale. To the

---

*San Francisco recently has been involved in a case of alleged undercharging brought by the Port of Oakland, which complained that San Francisco's lease of 21 acres at the new Army Street Terminal to States Steamship Company was "non-compensatory."

simple mind of an outside observer, a subsidy is a subsidy, whether it takes the form of cash, services, tax relief, non-compensatory rent or robbing of Peter to pay Paul. In this case, the subsidy consists in providing a public utility service (harbor facilities) to private users (the maritime industry) at less than true economic value. It is like building a structure and then offering it for rent at cost, neglecting to include any recompense for administration, depreciation or profit.

In the long run, the loss to the people of San Francisco will not be in cash but in extremely valuable public property leased out for private use; for the "subsidy" will come in the form of rents from Embarcadero City. To critics of the Port Commission, however, this is precisely the same as leasing part of Golden Gate Park to apartment house builders, using the revenues from this lease to build a cargo terminal — and then renting the terminal to private tenants for less than it is worth.

No elected official would dare to advance such an obnoxious proposal — yet this, in effect, is exactly what the Port Commission plans to do with the unique and extraordinarily valuable public shoreline near the Ferry Building.

6. Putting the Plans on Paper

There has never been any question that the Port Commission's domain along the northern waterfront would find enthusiastic reception in the private real estate market.

These acres of shoreline lie right at the edge of the downtown financial district, adjoining the Golden Gateway redevelopment project, North Beach, Embarcadero Plaza and Fisherman's Wharf and overlooking a dazzling uninterrupted vista of the north bay.

Rapid transit lines and automobile freeways feed commuters to the door. New city parks and plazas roll westward toward the downtown skyline. The existing buildings are flimsy and small; the terrain is dead-level; and the parcels are large.

This is exactly the sort of property that land developers seek out nowadays for the grandiose, multi-purpose urban projects that institutional investors adore — towering, joyless micropolises modeled on Rockefeller Center, complete with parking garages, retail shops, offices, living quarters and "amenities," all abound together like a bundle of concrete fasces by the financial strings of some vast and elusive underwriting syndicate. Sites for this sort of large scale development are rare, indeed, except in areas of urban renewal — and here, on the very shore of San Francisco Bay! Embarcadero City was a natural. This, essentially, was what Mayor Alioto meant when he called the northern waterfront "one of the hottest pieces of real estate that anyone could get."

A month after the Legislature passed the Transfer Act, the Port of San began to advertise for private developers to create Embarcadero City. The ads, prepared by the D'Arcy Advertising Agency, ran in the Wall Street Journal, the Sunday Examiner & Chronicle, the Western Real Estate News, the National Real Estate Investor and the California Savings and Loan Magazine. The pitch:

"Prime waterfront property in San Francisco is now available for commercial development. The Port can now offer downtown waterfront property from famed Fisherman's Wharf to the Bay Bridge. Much of it is zoned for hotels, motels, restaurants, entertainment, retail shopping, office buildings and apartments. Sites are available on long term leases with flexible terms specifically designed to be attractive to private capital. Our Director of Development will give you complete details."

Even before these ads appeared, however, the Port had occasion to welcome a group of private developers to the northern waterfront. The project was a multi-million-dollar complex of wholesale showrooms and hotel space in a former industrial area at the foot of Telegraph Hill, and the sponsors, who called themselves "Northern Waterfront Associates," were a syndicate of prominent San Franciscans including Roger D. Lapham Jr., former president of the City Planning Commission. Lawrence Halprin, a highly successful landscape architect, had prepared the preliminary designs.

Mayor Alioto, like his Port Commission, was delighted with the International Market Center.

"The Northern Waterfront Associates plan is very important to us," he said. "It is going to be complimentary to some larger plans we have for that whole waterfront."

But the International Market Center, despite its prestigious backing and its expensive campaign of public relations, ran into stiff political opposition. The Telegraph Hill Dwellers, who had been assured by the Mayor that he would uphold a 40 foot height limit on the waterfront, discovered that the Center's 550-room hotel would tower 180 feet, dwarfing the small hill and cutting off its celebrated views of the bay. They organized a campaign to challenge the project on legal and environmental grounds.

This controversy was never resolved, because the International Market Center failed to generate financial support. The "larger plans," however, continued to loom over the waterfront, causing uneasiness and apprehension to many San Franciscans. It was obvious that real estate speculators were closing in on the Embarcadero and that the Port lacked the staff, experience and breadth of vision to control the redevelopment of this priceless public resource.

To calm these natural (and evidently justified) misgivings, the city authorized its planning department to prepare a master plan for the future

STOP THEM FROM BURYING OUR CITY UNDER A SKYLINE OF TOMBSTONES

Both the above pictures are of downtown San Francisco. Same spot. Same time of day. Same weather conditions. The top one was twelve years ago. The bottom one, last year. San Francisco was once light, hilly, pastel, open. Inviting. In only twelve years it has taken on the forbidding look of every other American city. Forty more skyscrapers are due in the next five years. They are as great a disaster for the city economically as they are esthetically. Ask a New York taxpayer.

What can you do to stop it?

Contact SAN FRANCISCO OPPOSITION, 520 Third Street (second floor) or telephone 397-9220.

This ad, first appearing in the Examiner and Chronicle in October of 1970, was the first step in Alvin Duskin's campaign to enlarge the citizen assault on the U.S. Steel Building into a general attack on highrise development throughout the city. More than 10,000 newspaper readers clipped coupons from the ad and sent them to City Hall.

development of the entire north waterfront area, from the Army's Fort Mason to the Channel Street estuary. John S. Bolles, who was rapidly becoming the Port's house architect, contracted to prepare the basic plan, and Arthur D. Little, Inc., again took on the economic research. This lineup of hired consultants gave the public the impression that the plan would be, not just the wishful thinking of visionary esthetes, but a workable guideline for change, adjusted to the economic needs and capacities of the Port and the city.

The plan turned out to be exactly what one might have expected — practical rather than romantic, realistic rather than imaginative, predictable rather than surprising. It contained specific suggestions for public works to improve parking and traffic flow along the Embarcadero, for pedestrian catwalks and strips of greenery, for peephole parks at water's edge and building height limits on public and private land.

The most serious defect in the plan was that the burden of the architectural restrictions would fall on one "property owner" (the Port Commission) which would be under extraordinarily heavy pressure — political, economic and psychological — to *break* those restrictions. With considerable foresight, the Little Company pointed this out in its commentary on the Plan:

"When a builder's scale of development is restricted by height limits or design criteria, he will try to have some of those restrictions changed. This is nothing new ... Therefore, we have a potential source of conflict between any agency that attempts to enforce conformity to a plan, and another agency seeking to maximize the revenue generated on a particular piece of land."

In this case, the agency attempting to "enforce conformity" would be the Department of City Planning, backed up, more or less, by the Board of Supervisors; and the agency chafing under the restraints upon its money-making efforts would be the Port Commission, which, as we have seen, regards the enforcing agencies as interlopers.

Conflict between the Port Commission's short-term real estate speculations and the Planning Department's long-range aspirations seemed almost inevitable; and the Arthur D. Little report therefore proposed that the fate of the waterfront be entrusted to a single, overall agency that would be able to actually plan and carry out the anticipated developments entirely on its own.

But this important suggestion, filled with significance for the future of the entire Bay Area, never received serious consideration. Like the whole concept of regional port development, it was brushed aside; for the Port Commission had no intention of carrying out the provisions of the city's northern waterfront plan, much less of accepting Little's advice on how to accomplish this.

Instead, the Commission, abetted by the Mayor and egged on by the Chamber of Commerce, the Building and Construction Trades Council and other "progressive" elements in San Francisco's business-labor-political elite, blithely proceeded to disregard years of study and hundreds of thousands of dollars in professional advice in their overriding desire to peddle the choicest properties on the waterfront to real estate developers.

Within a few months after the City Planning Commission had completed its hearings on the northern waterfront and had adopted a slightly diluted version of the Bolles Plan, the Port Commission suggested junking the most important developmental restriction in the plan — the height limit on new structures in the vicinity of the Ferry Building — to accommodate corporate investors who wanted to construct highrise office buildings at the edge of the bay.

7. Tearing up the Blueprints

Those who have watched San Francisco's development crisis grow from a neighborhood squabble into a major political showdown remember this as the moment when the pot began to boil. It seemed that the Port Commission had been propositioned and was delighted to say "Yes."*

The propositions, in fact, were coming from all directions: The Hawaii-based Dillingham Corporation was interested in putting up a 450-room hotel; an Italian real estate consortium, said to embody financial interests of the Vatican, had ideas for a hotel-apartment-retail-office complex near Fisherman's Wharf; an Eastern syndicate presented elaborate plans for a hotel with commercial appendages on Piers 1 through 7; and there were nebulous plans for a STOL airport. The most majestic proposals of all came from the Ford Motor Company and the United States Steel Corporation, both of which wanted the same prime site, just south of the Ferry Building, for a skyscraper of Wall Street scale.

These propositions did not materialize out of ether, of course. They were solicited. The chief matchmakers, by their own proud admission, were the Mayor and his close friend Magnin, aided by Walter Shorenstein, a San Francisco real estate man who was in line for substantial profits as leasing agent for the Steel project and John Merrill, of Skidmore, Owings and Merrill. Magnin and Shorenstein, in particular, worked in close association to peddle the San Francisco waterfront, and the city's angry reaction was a harsh blow to their joint ambitions.

*A high official of the city government muttered in disgust, "San Francisco has always been an easy lay for anyone who came along with a few bucks in his hand." In evidence of this, he pointed to the city's supine acceptance of the hideous, double-deck freeway along the Embarcadero; the unconscionable defacement of the city's historic center, Portsmouth Square, first by a semi-private garage project and later by a graceless footbridge over Kearny Street; and the destruction of Bayview Park in an ill-starred quarry-and-fill arrangement that led to the construction of Candlestick Park Stadium.

Magnin, a wealthy and respected retired business executive (Joseph Magnin Stores), is a man of great cultural and political influence in Northern California. He has been at various times the city's official host, president of the Chamber of Commerce, and chairman of civic and political committees beyond number. Like his close friend, Ben Swig, owner of the Fairmont Hotel, Magnin is a major contributor and fund raiser for local, state and national candidates, primarily Democratic. The combined support of Swig and Magnin (sometimes playfully called "The Fairmont Cabinet") was crucial to the election of Mayor Alioto, a late entry in a divided field, in 1967.

Whether Shorenstein is also a member-in-full-standing of the Fairmont Cabinet or only its errand boy is a debated question. His position as president of Milton Meyer & Company, his professed interest in civic affairs, his ability to raise money, his contributions to Democratic causes and local elections have given him a certain amount of personal political leverage — not equal to that of the senior cabinet members, but not without importance.

In any case, both Magnin and Shorenstein had almost instant access to the ears of the Mayor and several members of the Board of Supervisors. Magnin's son-in-law, Walter Newman, is a member of the City Planning Commission; and the close working relationships between the Fairmont Cabinet and the local chieftains of organized labor made it almost certain there would be official union endorsement for any Magnin-inspired program of waterfront remodeling.

The negotiations that preceded public announcement of the various Port projects were carried on with as much privacy, even secrecy, as any high-level business dealings. Spencer Gilman, a former director of development for the Port, has said that by the time Port leases become public knowledge, "the decisions are already made . . . You can't do business in the public eye."

According to officials of the U.S. Steel Corporation, representatives of the Port of San Francisco first approached them with an offer of waterfront acreage in the spring of 1969. Whether this representative was an employee of the Port or Shorenstein, acting in his own and the Port's behalf, is not clear; but Shorenstein shortly became the representative for the corporation in presenting its lease proposals to the city.

A knowledgeable observer, familiar with the project from the onset, suggests that U.S. Steel "probably looked around the city for a real estate man who could also operate politically. Hell, they could look at the proposed zoning down there and know they were going to have trouble. They needed a little political muscle and Shorenstein was the man."

The steel company's attitude toward the waterfront site seems to have been casual almost to the point of indifference. It was Magnin, Shorenstein and the Mayor who were determined to pin U.S. Steel to the Ferry Building area. According to Edward ("Church") Bassett of Skidmore, Owings & Merrill, project architects for the tower, the company "was under some pressure from Washington to use some of its capital for redevelopment in large cities around the country. They also, of course, saw the project as a good investment. The complex was a speculative venture for the company, and a fairly certain one."

In preparing its offer to the Port Commission, U.S. Steel asked SOM to plan a rough mock-up of a $200 million complex, comprised of an office tower (most of which would be leased to tenants other than U.S. Steel), a large hotel and a shopping center.

"We batted ideas around, between different designs and different proportions of each," Bassett recalls. "We just billed them for the hours worked. It never reached the stage where we talked about a fee for the entire project."

From this seemingly informal beginning developed a major assault on the city's planning and zoning regulations, with political repercussions that have not yet ceased. The campaign by and on behalf of U.S. Steel was described privately by one supervisor as "the most terrific pressure I've felt in ten years of public office." That it failed was not for lack of effort, imagination or money.

The chosen site for the U.S. Steel tower, on the waterfront between the old Ferry Building and the approaches to the Bay Bridge, was in an area of 84-foot height limitation. On ten percent of the site, the ceiling could be extended to a maximum of 175 feet under provisions of the city's Northern Waterfront Plan.

U.S. Steel and its local sponsors (i.e., Magnin-Shorenstein & Co.) had no intention of building within these restrictions. The proposed U.S. Steel tower would top out at 550 feet, slightly taller than the pylons of the Bay Bridge. To break the local barriers would require a majority vote in the City Planning Commission, followed by a majority vote by the Supervisors.

In planning its strategy, the highrise faction had the encouraging precedent of Transamerica Corporation, which had mounted a brilliantly successful public relations campaign the year before to diffuse and dilute local opposition to its new headquarters building. This arrogant, pyramidal structure, tallest west of the Mississippi, was implanted in a neighborhood of relatively small commercial structures on the edge of North Beach over the agonized protests of a handful of citizen groups. John Krizek, Transamerica's public relations manager, published a remarkable article not long ago in which he discussed with evident pride the tactics he had used to maneuver the Pyramid past the shoals of two dozen public hearings. *(See page 167.)*

Before the public had learned of the building, Transamerica took the precaution of inviting Mayor Alioto and Chief Administrative Officer Mellon "to take a look and to advise us as to the proper steps for approval." Next, Allan Jacobs, director of city planning, and other city officials enjoyed a similar sneak-preview.

The publishers of San Francisco's several newspapers and the general managers of major local television stations were guests at a "special luncheon," after which the papers ran "favorable editorials." Similar luncheons honored the heads of all city departments, Supervisors, leaders of organized labor and 200 representative members of the Chamber of Commerce.

With the major media and city officials well briefed on the merits of the Transamerica project, it was relatively easy for the proponents to paint such critics as the Telegraph Hill Dwellers and the Environmental Workshop as obstructionists and cranks. When a self-appointed group of "Artists Against the Pyramid" picketed Transamerica headquarters, an ad hoc contingent of "Artists FOR the Pyramid" countered with a demonstration by "hippie-looking young men."

"No one was aware that the counter demonstrators were led by two young men who comprised an ad agency, who had come to us a week earlier with an idea," Krizek confided later.

Transamerica regularly sent representatives, incognito, to take notes at strategy meetings of conservation organizations. When the anti-Pyramid forces succeeded in packing a public hearing with opponents of the project, Mayor Alioto dropped in for a "surprise visit." The Mayor's favorable testimony dominated the news reports of the meeting.

"The effect of all this was (that) the intent of the demonstrators was diffused," Krizek relates. With "both sides of the question apparently equally represented," the media went on presenting Transamerica's position in full and slighting the arguments of the opponents.

By a 10-1 vote, the supervisors removed all legal obstacles to the Transamerica Building.

U.S. Steel elected not to mount a campaign of overt public persuasion.

"In the first place," an official of the company explained, "we weren't building a corporate headquarters, as was Transamerica. We didn't have as much at stake. Transamerica, you see, already had its headquarters in San Francisco and was more or less rooted here. We weren't."

Instead of seducing Supervisors and coddling commissioners the corporation stood aloof — or appeared to do so — while the Port Commission carried the torch for the gross and illegal skyscraper that was allegedly to bring a golden bounty to the waterfront. U.S. Steel, in Chuck Bassett's words, remained "rich, sophisticated and very, very cool. Their financial investment was not large, and they could well afford to lose it. Mostly, they let the city fight it out."

And it turned out that there were any number of local pugilists willing to do the fighting while U.S. Steel held the coats. The Mayor saw the project as a boon to the city and a credit to his administration. Magnin regarded it as the keystone of his Embarcadero City, the "anchor" that would tie down smaller, subsidiary developments. Shorenstein could anticipate prestige and profits as leasing agent for one of the largest and best-situated office buildings in the West.

The Greater San Francisco Chamber of Commerce and the Downtown Association (retail merchants) naturally endorsed the Tower, as they would have done had it been 1,550 feet tall. (It is almost impossible to remember a time when these bastions of boomerism failed to welcome any sort of private undertaking that involved an expenditure of money within the city limits.)

Nor was it surprising that the unions allied in the Building and Construction Trades Council also welcomed the Steel Tower. To the officials of the Council, the skyscraper offered a promise of jobs for craft union members idled by a slowdown in residential construction. As one union agent put it: "Eight hundred guys sitting in our hiring hall waiting for work . . . a lot of them black . . . and the conservationists are screaming about the U.S. Steel project blocking the view. View? How many working people have a view? The project means jobs, and that's what counts."

More surprising was the unqualified support of the International Longshoremen and Warehousemen's Union (ILWU), which has seldom seen eye-to-eye with the downtown establishment on the proper use of public resources. The ILWU's position has been attributed, in part, to the personal influence of the union's long-time president, Harry Bridges, who, as an Alioto appointee to the Port Commission, was convinced that revenue from a U.S. Steel land lease was essential to assure construction of new maritime facilities, and in part to the close working relationship between Mayor Alioto and David Jenkins, the ILWU's skilled political organizer and an Alioto placement on the redevelopment staff at about $1,575 a month.

The combined influence of organized labor and organized business was difficult for any Supervisor to resist.

"It works like this," Supervisor Robert Mendelsohn explained. "Someone from the trade union calls you up, or pays a visit, like Ken Edwards, president of the Building Trades Council, and they say, 'We'll be watching this vote. This vote is the one we'll judge you by next election.'"

From the standpoint of planners, conservationists, neighborhood businessmen and homeowners, the most distressing endorsement of all — tantamount to a betrayal of principles — was that of SPUR, the moderate, privately financed citizen group that had purported to reflect the conscience of the community in matters of design, land use and environmental planning for several decades.

When SPUR was founded in 1943, it was called the San Francisco Planning and Housing Association. It was a gadfly organization of architects, planners and political liberals, constituting a permanent lobby for slum clearance, public housing and other supposed "urban improvements." In the late 1950's, the Association became San Francisco's official "citizen participation" organization under the federal government's urban renewal program. The new name, with its pugnacious acronym, reflected the Association's broader interests and tougher attitudes.

Although SPUR was powerless to save San Francisco from such catastrophes as the Embarcadero Freeway, Candlestick Park and the Transamerica pyramid, the Association has had, in general, a benign influence on the physical development of the city. Confronted by the Port Commission's deal with U.S. Steel, however, SPUR went into a peculiar and quite unprecedented collapse.

Apparently, a majority of SPUR directors accepted whole-hog the Port Commission's specious argument that large-scale commercial development of the northern waterfront was the only way to finance essential maritime facilities. Sizing up the formidable political lineup on Steel's side, SPUR concluded the rape of the waterfront was inevitable and therefore might as well be enjoyed — or, to put it more elegantly, that it might be possible to gain a little by yielding a lot.

In February, 1970, SPUR announced its endorsement of the Steel project and urged the city to lift the height limit it had imposed on that part of the waterfront. In return for this capitulation, the Port Commission secretly promised SPUR to respect lower height limits on the rest of the northern waterfront. Later, Cyril Magnin publicly offered to deed air rights above the 40-foot level to the city's Recreation and Park Commission in return for a go-ahead on the Steel and Ferry Port projects.

SPUR's acquiescence confused and divided the conservation bloc and the small but articulate planning lobby. For the moment it seemed that all San Francisco would accept the assault on the Embarcadero without political resistance.

"It was a mistake, I guess," says John Jacobs, SPUR's executive director. "We thought the project was sure to be passed by the Supervisors, that there was no chance of stopping it, so we tried to get something in return."

8. The Price of Compromise

At first SPUR's tactic appeared to be sound. There was no salient, no bastion from which to mount a defense against the developers. The City

The Price of Compromise

Planning Commission, overwhelmed by external pressures, rejected the advice of its professional staff and voted to raise the height limit to 400 feet to accommodate a 42-story U.S. Steel building. Just before the crucial vote, Mayor Alioto called each commissioner to his office to have what one Supervisor called "a little chat." Two small organizations (San Francisco Tomorrow and the Telegraph Hill Dwellers) opposing the height increase were left to chat with one another.

"We sent dozens of letters to the Supervisors but no one seemed interested," one of the founders of San Francisco Tomorrow recalls. U.S. Steel and the Port appealed to the Planning Commission a second time and got the height limit raised to 550 feet.

At this point, however, when it appeared that the issue was settled, there was a remarkable upsurge of conservationist opposition to both the Steel Tower and the nearby Ferry Port Plaza. Many persons can (and do) take credit for inspiring and directing this movement. Robert Jones, the Guardian's environmental editor, after numerous interviews, prepared the following account of the birth of the Highrise Resistance.

"At some point in almost every environmental campaign there comes a time, in the dark of night, amid tea and cookies, when a group that is usually described as 'a small band of concerned citizens' meets and maps out its plans. In this case, the meeting took place in September, 1970, at the home

Kids on a raft off Hunters Point, one place you can get to the waterfront. Port would close off these sections—no parks—and pack in cargo handling.

of Dr. Frank Gerbode. It was attended by many of the conservationist establishment of San Francisco, including Gardner Mein, former president of the Planning Commission ... John Ritchie, one of the two planning commissioners who had voted against raising the height limit ... Frieda Klussmann, who almost single-handedly organized the campaign to save the cable cars some years ago ... and leaders of a number of conservation groups such as the Sierra Club, San Francisco Tomorrow and the Environmental Workshop ...

"These people are wealthy, sophisticated and powerful. Nobody had to warn them about the difficulties ahead. Many of them had been involved in the fight against the Transamerica Pyramid, and they knew the sting of that defeat, 10 to 1, in the Board of Supervisors ...

"This time, however, they had a new ally: Herb Caen, whose newspaper column is of incalculable influence throughout northern California. Caen's daily mix of anecdotes, exclusive news tips and personal opinions is a newspaper within a newspaper, free of restraint from the management of the Chronicle. To a politician, artist or crusader, a word of praise in Caen's column is worth a paragraph of endorsement on the editorial page.

"On the day after the strategy meeting in the Gerbode home, Caen devoted an entire column to the Steel project and its promoters, lashing out at 'the old gaffers who squirm with delight at the thought of another towering erection.'

"At once, the issue commanded intense community interest. No longer was it just another round in the long fight between well-heeled Pacific Heights posey-pluckers and Chamber of Commerce boosters: it was a major political showdown over the future of San Francisco. With his network of informants, his acid wit and his tremendous readership, Caen was a formidable critic for even The Fairmont Cabinet.

"As one of the founders of San Francisco Tomorrow put it: 'What Caen did, really, was to make the whole issue count in terms of votes at the next election.' As the anti-highrise movement gained respectability, it also began to pick up adherents at City Hall. Supervisor Roger Boas, a seasoned and articulate member of the Board, was the first to declare his open opposition to the Steel Tower. Boas usually plays a lone hand; but in this instance he went to talk over his feelings with his colleague, Supervisor Ronald Pelosi, who had been hospitalized with a broken hip.

"'Life is short,' Boas remembers saying. 'I've got to do the right thing for the city ... I didn't give a damn politically. I knew I was going to upset labor's applecart, and that's hard when you've been a member of their establishment so long ...' It was a difficult step for a man of ambition. 'Even though I was State Democratic Chairman, I badly damaged my image. If I were to run for mayor now, I'd have a very hard time of it.'

"Damaged or not, Boas soon had another ally in Supervisor Dianne Feinstein, president of the Board. Although Mrs. Feinstein had been a Supervisor only nine months, she had observed the battle over the Transamerica building as an outsider. 'I thought, the city's going to die if someone doesn't fight this.'

"But the other nine members of the Board had yet to be counted. Supervisors Terry Francois, Peter Tamaras, Dorothy von Beroldingen and John Barbagelata were presumed to favor lifting the height limits on the Embarcadero to accommodate U.S. Steel. Supervisors Robert Mendelsohn, John Ertola, Robert Gonzales, James Mailliard and Pelosi had still to speak out one way or the other.

'The conservationists, meanwhile, were falling prey to some of the squabbles that often beset volunteer groups. The Citizens Waterfront Committee, an ad hoc organization formed out of the Gerbode meeting, undertook to coordinate and command the various factions, but it suffered from internal disagreements, notably between the president, Richard Goldman, and the secretary, Fred Selinger.

"'It was not a happy combination,' says one of the original members of the CWC. 'Dick wanted to educate the masses and Fred wanted to be mayor.'

"Furthermore, there were factions within the conservationist opposition that did not wish to be commanded by Goldman, Selinger or anyone else. Among these was Alvin Duskin, the San Francisco clothing designer-manufacturer, who suddenly splashed into environmental politics a few months earlier with a campaign of full-page newspaper advertisements to stop the commercial exploitation of Alcatraz Island. Duskin had attended the Gerbode meeting, but he did not seem willing to subordinate his own efforts to those of a Pacific Heights tactical command.

"'He came and told us what he was going to do,' Jerry Cauthen, a founder of San Francisco Tomorrow, says. 'He didn't want to work with anybody. He didn't ask anybody to work with him. He was, I think, staking out his turf, saying, here's my bailiwick, you can do what you like, just don't inter-fere with me.'

"Both San Francisco Tomorrow and the Telegraph Hill Dwellers also were supposed to be under the umbrella of the Citizens Waterfront Committee. SF Tomorrow gradually withdrew, however, on grounds that its members were not invited to meetings of the CWC; and the Hill Dwellers also went their own way, confounded by the harem politics of the waterfront group.

"'They spent all their time jockeying for positions inside the organization,' a Hill Dweller said in disgust.

"Within a month after the Waterfront Committee was formed, the Board of Supervisors was scheduled to vote on the Planning Commission's proposal to raise the height limit for the Steel Tower.

"'There was little we could do,' Goldman recalls. 'We had only two votes for sure against the project, maybe three. The people supporting the project saw that, and, thank god, they got greedy.' Instead of accepting a 400-foot height limit, which would have been acceptable even to Boas and Feinstein, the proponents of the project decided to push for a 500-foot ceiling.

"As Boas tells it: 'A couple of Supervisors came to me and said, Look, if you'll go for 400 feet, we'll come down from 550. I was ready to go along. It seemed the best we could do . . . But at the meeting, Mendelsohn proposed a 90 day postponement. I am sure the Port had decided against the 400-foot compromise and wanted the three months to gather support for the full 550.'

"The postponement carried, 6 votes to 4. Pelosi and Mailliard joined Boas and Feinstein in voting against delay.

"'We turned out to be stronger than I had believed, Boas admits, 'but I thought we were finished, all the same. The three months, I thought, that's long enough to dilute the opposition to the project. The public is very fickle about such things, you know. At that point, you must realize, U.S. Steel had never lost a vote. They thought, and we thought, that U.S. Steel would get all it wanted.'

"Mendelsohn has since explained that he had quite another reason for proposing a delay.

"'You'll remember that I am also a member of the Bay Conservation and Development Commission, and I knew the issue was not resolved with the BCDC, as everyone believed. I wanted to give us – the Supervisors – time to see how the BCDC would act.'

"The BCDC, a regional organization with power to regulate dredging and filling projects in San Francisco Bay, was reviewing application from both the U.S. Steel and Ferry Port Plaza projects. Several points were at issue in both

SAN FRANCISCO LEASES US THIS WATERFRONT LAND....

...THEN WE BUILD THIS MODEST 10 MILE HIGH BUILDING AND IN TURN LEASE IT OUT AND MAYBE MAKE A FEW BUCKS HEH HEH

U.S. Steel

TO SHOW OUR GRATITUDE, WE BUILD THIS PASSENGER TERMINAL WHICH NOBODY NEEDS.

cases. Were these projects appropriate to the waterfront? Were they "water-related" projects that could legally be built on fill or pilings? (The Steel complex included a passenger ship terminal adjoining the hotel and office tower.) Would the replacement of the old piers involve a net loss of water area in the bay?

"Crucial to the BCDC was a theory called the "rule of equivalencies," which had been advanced by attorneys for the Ferry Port Plaza with the support of the Port Commission. Under this theory, it would be all right for the Port Commission to go ahead with a project that involved a net loss of water area so long as an equivalent water area was opened up elsewhere (i.e., at Pier 45) by tearing down an old pier.

"Joseph Bodovitz, executive director of BCDC, felt the rule of equivalencies had merit — 'otherwise, those old piers will stay there forever' — and he believed the commission should adopt the rule. Anticipating legal challenges, however, the commission asked Att. Gen. Thomas Lynch to study the proposed rule of equivalencies and give an opinion as to whether it conformed with the basic law establishing the BCDC.

"In December Lynch decided that the so-called rule of equivalencies would violate the fundamental principles of the bay commission. The commission had little choice but to accept his advice. Two weeks later, BCDC voted 22 to 1 to refuse to allow fill permits for Ferry Port Plaza under the rule of equivalencies.

"Mayor Alioto, who had urged the BCDC to defy the attorney general's ruling, now threatened to sue the Commission and to lobby in Sacramento for changes in the bay conservation law.

"'The law is no permanent thing,' the Mayor said, and he strode out of the hearing room.

"In effect, both Ferry Port Plaza and the U.S. Steel complex were killed by action of the BCDC.

"'It was something of a miracle,' says Jerry Cauthen of San Francisco Tomorrow. 'It came out of nowhere and saved us for a while. Because we were just too disorganized, too petty and too poor to really stop those projects. A lot of people are taking credit now for saving the waterfront, but really, it was that technicality. For once, the technicality worked for us.'

"The labor unions, business organizations and conservation activists who had been whipsawing the Board of Supervisors with threats and promises, realized that the controversial projects were illegal, at least temporarily. But the Board's vote on the height limit had not lost its urgency. The Supervisors, themselves, felt a need to prove to the city that they would not evade a controversial issue on a technicality. Moreover, there was the distinct possibility that the height limit would again be at issue if BCDC should change its position. The Port Commission was still fighting for its grandiose scheme.

"'They called in all their cohorts,' Mrs. Feinstein says. 'The Labor Council, the Chamber of Commerce, the Downtown Association. They knew they would need 500 feet if the BCDC ever accepted the rule of equivalencies or anything like the rule of equivalencies.'

"During the three month delay, the mood of the Supervisors had changed, however. The strength of the highrise opposition had grown incredibly, whereas the position of the Port Commission had deteriorated. At the last minute, the Port Commission decided to ask for another delay.

"'We almost lost it right then,' Boas recalls. 'Up to the very day of the vote, Mendelsohn was lobbying for another delay. I knew that our strength was at a peak and that a delay would be fatal. Then, out of nowhere, the Citizens Waterfront Committee decided to go along with the delay. I couldn't believe it — I never understood what went wrong. It seems some faction seized the mimeograph and cranked out an unauthorized release, supporting the delay.' Boas called the Committee and asked them to change and clarify its policy. Mendelsohn dropped his effort to gain a delay, and the Board faced three alternatives: to accept the Planning Commission's 550 foot ceiling, to compromise at 400 feet or less or to go back to the 175 foot height limit recommended by the professional planning staff.

"Before the meeting, Boas, Feinstein, Pelosi and Mailliard agreed they would vote against the top limit. As for Francois, Von Beroldingen, Tamaras and Michael Driscoll (appointed by Mayor Alioto to replace John Ertola,) they had decided, individually or collectively, against compromise. Francois says: 'We had been told by the Port that 400 feet would not be enough height to assure the financial success of the project, so we believed the Port should receive the full 550 feet.'

"To test the strength of the opposition, Francois decided to move another postponement. His motion failed.

"'That made Francois mad,' one of his colleagues said later, 'and he pulled a stupid trick. He said, If we're going to kill the Port, let's really kill it, and he moved for a 40 foot height limit. It was childish, and it turned the tide against the Port.'

"Angry at being accused of trying to 'kill' the Port, the other Supervisors struck down Francois' 40 foot proposal. Pelosi moved to adopt a 175 foot limit in the area. Mendelsohn and Gonzales joined the four anti-highrise Supervisors, and the motion passed 6 to 4. The Steel Tower was dead and double-dead."

9. Post Mortems

Immediately, the atmosphere of crisis that had electrified the city vanished. A mayoral election and a supervisoral election loomed ahead, and every office holder who had been buffeted by the waterfront controversy needed time and rest to bandage personal wounds and repair broken alliances.

But the factors that had brought the city to such agonies of doubt and self-examination remained; menacing not only the Embarcadero but half a dozen other neighborhoods: the relentless desire of real estate developers to seize large, well-located parcels of urban land and build on them to the legal limits of height and density; the short-sighted tendency of the city administration to welcome all development as equally desirable; the public ignorance of the real costs — ecological as well as financial — of high density development; and the single-minded determination of such public agencies as the Port Commission to maintain their administrative satrapies by peddling land development concessions to eager corporations.

Joseph Sax, in his book *Defending the Environment*, warned that such a unique public resource as the San Francisco waterfront can never be entirely "safe" from offensive onslaughts of over-development.

"Money can always wait," Sax writes. "An issue may lie fallow for years, with the public thinking a project is dead, when suddenly it re-blooms. You see, the money didn't disappear, it was just waiting."

One month after the Supervisors had re-imposed the stringent height limit on the area of the Ferry Building, the Port Commission sued BCDC.

"It may take a year of litigation and $25,000," said Port Director Miriam Wolff, "but we will change this destructive situation with the BCDC."

At the same time, however, San Franciscans were awakening to a new political movement born out of the crisis on the Embarcadero. It is an ill-defined rebellion — an effort to express resentment against exploitation — the exploitation of public resources and public lands in the name of municipal progress, the exploitation of irreplaceable environmental amenities for private profit, the exploitation of a passive middle-class by spoilers who masquerade as civic benefactors.

An example of this movement is Alvin Duskin's campaign to enlarge the assault on the U.S. Steel building into a general attack on highrise commercial building throughout the city. During the civic debate on the Embarcadero height limit, Duskin bought a full page advertisement in the Chronicle, headlined: "Skyscrapers are economically feasible, but only if you own one."

At the beginning, Duskin's anti-highrise campaign was based primarily on intuitions and prejudices rather than economic facts. His fellow conservationists termed it "naive" and "unsophisticated," and they were right.

But more than 10,000 newspaper readers clipped coupons from the anti-highrise ad and sent them to City Hall to show dissatisfaction with Port Commission policy.

"Say what you like about Alvin Duskin," says Supervisor Dianne Feinstein. "Those ads work. They are the best mobilizing tool anyone's come up with yet."

On the Waterfront: Piggybacking and Thimble-rigging

It was the U.S. Steel/Ferry Port Plaza threat to the northern waterfront that ignited San Francisco's highrise crisis. The same threat still hangs over the waterfront area, despite the decision of the Board of Supervisors to maintain height limits on the Embarcadero and legal actions by the Bay Conservation and Development Commission and Attorney General.

The threat is both political and economic, for there are powerful private interests that would profit from overdeveloping the public waterfront. Fortunately, there also are strong political and economic arguments against overdevelopment. Once these counter-arguments are generally known and understood, the city will be able to protect this irreplaceable area from destruction. Meanwhile, the Port Commission's mistaken policies continue to present a grave hazard to the future of the city.

The basic fallacy of the Port Commission's "piggy-backing" policy — the policy that led the Commission to sponsor the U.S. Steel and Ferry Port Plaza projects — is the wickedly stupid assumption that it is possible for cities to get something for nothing by handing over public functions to private interests. Generally speaking, the worst deals San Francisco or any other city has blundered into have been "arrangements" under which a public service facility (such as a stadium or parking garage) has been built as a private franchise or concession "at no cost to the public."

The "no cost" pitch was offered as an excuse to bring private capitalists and concessionaires into the city's program of downtown parking garages. Supposedly, the city would be spared the political effort and financial burden of raising money to build the garages, and private enterprise would do a "more efficient" job of building and running the facilities.

What actually happened was that each garage cost considerably more, in the long run, than it would have cost under public financing. The users pay more, over the years, to enjoy the benefit of this "public improvement" on publicly owned land; the private developers take a comfortable, tax-free interest on their capital; the private operator takes a profit on his concession; and the city gets a pittance in rental and the assurance that it will inherit the facility some day in the future when all the debts have been paid off.

Obviously, if a private entrepreneur is willing to take on the construction and operation of a public convenience, there has got to be a profit in it. The very words "at no cost to the public," popping up in a news story or a political speech, should be fair warning to any sagacious citizen to take a firm grip on his wallet.

The process of municipal giveaway has seldom been illustrated in a more subtle and insidious form than in the passenger ship terminal that served as a carrot-on-a-stick in the proposed U.S. Steel complex on the Embarcadero. In this case, the construction of a relatively useless public facility by private capital became the excuse for bestowing a land lease of tremendous value upon the capitalists *with virtually no cash return to the city.*

To begin with, the proposed passenger ship terminal is of dubious value. Although Port Director Miriam Wolff has said the Port "desperately" needs a new terminal for passenger ships (Chronicle, March 4, 1970), ship operators do not agree that San Francisco needs such a terminal *at all.* Unquestionably, it would be pleasant for trans-Pacific and coastal passengers to pass through a trim, clean, modern terminal at San Francisco's water gate — but are there enough passengers to justify the cost of the building, which has been variously and vaguely estimated at $10 million, $15 million and $30 million?

Businessmen do not think so — or the terminal would have been built years ago. At last count, only three passenger lines (Matson, American President and P & O) regularly called at San Francisco. Only a few others — Princess, Holland-American and a few mixed service passenger-freighters — called on an irregular schedule.

The passenger terminal has been discussed on the Embarcadero for years. Neither private enterprise nor the former management of the Port ever concluded the project would be viable. Yet, Cyril Magnin's Port Commission and staff, in their eagerness to consummate the commercial redevelopment of the northern waterfront, tried to convice the people of San Francisco that (a) the terminal was a desperate necessity to the life of the Port and (b) the Port should be allowed to negotiate an agreement with a large corporation, in violation of the northern waterfront plan, for a skyscraper hotel-office complex that would include as an auxiliary feature a passenger ship terminal to be built and paid for by the corporation *in lieu of rent.*

In other words, the passenger terminal, which could not justify itself, was used to justify a $200 million commercial development cheek-and-jaw with the towers of the Bay Bridge. Each year, U.S. Steel would be permitted to apply the total of its rental fee to the Port toward paying off the principal and interest on the construction of the terminal.

Fiscal experts calculated the Port would not receive a penny in cash income from U.S. steel for at least 25 to 30 years — only a passenger terminal that could never pay for itself.

The Port management never explained how this passenger terminal, which was not practical for the state or city to build with low interest, public bond funds, had suddenly become economic for a private corporation to build with high interest, private capital. The answer, of course, is that there was a hidden municipal subsidy: the city, itself, would actually be paying the cost of the terminal by giving up the use of choice waterfront land at no cash return.

Get it? Is your hand on your wallet now?

The Great Passenger Terminal Money Trick is only one example of the Port Commission's economic thimble-rigging. On close examination, most of the Port's arguments for its development policies turn out to be equally fallacious, flimsy or false.

1. **Argument:** Most of the finger piers along the northern waterfront are obsolete and could therefore be eliminated without harming the Port.

Fact: Most of the finger piers are not obsolete, except for use by container-carrying vessels. All but a few of the oldest piers are quite adequate to handle traditional, break-bulk cargo for many years ahead.

The Arthur D. Little Company, in reviewing the city's master plan for the northern waterfront, advised the Port Commission to relinquish its older piers *only if the proposed use of the land would generate enough revenue to finance the construction of new, more efficient cargo facilities.*

"The 'if' in the previous sentence should not be ignored," the consultants warned. "It is economically sound for the Port to trade old piers for new revenues; it is not sound for the Port merely to give up old piers."

2. **Argument:** Revenue from the proposed highrise developments on the northern waterfront will be sufficient to pay the cost of financing new facilities elsewhere.

Fact: Revenues from the proposed developments would not be adequate for this purpose, either during the construction or after the completion of the highrise buildings.

After an independent study of the Port's economic needs, Supervisor Roger Boas and Planning Commissioner Mortimer Fleishhacker, Jr. reported that the proposed highrise buildings could not be constructed soon enough to produce revenues for new shipping facilities and that the annual rents to the Port after completion of the office buildings would not cover interest and principal payments on the revenue bonds for construction of the cargo piers.

The consultant on this study was Dr. Claude Gruen, formerly of the Arthur D. Little Company. Dr. Gruen was chief economist in the original report on the harbor.

3. **Argument:** The Port's scheme of financing new facilities by revenue bonds will save the taxpayers money.

Fact: Financing port improvements by revenue bonds is more expensive (by millions of dollars) than financing with general obligation bonds because revenue bonds pay a higher rate of interest. Dr. Gruen estimated that the proposed $32 million cargo terminal at Islais Creek, for example, would cost $5.5 million *more* if financed with revenue bonds than it would if financed with general obligation bonds. This additional cost would be passed on to shippers or non-maritime tenants of the Port and would ultimately result in higher costs to consumers.

4. **Argument:** Construction of highrise real estate projects on port properties will bring tax subsidies to homeowners.

Fact: New construction generally adds to the total assessed property value or tax base of a community, but this increase does not necessarily result in a higher net return in tax revenues because the new construction may also bring added costs of service and dislocation to the local government.

Suburban communities have long been aware that certain residential tracts actually increase the local tax burden. As the Livingston & Blayney report showed for the Palo Alto foothills, they cost more in services (schools, streets, sewers, police and fire protection, etc.) than they generate in tax revenues.

There is growing evidence this may be true of highrise office buildings. Large office buildings draw a flood of 300,000 commuters into the central city five days a week creating a tremendous demand for public transportation, parking facilities, sewerage lines, street lighting and general government services.

5. **Argument:** Highrise construction on the Northern Waterfront will create jobs for San Franciscans.

Fact: While no one can deny that building projects provide jobs for

Threats to the Shore

1. Area: Ocean Beach--San Francisco's breezy salt water playground. Publicly owned beach and bridle path runs clear from the Cliff House to the San Mateo county line. A great place to drive, walk, bike, breathe.
Threat: Residential towers-- Developers would like to put up tower apartments in the Sloat Boulevard-Great Highway area. Potential redevelopment of old Playland-at-the-Beach might involve cliff-hugging highrises of the type now defacing Santa Monica's famous palisades.

2. Area: Point Lobos--Magnificent view point, part city-owned, part private.
Threat: Highrise apartments-- Views from city parkland would be blocked entirely by proposed multi-story apartments on site of old Sutro Baths.

3. Area: Seacliff--Golf course, beaches and one of the city's finest residential neighborhoods on the headlands of the continent.
Threat: Army developments-- Public access to open areas and beaches could be severely curtailed by housing projects, schools, other building plans of U.S. Army at Presidio.

4. Area: Presidio Shoals-- Sheltered, level shoreline from Old Fort Point to the Marina commands one of the world's superb marine vistas.
Threat: Army institutional expansion-- Massive Letterman Hospital is an example of potential overdevelopment of Presidio lands. Army has recently expanded Crissy Field airport, uses prime shoreline land for warehouses, parking lots.

5. Area: The Marina-- Emerald grass at the water's edge--and an incomparable view of the bay, its islands and surrounding hills. A daily delight for frisbie-tossers, dog-walkers, softball-pitchers.
Threat: Trafficways-- Second crossing to Marin county or freeway links to Golden Gate Bridge could despoil entire area. Powerful local resistance to highrise.

6. Area: Black Point - North Point--Shops, museums, restaurants clustered in a world-famous center of commercial recreation.
Threat: Bridge Building-- Marin bridge anchored on Russian Hill or Fort Mason would turn beloved Aquatic Park area into a swirling tangle of freeway ramps, exhaust fumes, automobile noise. Developers would love to grab onto Army's Fort Mason, "improve" it with clusters of highrise luxury apartments like the Fontana.

7. Area: Northern Waterfront-- Fascinating historic center of San Francisco's maritime industry.
Threat: Commercial highrise construction-- Port Commission's ambitious designs for an "Embarcadero City" would transform old piers into massive commercial structures at water's edge, blocking access, views, light and air--and dooming the city to Manhattan-like congestion.

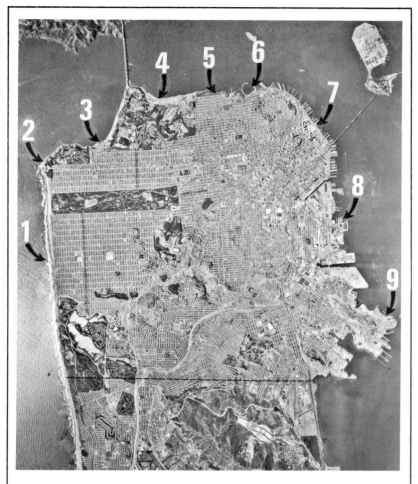

8. Area: Potrero Coast--Inaccessible and badly defaced industrial district with a few delightful peep-holes for boating, fishing, strolling.
Threat: Expansion of maritime terminals-- Port Commission plans for fenced container cargo terminals would destroy few remaining access spots. Neighborhood desperately needs more,not less, parkland along the bay.

9. Area: South Bayshore-- Working class homes, housing projects, commerce and industry mingle in an area of fine weather, refreshing views and exciting human potentialities.
Threat: Freeways, bridges, port terminals-- State and city join private owners in filling tidelands, forcing further industrial and transportation use of shoreline and thwarting neighborhood hopes of improved conditions.

carpenters, concrete finishers, electricians and other craftsmen, this does not constitute an argument to put buildings on every square inch of land — nor to permit skyscrapers in inappropriate locations.

A well located project provides just as many union jobs as a badly located one. So does rebuilding schools and public facilities to earthquake standards or "face-lifting" aging neighborhoods.

As for the argument that office towers create permanent new employment for white collar workers, this has never been proved. It seems more likely that a new waterfront office center would merely draw office workers from downtown buildings — or bring in more commuters. San Francisco now has about an 11% vacancy factor in its office buildings. More: highrise buildings create jobs for commuters: a Wells Fargo study showed that from 1963 to 1968 jobs for San Franciscans in the downtown increased by just 1%, while jobs for commuters increased by 23%.

6. **Argument:** If one or two over-sized projects are permitted in the vicinity of the Ferry Building, the rest of the northern waterfront can be protected from highrise development.

Fact: This political compromise was proposed by SPUR, (the San Francisco Planning and Urban Renewal Association). In return for permission to over-exploit the Ferry Building area, the Port Commission would relinquish air rights above the 40-foot level over the rest of the northern waterfront. Thus, the Port would be "saved" and most of the waterfront protected.

The SPUR compromise was based on the mistaken assumption that rental income from massive commercial developments is the best — and perhaps the only — way for the Port to meet its obligations under the Burton Act. According to Dr. Gruen, however, the Port cannot hope to be rescued from its economic crisis by revenues from complex projects that are not yet at the stage of working drawings.

The need for new capital is immediate; and the rental income is far in the future. Thus, piggy-backing schemes will not solve the Port's present dilemma nor relieve future developmental pressures on Port lands. There are other and better financial courses for the Port.

Furthermore, the SPUR compromise would not guarantee satisfactory development of those portions of the northern Waterfront that would be placed under the 40 foot ceiling. To the contrary, by endorsing a major violation of the city's waterfront plan, it would weaken all parts of that plan and probably accelerate more big waterfront projects.

It is neither wise nor necessary to bargain away the height controls in the vicinity of the Ferry Building in an attempt to guarantee the enforcement of controls elsewhere. In diplomatic terms, this SPUR compromise is a "Munich Agreement."

7. **Argument:** The Port's development program will benefit the southern bayshore.

Fact: There is a disturbing vagueness about the Port's long-range plans; but, generally speaking, these call for building dozens of acres of fenced storage yards along the water's edge on the Southern bayshore.

If the Port completes all its projects there won't be much recreation space and access left along this stretch.

Throughout the public debate on the proposed development of the northern waterfront, nobody has said much about the effect of the Port Commission's expansion program upon this neglected area of San Francisco. Yet, the Port Commission's activities will have a strong, potentially detrimental effect on neighborhood life, especially in South Bayshore, a troublesome, disfigured area between India Basin and the San Mateo county line.

South Bayshore suffers today from many forms of social and economic distress that are summed up in the term "ghetto conditions" — unemployment, poor education, discrimination, a general feeling of hopelessness. The human problems are compounded by the isolation and physical deterioration of the neighborhood. South Bayshore is simply not a salubrious, attractive place; one of its gravest defects is what the Planning Department euphemistically calls "the gradual deterioration and inaccessibility of the shoreline."

To South Bayshore residents, this means that mountains of sand and rubble and acres of smoldering rubbish lie between the people of the neighborhood and the shore of the bay. Blue water shimmers at a tantalizing distance, almost totally inaccessible to anyone who might wish to walk, fish, swim, bicycle or sit quietly in fresh air and sunshine.

The people of San Francisco would be enormously enriched if the South Bayshore could lay claim to its shoreline — and this is by no means an impossible dream. The City Planning Department, in consultation with representatives from the district, has drawn up a plan of neighborhood reconstruction that includes a system of waterside parks, marinas, paths and parkways.

Just east of Candlestick Park stadium would be an 88-acre park with a commercial marina, a small boat harbor and restaurants built around a man-made cove. North of Hunters Point would be a second, smaller marina on India Basin.

Critical to the success of this plan is the cooperation and enthusiasm of the Port Commission, but Commissioners have evidenced no interest in promoting the physical rejuvenation of the South Bayshore district. Instead, in their eagerness to develop new cargo-handling facilities, they have laid plans to fill nearly all of India Basin, surrounding it with a high chain-link fence and sealing off still another long stretch of shoreline to public access. The BDCD, in granting the Port the necessary fill permit, required that a 50-foot strip of "park" be created along the edge of a small, land-locked lagoon that will remain — but there is no guarantee the Port ever will find the money or the inspiration to landscape this property.

Rather than taking the lead in developing the human uses of the San Francisco waterfront, the Port Commission seems to regard humans as a nuisance and public access to the water as a special privilege, to be granted only where it does not interfere with cargo handling. Along the Potrero shore just north of India Basin, where the Port has grandiose plans to fill acres and acres of tidelands, virtually no locations are reserved for public access or recreation.

A group of residents on Potrero Hill, learning of the Port's designs on the shoreline, proposed a plan for half a dozen small parks, view-points and peep-holes in the solid cordon of fenced industrial yards along the bay; but even this modest proposal (it might better be called a prayer) depends upon the sufferance of the Port — (for the city has no master plan for this portion of the waterfront) and the Port is far more interested in building container yards than bicycle paths and fishing piers.

It is not that the Port Commissioners are hostile to recreation. They just don't see much profit in it. The Port's chief engineer and his staff have been working up a plan for some little access places among the cargo terminals; but greenbelts and esplanades are not the Port's compelling interest.

Most of its staff energies are fully absorbed by the inter-city struggle to attract maritime trade. Such problems as environmental quality and the enhancement of urban life take a remote second place to the more exciting business of large-scale real estate development.

Thus, it must be argued, Port plans for the southern waterfront will be distinctly detrimental to residents of those neighborhoods unless the allotment of recreational space is substantially increased. As for the effect of the proposed container cargo terminals upon adjoining industrial properties, no evidence has been offered to show that the new maritime facilities will either enhance or depress adjacent areas.

8. **Argument:** The Port-proposed commercial projects will not interfere with continued maritime activities on the northern waterfront.

Fact: Although the Port's most recent policies call for continued maritime use of piers between Fisherman's Wharf and the Ferry Building, it seems likely that further highrise commercial development at the water's edge would generate traffic that would seriously interfere with the movements of trucks and trains near the piers.

The Search For Workable Alternatives

Up to this point, we have discussed the development policies of the Port of San Francisco and how these policies threaten the comfort, convenience and economic well-being of the city. Now it is necessary to consider whether there are any realistic alternatives to these wrong-headed policies — whether there are, in fact, policies that would not only vitalize the maritime industry but also enhance the beauty and usefulness of the waterfront.

At the outset, one has to accept two basic assumptions: first, that the Port *does* need new cargo handling facilities; and second, that the Port *does not* have funds to finance these facilities out of accumulated surpluses or current revenues. From there on, practically everything is conjecture. Port management has never been specific about the amount of non-maritime revenue it would need to support its expansion program. For this reason, no one can say for certain whether the rentals on the U.S. Steel and Ferry Port Plaza projects would be more or less than adequate.

Despite this vagueness, it is obvious that several sources of capital are available to the Port. Besides its own revenue bonds, the Port can raise money from general obligation bonds of the City-County of San Francisco, federal urban renewal funds or tax increment bonds.

The former director, Rae Watts, favored using general obligation bonds (the same sort of city-backed bonds that are used to construct new airport facilities, water lines, sewers and other municipal improvements) to build a 33-acre cargo terminal at the former Bethlehem shipyard site. Early in 1970, he asked the Planning Commission to approve submission of a $14.1 million bond proposal to the voters that autumn. He admitted the terminal would not pay for itself —that some, if not all,of the cost of paying off the bonds would fall on the taxpayers — but he hoped that within a few years the Port would have increased its non-maritime revenues so the tax subsidy would no longer be necessary.

Watts's approach apparently was too candid for the Port Commissioners. They were afraid the voters would reject a bond issue that required tax support.

The Commission abruptly withdrew the bond proposal from the Planning Department, fired Watts and gave his job to Miss Miriam Wolff, who had been the Port's legal counsel. At the same time, Commissioners stepped up their campaign to convince the public that San Francisco could get something for nothing by piggy-backing the cost of the new cargo terminal onto commercial developments near the Ferry building.

Watts, of course, was not an opponent of the piggy-backing concept. He, too, believed that the Port would have to develop non-maritime revenues to help pay for new terminal facilities. But he doggedly insisted on completing

How the Port Commission Wants to "Improve" the Waterfront

The Port Commission's so-called "master plan" for the San Francisco shoreline is a confusing mixture of daydreams, possibilities and pure speculation. Several projects shown on this map have been stalled by legal barriers. Others are merely glints in the eye of the port engineer.

But it is worth knowing what the Port Commission has in mind. Experience has shown that a mark on the map can be turned overnight into a disastrous threat.

A.   Hyde Street Pier — "Fish Alley" development of commercial canneries, shops, restaurants. A generally tourist extension of Fisherman's Wharf.

B.   Pier 45 — Slated for non-maritime use as a motel and shop development similar to Fisherman's Wharf. Italian investment syndicate proposed to build a 300-room hotel, luxury apartments, offices, shops.

C.   Piers 37 to 39 — Marked for private redevelopment as a hotel-motel-commercial complex. In September, 1969, Port Commission signed lease agreement with Dillingham Corporation for motel on nine acre site. Return to Port: $80,000-a-year or 3% of gross. An ice cream parlor at Fisherman's Wharf pays 8% of gross.

D.   Piers 1, 3, 5 and 7 — Site of temporarily stalled Ferry Port Plaza, a $110 million private project by Oceanic Properties subsidiary of Castle & Cooke; Kipco subsidiary of Kidder, Peabody; and the Ford Foundation. Involved building an over-water platform of about 14 acres, about the size of Alcatraz Island; a 2,400-car underground garage; a 1,200-room super-luxury hotel; a commercial "galleria" the length of two football fields. Port Commission proposed removing existing Pier 41 to compensate for loss of water area.

E.   Piers 14, 16, 18, 20, 22 & 24 — Site of U.S. Steel Tower, hotel, plaza and passenger terminal, a $200 million highrise project (550-foot office building, 1000-room hotel, 2000-car garage, $15 million passenger terminal). Port was to receive minimum $400,000 a year and up to $600,000 from gross rentals to tenants, but it was estimated all financial return for 27 years would actually go to pay off cost of building the terminal.

F.   Piers 34, 36, 38, 40, 42, 44 and 46A — All existing structures subject to rebuilding or reuse, possibly for industrial or aviation (STOL airport.) Port designates the area for "maritime, port support, industrial or aviation use."

G.   Pier 48 — Existing small pier at mouth of ship channel to be expanded to a 15 acre container cargo terminal. Major curtailment of public access likely.

H.   Berry Street Ship Channel — Berths for LASH barges and similar lighters contemplated on both north and south sides of estuary.

I.   Pier 56 — Major filling of existing China Basin to create 15-acre container-cargo terminal.

J.   Pier 70 (Bethlehem Steel Company Drydock) — Privately financed, 900-foot drydock at northeast corner of Bethlehem Yard, on long term lease from Port Commission. Facility to be built and operated by company.

K.   Pier 72 — A $14-$17 million, two-berth cargo terminal (break-bulk and container) on 33 acres of former Bethlehem Shipyard plus about 49 acres of bay fill in Warm Water Cove at the foot of 24th Street. Total site (82 acres) would accommodate four or five container berths. No financing or design plans. A long-range development.

L.   Islais Creek — Both sides of channel earmarked for Port use as storage area for cargo barges from LASH terminal at India Basin. Present limited public access to be curtailed.

    M. Pier 94 — Four berth container cargo terminal on a 114 acre site. Cost and development schedule uncertain.

    N. Pier 96 — India Basin LASH Terminal, a 48-acre fill project, with 20 acres of offshore water reserved for two cargo ships and their lighters. A $21 million project, now under construction, to be leased by Pacific Far East Lines.

    O. Pier 98 — A second, 48-acre fill project to create another two berth LASH facility. Not yet financed or designed. Cost estimated at $15 million.

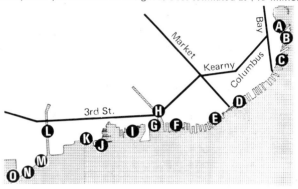

the prescription by admitting that most marine terminals lose money and that the Port would need a further public subsidy *even if the piggy-backing scheme went through.*

Watts apparently thought the public was entitled to a certain degree of candor from public agencies. There have been other, hard-nosed officials who have taken the same position — that if a plan cannot stand up under scrutiny, if it must be promulgated by subterfuge, by deeding away the permanent use of public property to private investors, then its value to the community must be questionable, and there is reason to ask whether U.S. Steel et al. is taking priority over the public interest. The Port Commission, however, prefers the type of financing that requires miniscule public review. This attitude is consistent with the Commission's "authority-itis," that pernicious species of government arrogance that precipitated the development crisis on the San Francisco waterfront.

Breaking the Mold

Without being unduly pessimistic, one may assume the recent crisis on the waterfront was not a unique or isolated phenomenon. The same exuberant desire for massive urban development still throbs in the icy corporate veins of the investment consortiums; the same esthetic insensibility still numbs the great architectural offices; the same monolithic provinciality still motivates the Port Commission.

To avoid a repetition, a dozen repetitions, of the 1970-71 assault on the northern waterfront, San Francisco will have to exert a firmer control on its urban destiny than most American cities have as yet been able to maintain. The control involves not only the adoption and enforcement of environmental standards (which is the customary, tried-and-failed technique of traditional city planning), but also structural changes in local government to assure a more rational approach to land use.

Repeatedly throughout this narrative of San Francisco's waterfront crisis, the competition among ports has been described as a major cause of developmental pressure on the bay shoreline. Obviously, anything that can be done to reduce this cannibalistic competition would help ease the resulting pressure and make it easier for all shoreline cities to make sensible decisions on waterfront development.

From San Francisco's standpoint, the first step is to recognize that the historic Embarcadero and its romantic gray piers are not THE port of San Francisco but only a unit within a geographic entity that shippers think of as "the San Francisco gateway."

This "gateway" consists of a number of more or less specialized harbors within San Francisco Bay and its navigable inland waters — plus the whole conglomeration of railroads, highways, bridges, warehouses, airports, etc. that transports goods and passengers in and out of the area. It is fourth in the nation in ship arrivals, exceeded only by the "gateways" of New York, Philadelphia and Los Angeles-Long Beach.

During and immediately after World War II, there was a startling growth of port and docking facilities throughout this "gateway." Most of these were specialized terminals, built to handle particular bulk commodities or raw materials such as petroleum, bulk grain or building materials. But there were also many new facilities, especially in Oakland and Alameda, that competed for the break-bulk general cargoes that historically had been monopolized by the Port of San Francisco.

The various harbors and transportation facilities comprising the bay gateway are located in a number of separate political jurisdictions that command the parochial loyalties of an approximately equal number of chambers of commerce, labor councils, boards of supervisors and city commissioners; but this local pride is of no particular significance to the maritime industry. Shippers are not motivated by sentiment, snobbery, tradition or esthetics in choosing among marine carriers or their berthing places. They select the bay gateway for cost advantages, and they choose among its several harbors for equally cold-blooded reasons: convenience, efficiency, specialized handling facilities.

Oakland is the leading container-cargo port on the West Coast, and its Seventh Street Terminal, used by Matson and other large carriers, is one of the largest such terminals on the Pacific.

The proliferation of ports in the bay gateway, and their tendency to offer specialized services based on the geographic and economic attributes of the surrounding area, are irrefutable facts. The SF Port staff recognizes this, and insists that its program of expansion and modernization is not in competition with the other ports of the bay gateway but with other gateways on the Pacific and the Gulf of Mexico. Yet, the economic studies on which this program is based ignored the plans of Oakland, Richmond, Stockton and Sacramento.

The Port of Sacramento, a growing entrepot for bulk cargoes, specializes in handling rice, wood chips, lumber, cubed hay, canned goods, clay, logs and pellets of copra meal. The Port of Stockton, free of the restrictions on tideland filling that inhibit the growth of some of the salt-water ports on the bay, is building a 10-acre, $3.5 million container cargo terminal.

San Francisco, meanwhile, remains the great receiving port for coffee, copra, wines and liquors, meat products, bananas, foreign cars, and the great export center for fresh fruits, industrial machines, tobacco products, electrical equipment, mining and construction machinery and farm machines.

Instead of coordinating its planning, administration, advertising and legislative representation with other bay ports, San Francisco operates like a jealous Hanseatic republic. Instead of exploring the possibilities of an association of Bay Area harbors, a central planning bureau or a Golden Gate Port Authority, the Port of San Francisco pushes ahead with its singular plan to exploit the public waterfront to raise funds for new terminal facilities that may duplicate those under construction elsewhere.

In the long run, regional government may be the only force that can save the San Francisco shoreline from the misplaced zeal of the city's parochial public officials. The San Francisco Port Commission, with its "authority-itis" and its 19th Century notions of civic destiny, is at the moment Public Enemy No. 1 threatening the public interest on the waterfront.

For this reason, the controversy over highrise building on the Embarcadero is one of the healthiest political fights in the Bay Area in many years. Translated into political action, it could lead to the creation of a Golden Gate Harbor District that would rationalize and direct the development, operation and promotion of the several ports within the bay gateway.

More important, it could force San Francisco to refine and strengthen the plans it has made for the future use of its incomparable northern waterfront. And, most important of all, it could set off a major re-examination of the policies and prejudices toward real estate development that make the Bay Area and other urban centers continual prey to environmental destruction disguised as "civic progress."

5.

Highrise Miscellany

What Happens When the Earthquake Hits
By Peter Owens

In 1957, San Francisco was rocked by a 'moderate' earthquake measuring 5.3 on the Richter Scale. In downtown San Francisco, ten miles from the epicenter of the quake, a 14-story steel-frame building, with structural supports driven to a depth of 125 feet, experienced "considerable partition damage and a number of windows broken," a federal damage survey reported. The energy of that mild quake was about equal to 500 tons of TNT.

The great earthquake of 1906, a thousand times more severe, shook San Francisco for about 40 seconds, measured 8.2 on the Richter Scale and produced an energy equivalent to 12,550,000 tons of TNT. And the great SF quake was only one-third the size of the 1964 Alaska earthquake, which shook for about three minutes, measured 8.5 and equaled about 31,550,000 tons of TNT.

Because of the tensions accumulating on the San Andreas Fault, San Francisco is now overdue for another monster quake. Louis Pakiser, U.S. Geological Survey physicist, believes a quake the size of the Alaska experience is "quite possible." Robert Brown, USGS geologist, would not predict the size of the quake, but said he could only say that it would not exceed a Richter magnitude of 9.0 — which is as big as earthquakes ever get. A 9.0 quake would be five times larger than Alaska's, eight times larger than the 1906 disaster.

Moreover, recent findings and measurements indicate that so-called 'moderate' quakes pack considerably more wallop than expected. In a report following the 'moderate' 1969 Santa Rosa quake, earthquake expert Karl Steinbrugge wrote: "The amount of damage to publicly owned, newer earthquake-resistive structures was a surprise and dismay to large elements of the public." Steinbrugge is a structural engineer who works for the Pacific Fire Rating Bureau.

Steinbrugge went on grimly, "There is an increasing number of highrise reinforced concrete frame structures being built throughout metropolitan San Francisco, Los Angeles and other Western cities. Based on the 1969 Santa Rosa experience and the 1964 Alaskan experience, collapse of one or more of these modern highrise reinforced concrete frame structures in a great earthquake would not be a surprise. (No comments are made for modern highrise steel frame buildings due to insufficient recent experience.)"

Steinbrugge, government geologists and other earthquake experts are extremely discouraged with San Francisco's lack of progress, even interest, in the impending earthquake disaster. "The city must be put on notice," Steinbrugge said in an interview. "There must be a crunch." All the scientists and engineers I talked with felt fairly confident that a disaster would turn the city around. But this grim "hope" indicates earthquake specialists have already become complacent and resigned to official indifference.

The tragedy of this assumption is underscored by the Alaska experience. Following that disaster, businessmen and federal officials got together and agreed to zone off dangerous lands in the destroyed downtown business district of Anchorage. But once the federal funds came in and the shock and fear of the quake wore off, the same businessmen talked the government into allowing reconstruction on the extremely hazardous ground which had already ruined them once. Relocation of the business district in another part of town, they claimed, would be "disruptive" to the local economy. Earthquake zoning was forgotten.

Reconstruction of devastated downtown San Francisco after 1906 paralleled the 1964 Alaska experience. The word 'earthquake' was taboo and the disaster became "the great fire," according to the Chamber of Commerce/downtown promo. Irrefutable geologic evidence indicated that buildings constructed on artificial fill over bay mud and sand were prone to great earthquake damage (see 1906 damage map). But city, state and federal officials ignored this knowledge, and San Francisco haphazardly rebuilt itself on those same hazardous lands.

Believe it or not, it wasn't until 1947 that the City finally required special earthquake bracing standards in its building code. Even these specifications are of dubious effectiveness — five modern steel-and-glass highrises, built to specifications stronger than those in the 1947 code, collapsed in the 1969 Caracas, Venezuela quake.

During a 1969 symposium on earthquakes at Santa Rosa, structural engineer Henry Degenkolb said that, "the state of the art in earthquake engineering has not developed to the point where it can be defined for code use. It is still an art, not yet a science."

This standard apologia has not discouraged Degenkolb from leading the field in condemning a number of S.F. public schools as earthquake hazards

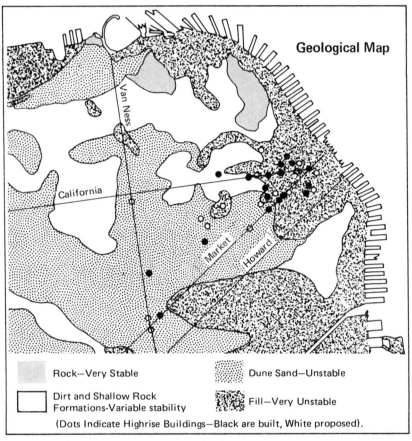

Geological Map

Rock—Very Stable

Dune Sand—Unstable

Dirt and Shallow Rock Formations-Variable stability

Fill—Very Unstable

(Dots Indicate Highrise Buildings—Black are built, White proposed).

according to provisions of the Field Act. While Field Act provisions are stringent and leave little room for vague interpretation, similar guidelines can and must be established for public facilities like hospitals and high density, 'publicly occupied' structures, including privately owned highrise offices and apartments. Moreover, the present code provides for condemnation of unsafe buildings, and a state report called *Dangerous Buildings* (Uniform Building Code, 1967 Vol. IV) offers guidelines which could be modified and enforced if the city wanted to move.

Also, in a short form of the Pacific Fire Rating Bureau Tariff Rules, Karl Steinbrugge provides general building-type guidelines to determine the relative "damageability" of "most older structures."

The most hazardous buildings are those with "bearing walls of unreinforced adobe, unreinforced hollow concrete block, or unreinforced hollow clay tile. "These," according to Steinbrugge, represent "collapse hazards in *moderate* shocks." (My italics). Also on the list are "buildings with

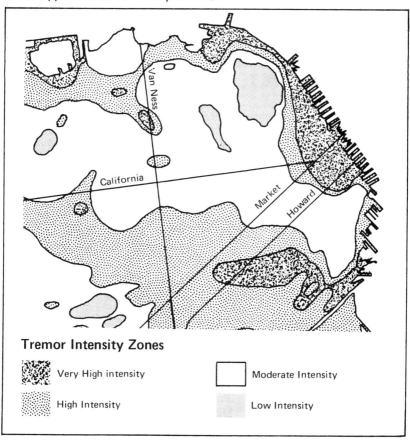

Tremor Intensity Zones

Very High intensity   Moderate Intensity

High Intensity   Low Intensity

unreinforced brick masonry having sand-lime mortar ...'' and of these buildings Steinbrugge says, "Many of these will suffer a partial or total collapse in a great earthquake." Steinbrugge has written that there are hundreds of these structures in San Francisco.

Also included as relatively high risk structures are those highly rigid buildings with "reinforced concrete bearing walls with supported floors and roof of any materials (usually wood)," and also both reinforced concrete and steel-frame buildings "with unreinforced masonry exterior wall panels; concrete floors and concrete roof." (See our rundown on reinforced concrete frame structures built prior to code: we rate them 'x' and call for immediate investigation of their "structural soundness" — p. 143)

Chairing a Presidential Task Force last year, Steinbrugge and his committee called for a "survey of dangerous buildings in the high risk areas." The intent of the recommendations was absolutely clear: "If the hazard is deemed very serious, the building or structure should be condemned ... If adaption is infeasible and the hazard is not deemed serious enough to merit immediate removal, rapid tax write-off and other incentive programs should be devised to encourage early elimination of the hazard."

As might be anticipated, these recommendations have not been acted upon in San Francisco. The city and the federal government have consistently blocked them. The task force report continues: "Local governments are the principal agents for carrying out earthquake hazard reduction policies but they are in a difficult position to do so, so long as they remain dependent upon the present property tax system as their principal source of income. The property tax inhibits local government from enforcing seismic hazard restrictions that might substantially reduce their tax base."

In other words, San Francisco has chosen to support a dubious economic concept over what physicist Pakiser says could be as many as 50,000 deaths. If the alliance between private developers and the city is not broken, city officials must be held accountable for what could be one of the greatest natural disasters in this country's history. By refusing to demand an immediate study of dangerous buildings, the city fosters ignorance about buildings which could be death traps during the next great earthquake.

The poor soil conditions beneath many highrise structures in downtown San Francisco would be a key contributor to earthquake damage. In his book *Earthquake Hazards in the San Francisco Bay Area: A Continuing Problem in Public Policy*, Steinbrugge provides general guidelines for a program of "Risk Zoning" on earthquake-hazardous lands. In a similar study by the BCDC Board of consultants, more detailed guidelines were determined for "bay fill" areas. Sadly lacking are specific labeling of dangerous downtown locations and any mention of retroactive "hazard zones" within which it would be possible to require the removal of dangerous buildings which lacked structural and foundation correctives for bay fill.

Despite this official pussy-footing, the Steinbrugge/BCDC message is clear enough. In three of their four proposed hazard zones, high density and multi-story buildings would be prohibited unless "special design" factors were taken into consideration, many of which would be prohibitively expensive, according to the BCDC report. The report recommends open space or park lands in zone 4, the worst of the bad lands, and low density predominately single story structures for the less dangerous fill areas.

The key variable is the depth of the soil, and engineering geologists claim there are not enough readings or cores to formulate adequately a dangerous-ground zoning map for San Francisco. Nonetheless, such a zoning map was compiled for undeveloped lands in Santa Clara County with much less complete information than present available information for downtown SF. But city officials here are afraid of lawsuits and reluctant to take on the

Dangerous Old San Francisco Highrises

Guardian investigators buried themselves for more than a week in the archives of San Francisco's Central Permit Bureau and examined hundreds of yellowing, dog-eared building permits. The permits provided information on structure, foundation and building material that show all buildings listed below — or almost all, since some permits were inexplicably missing, as noted — are unsafe according to structural specifications of the city's 1947 earthquake code and the State of California report, *Dangerous Buildings* (Uniform Building Code, 1967 Vol. IV).

All buildings on the list stand on highly unstable Bay fill soil and all were built before 1947, which is when the first earthquake safety sections were written into the city code. It is highly unlikely any of these buildings are structurally as sound as the five San Francisco schools recently closed because of their failure to meet structural standards set forth in the 1933 Field Act — which applies only to schools.

It might be instructive to remember, as you look through the list, that many experts consider that even buildings built according to the post-1947 code — such as modern glass-and-steel highrises in the Bay fill area — would be unsafe in even a "moderate" earthquake.

Building Name	Address		Year Const.	Stories	Code
R. Stanley Dollar	141-115	Battery	1917	6	xp
Hilp	601-05-15	Battery	1907	6	
Shell	63-33-31	Battery	1930	10	sf
Bank-offices	635	Battery		6	x
Offices	124	Beale		6	x
Phillips & Van Orden	135	Berry		6	xp
Standard Oil	200	Bush	1912-15	12	pf
Mills Tower	220	Bush	1931	22	o
Standard Oil & Annex	225	Bush	1922	22	sf
230 California	230	California		6	pf
S.F. Natl. Bank	262	California	1910	11	f
320 California	320	California	1946-48	8	f
Robert Dollar	301-333	California	1928	10	f
Balfour	365-341	California	1920	15	pf
Insurance Exchange	441-427	California	1913	11	f
The Merchants Exchange	447-451	California	1904-06	15	o
Offices	15	Drumm	1907	8	x
Hotel	132	Embarcadero	1906	6	f

Building Name	Address		Year Const.	Stories	Code
The Kennedy Hotel	225	Embarcadero	1912	7	o.
grocery warehouse	400	Embarcadero	1918	6	
Hills Bros.	30	Harrison	1924	6	xs
Calif. Packing Corp.	345	Howard	1928	11	xs
Blackfield	612	Howard		6	o
Matson Navigation	480	Main	1926	6	xp
Southern Pacific Co.	65	Market	1917	14	pf
110 Market St.	110	Market	1907	7	pf
Santa Maria	114	Market	1907	8	px
Lincoln Hotel	115	Market	1913	7	f
Hotel Whitcomb	201-31	Market	1911	15	pf
P.G.&E.	245	Market	1924-47	17	pf
Union Carbide & Carbon	470	Market	1908-25	11	pf
Executive Tower	503	Market	1908	10	f
offices & shops	583	Market	1910	6	x
Balboa	593	Market	1906	11	sf
lofts	101	Minna	1908	6	sf
offices	315	Mission	1922	6	xp
P.G.&E.	345	Mission	1922	8	sx
Western Pac. RR Co.	526	Mission	1921-54	7	sf
DN&E Walter & Co.	502	Mission	1919	6	xs
lofts	576-77-79	Mission	1912	6	sf
lofts	609	Mission	1908	6	sx
garment factory	611	Mission	1907	6	sf
Jeweler's	657	Mission	1907	6	sx
Williams	693	Mission	1907	8	pf
Mills	220	Montgomery	1892-1907-14	10	sf
United Calif. Bank	405	Montgomery	1926	15	sf
Kohl	412-00	Montgomery	1909	11	o
Richfield	425-17	Montgomery	1935	10	x
L Scatena	552-40	Montgomery	1909-31	10	sf
Standard	109	N. Mont.	1908	7	o
Rialto	110-18	N. Mont.	1911	8	o
Pac. Coast Division Off.	140	N. Mont.	1924	30	sf
Greenwood Black	149	N. Mont.	1907	6	sx
New Mont.	180	N. Mont.	1920	8	sx
Spreckels'	2	Pine	1906-18	8	pf
64 Pine St.	64	Pine	1917	7	x
Liberty Mutual	228-00	Pine	1906	8	x
offices	201	Pine		6	f
Fireman's Fund	344-26	Pine	1928	8	f
Dividend	354-48	Pine	1907	7	o
Phoenix	360-58	Pine	1929	6	o
Exchange Block	378-69	Pine	1918	8	sx
office	353-49-45	Sacramento	1922	6	spf

Building Name	Address		Year Const.	Stories	Code
Adam Grant	130-00	Sansome	1907	14	spf
Indust. Indemnity	155	Sansome	1929	12	spf
Amer. Internat.	200	Sansome	1926-27	15	pf
Royal Insurance	201	Sansome	1909	11	psf
office	231	Sansome	1924	6	o
Fireman's Fund Co.	241-35-33	Sansome	1924	12	x
Alaska Commercial	324-00	Sansome	1908	12	pf
Federal Reserve Bank	400	Sansome	1922-24	8	f
Sansome	500	Sansome	1929	8	xp
office	545-31	Sansome	1930	10	o
U.S. Appraisers' Store & Immigration Station	630	Sansome	1941	18	o
office	21	Stevenson	1917	7	o
Underwood	30	Stevenson	1912	7	sf
Holbrook	58	Sutter	1913	7	sx
Sheldon	9	1st. St.	1908	8	x
offices & lofts	16	1st. St.	1906	6	sf
offices	25	1st. St.	1917	6	x
offices	42-48	1st. St.	1927	7	sx
offices	50-60	1st. St.	1906	7	sx
rest lofts	76-78	1st. St.	1917	6	sf
Bank shops	90-92-98	1st. St.	1907	6	sx
85 2nd. St.	85	2nd. St.	1907	8	o
Jackson	156	2nd. St.	1908	6	o
Electric	165-73	2nd. St.	1908	6	sf
Hotel Alto	161	3rd. St.	1907	8	sf
Odd Fellows	14	7th. St.	1910	7	x

CODE LEGEND/all buildings pre-1947 over artificial fill and poor sub materials.

x. . . . these are reinforced concrete structures and frames; many contain brick and represent a class of structures even the best of which are causing mounting concern and are the most likely to fall during a great quake.

s. . . . permits specifically state they are on "solid" ground; this is geologic fantasy in downtown San Francisco.

o. . . . either no permit on file or no information on permit.

p. . . . permit specifically states building on pile foundations. Experience suggests piles may be helpful.

f. . . . steel frame structures. Contrary to myth, steel frames do not necessarily make a building safer in a quake. Structural engineers would find some of the most dangerous among this class.

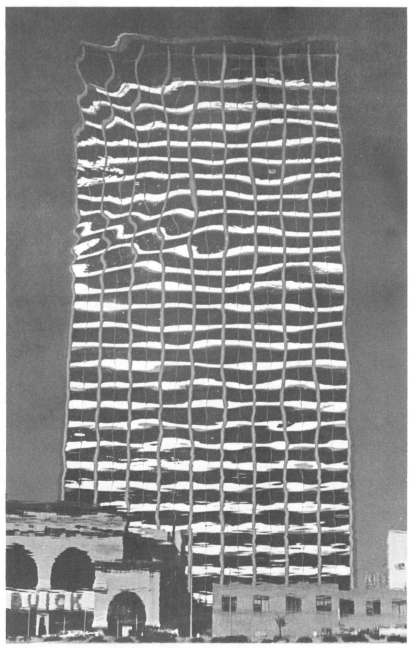

What will a tall building look like when the earthquake hits? Perhaps like this: the Ordway building in Oakland as reflected from Lake Merritt.

146

Chamber/Downtown Association/realtor bloc, so all that can be certain is that most artificial fill lands are highly dangerous.

During a major quake these soils will liquefy or, at the very least, amplify vibrations many times. The ten miles between downtown San Francisco and the San Andreas fault would mean little during a major earthquake: tremors would be as strong on these soils as if the same buildings were located on the fault itself. All buildings on the preceding list are situated on fill and poor soils.

Soil, structural and magnitude variables are only part of the earthquake picture. We have never had a major quake in this country which has occurred in a metropolitan area at rush hour. The 1906 and recent San Fernando disasters occurred very early in the morning when most people were asleep in generally safe single-story wood frame buildings.

Moreover, a highrise structure need not collapse for it to be considered extremely hazardous. Many steel frame structures on our list are constructed with interior hollow tile or concrete partitions, many with plaster ceilings, and walls of brick; in all probability, a detailed study of blueprints would reveal badly anchored stairways, light fixtures and parapets; unanchored or could anchored facades; highly lethal exterior ornaments; walls of glass that poorly cascade down in deadly shards, and giant water storage tanks on roofs.

During a major destructive quake at rush hour, many people in the streets could be crushed by a vast array of falling objects. People inside the buildings would be at the mercy of toppling objects, collapsing ceilings and innumberable other hazards even if the structure itself were to remain solidly intact. The city's own parapet resolution, which could help reduce external hazards, lies fallow without the funding necessary to carry out its modest size.

Almost all of the city's constructive efforts have sought to toughen provisions of the 1947 code. However, these provisions apply only to the newest buildings. In its mad plunge forward, the city has left a wake of potential disasters, of buildings which would be defined as extremely hazardous if the code were applied retroactively.

San Francisco also has no non-structural inspection program for earthquake hazards. Such a program could be analogous to fire safety inspections and relatively easy to initiate. However, the city attempts to enforce its "toughened " code without bothering to hire a single engineering geologist. Often, builders shop around for consultants who can find technical loopholes and know how to skimp on safety, cut costs and still meet code. At the Santa Rosa conference, Degenkolb said: "As the matter now stands, the public has to rely on the skill and integrity of the structural engineer who prepared the design in the first place."

As for the builder's interest in safety or durability, the presidential task force found that "the developer may find it profitable to build on a disaster-prone site because any losses would be borne by other individuals and by the public." Unbelievable? The Alaska experience indicates otherwise. With private property losses estimated at $77 million, the federal government provided $114 million in relief, nearly a 75 percent mark-up for those fortunate enough to be wiped out. The only losers in Alaska were U.S. taxpayers and the 131 people who died.

Despite their vested interest in keeping skyscrapers going up, a few consulting firms of engineers and engineering geologists have been instrumental in pointing up stark realities of San Francisco's earthquake danger. They are extremely timid about pointing their fingers at negligent colleagues: they live in dread of lawsuits by private owners; they refuse to say publicly which buildings are deathtraps. But there is no question that, however cautiously, they have been telling the city for many years that a serious disaster is imminent.

Citizens must demand to know the odds that the buildings they inhabit will survive the next great earthquake. This burden of proof must be put on the city. We challenge the city to prove the safety of those downtown, pre-code structures on our list. Not only has the city been negligent in doing something about the earthquake problem, but it has failed to assess the extent of the dangers.

As the controversial BBC documentary so aptly puts it, San Francisco is a city that waits to die.

Holacausts Above the 35th Floor

By Michael J. Cussen

They don't look flammable, of course, gleaming in the afternoon sun, monuments to the American economic empire. But the modern highrise building, contrary to appearances, is a potential inferno. Last November, the Bank of America skyscraper narrowly escaped real tragedy when fire erupted in its upper stories. And it's only a matter of time, say the many authorities I interviewed, before a major fire disaster hits a San Francisco highrise.

The problem is not new. Skyscrapers have been around since the early 1900s. Over the years, however, fire control and safety procedures for the older highrises have become so effective that city fire departments have been able to reduce their services to the highrise areas.

San Francisco has many of these virtually fire-proof buildings. The old Standard Oil building, the Russ building, the Shell building — all were built almost exclusively of steel and concrete. They had high ceilings and a

Highrise buildings are no safer from fire hazards in 1971 than they were in 1906. Here, the Call Building on Market Street is ablaze after the earthquake.

minimum of electrical circuitry and telephone cables. The air conditioning system was called "windows."

But times have changed. Under the familiar banner of cost efficiency, modern technology, in the form of flammable plastics, came stomping through the building industry. During the mid-1950s, a whole new kind of skyscraper began to appear. Considerations of fire safety took a back seat to cost accounting. Buildings have to be built quickly for maximum profit, and speed means corner-cutting and corner-cutting means danger.

There are four major highrise fire hazard problems:

1. Highrise fires are inaccessible to firefighters.

2. The new highrises are furnished with plastics that make the interiors extremely combustible.

3. The fireproofing requirements are inadequate — jeopardizing not only the lives of the people living or working in the building but also its structural integrity. Highrise fires are so hot some engineers wouldn't be surprised to see steel frames begin to bend in the heat of a blaze.

4. The vertical arteries — stairwells, elevator shafts and air ducts — serve to contaminate other parts of the building with smoke, gas and heat.

Let's consider these points individually. First, the extreme height of a highrise precludes firemen from effectively using aerial ladders. The ladders in San Francisco extend to 100 feet, or about eight stories.

To complicate matters further, the firemen are "loathe to use elevators," as one put it, for fear of getting stuck in them or, worse yet, having the elevator open on the fire floor, as happened in both of the New York City highrise fires which occurred a year ago. This means the firemen's only safe access to the fire is through the stairwells — and even these are of dubious value. Besides being difficult to climb, the stairwells are major arteries for smoke and gas transfer between floors.

The danger of the blaze can be looked at from a different point of view: that of the occupants, who are too close to the fire and want to get away. They are faced with the same problem going down as the firemen are faced with coming up. It takes approximately two hours to evacuate completely a 50 story building using the stairways only. Think about this the next time you venture into the B of A World Headquarters.

To complicate the evacuation problem even further, there is a very good chance the occupants will find the exit doors chained shut as a security measure to protect the building. This was the case in New York City during the famous black-out of 1967. Employees of the Time-Life Building, after descending the 40-odd stories seeking fresh air and light, found that the street doors had been chained shut. Several people were trampled and injured.

The same situation exists in San Francisco. Building owners are overly security conscious and want only "authorized" personnel about the building. So they often have taken unsafe measures to protect the property — but not the people working and doing business in the property.

What all this adds up to is that evacuation of a highrise is neither practical nor feasible. This is quite a departure from the traditional view that the best way to insure fire safety was to have many well-spaced exits. Indeed, an international conference of fire protection procedures in highrises held in San Francisco by the General Services Administration concluded: "The occupants of the highrise building will have to find their safety within the structure." In brief: there's almost no way out.

There are some stop-gap safety measures. Chief Keith Calden of the San Francisco Fire Department has prepared and distributed a detailed set of instructions and recommendations which could easily be carried out in any existing highrise buildings. Color coding the stairways and exits, designating floor captains and monitors, the installation of a total communication system for the entire building — were recommended as life-saving ideas by the Chief and unanimously supported by the GSA conference. In the future, however, fire protection should become a matter of design rather than a haphazard set of rules and control measures that might have a chance of working if no one panicked.

A highrise building burns for several reasons. The primary one is that the new buildings are essentially sealed boxes filled with tons of highly combustible plastics. Fires start, travel and propagate themselves according to the law of aero-dynamics, thermal analysis and chemistry. Fires in highrises could be controlled if the situation were attacked in a scientific manner. But economics seem to have more say than fire control policy science.

The modern highrise is totally closed to the outside environment and the air conditioning-fed fires which rage in them often approach 1500° F, making the fire floor much like a blast furnace. In New York City, fire investigators found that the fire at One New York Plaza last August had melted aluminum chairs.

The fire investigator making the report was astounded by the ferocity of the inferno. The damage to the building was incredible. Not only was the aluminum skin of the building melted on the fire floor but also on the floor above. Steel beams were twisted and deflected out of plumb several inches and connecting bolts had either been sheared off or failed to hold in the heat of the fire. The fire was spread by the air conditioning system and also through the walls and ceiling spaces.

W. Robert Powers, Superintendent of the New York Board of Fire Underwriters, wrote later that "buildings of this type (the modern highrise) erected in this Plastic Age should more correctly be called semicombustible!"

Holocausts Above the 35th Floor

Except for the concrete and steel, almost everything in the modern highrise is combustible to some degree.

The plastics used for wire insulation, cushions, furniture and office equipment are usually poly-urethane or a similar plastic. The foam insulation board in the ceiling spaces is poly-styrene. Both of these plastics ignite at a little over 200° F, giving off a thick black smoke which reduces visibility and makes the fireman's job extremely difficult.

Complicating the problem, according to a fire insurance underwriter, is a prevalent practice called "poke through." Subcontractors, usually because of sloppiness on the part of the architect, are forced to peel away the asbestos insulation to make room for phone cables, electrical conduits and air conditioning ducts. Fire can also be spread by the packing boxes and lunch bags tossed into wall and floor spaces "where they won't show" by lazy workmen.

The best way to extinguish a fire is to throw water on it. So a simple solution to the fire problem would be to install a total automatic sprinkler system in every building. But the simplest solution is also the costliest.

Failing laws which require complete automatic sprinkler systems in highrises, the next best way to control fires in skyscrapers is to control the air handling system, which is primarily responsible for spreading the blaze throughout the fire floor and transmitting smoke and gas to other floors. But here, too, there are problems.

The excessive vertical arrangement of highrise architecture causes an air pressure phenomenon known as "stack effect." The "stack effect" creates the air movement within the building, depending on the differences between the outside and inside temperatures of the building.

For example, on a very cold day, the outside air is pressing down on the ground and forces itself into the building at ground level. Once inside the building, it warms up slightly and rises through the building. So if a fire starts on the fifth floor the smoke can easily spread to the floors above just on the air pressure differences alone. On a warm day, the situation is reversed, so that fire on the 40th floor will cause smoke to move to the floors below.

Another method to control the air in a building is a "smoke tower." The smoke tower can be a stairway, shaft or series of balconies on the exterior of a building which gives every floor access to fresh air. It also provides a safe refuge for occupants trying to escape the fire.

Ironically, in New York City, shortly after the building code had been changed to eliminate the requirement for smoke towers, a fire broke out at 919 Third Ave. and claimed three lives. A smoke tower would have given the occupants fresh air and probably saved them. The requirement for smoke towers was dropped after the building owners successfully lobbied for a change in the code. Smoke towers, you see, are situated on the exterior of the building, the most valuable rentable space.

What highrise then, is the ultimate answer to fire safety in the new highrise buildings? Obviously, changes in the fire code. The San Francisco Fire Department is currently sending several code changes a week to the Bureau of Building Inspection. But the trick is to get these revisions accepted and implemented. And that isn't easy.

Each proposed revision is sent to every group, individual or agency — municipal, state, federal or private — who might be concerned by the change. Each group is expected to reply and recommend changes — including the Chamber of Commerce and its influential 41 member committee on code enforcement. The changes don't go to the Supervisors, several city officials said, until they've been passed by the Chamber.

Some changes generate much opposition, often from the Chamber. In fact, the one item most wanted by the SF Fire Department — total automatic sprinkler systems — an almost foolproof method of fire protection, has drawn strong Chamber opposition on grounds of its "excessive cost." (Only the Transamerica Building will have this sprinkling system.)

The S.F. Fire Department has made eight major recommendations for code changes. They are:

1. Installation of an automatic fire suppression system (AFSS) must be mandatory.

2. Every window must open. Mechanically-operated sliding windows must be provided as necessary to allow the Fire Department to set up cross ventilation on fire-involved floors. Power ventilation systems must be installed and control panels for them must be provided for the Fire Department. Smoke detectors which activate dampers in air conditioning ducts should be installed so that the fire area is effectively cut off from the rest of the building.

3. Elevators, the most used means of egress from a burning building, must be foolproof.

4. A combined fire alarm (which alerts the Fire Department as well as a security facility somewhere in the building) and a house phone system should be installed.

5. The "vertical lapse," the distance between openings on adjoining floors, must be made greater.

6. The ceiling space should be properly fire-stopped.

7. "Poke through" construction practices should be stopped.

8. Auxiliary power systems should be ready to take over if city power fails.

Holocausts Above the 35th Floor

The point: Almost all new skyscrapers in San Francisco have been built without these basic fire-safety features. Many more may go up before they are adopted and the Chamber/skyscraper interests will undoubtedly oppose to the bitter end the only system firemen say will work (the water sprinkler).

SOUTH EAST FROM PINE & MASON STREETS.
APRIL 18, 1906.

April 18, 1906: The earthquake and fire looking southeast from Pine and Mason in downtown San Francisco.

The Chamber's Bull Market for Pro-Highrise Studies

By Greggar Sletteland

Scene: Board Room of the Press Club, 9 a.m. Aug. 26, 1971, girls scurrying about with coffee and donuts, anonymous men in neat suits (certainly not reporters) hovering in corners, "the best turn-out for a P.R. press conference in a long time," according to KQED's Scott Blakey.

For good reason. In early April, filing of Alvin Duskin's 45,000 name initiative petition calling for a city-wide 72-foot height limit on all new buildings brought yelps of pain and outrage from downtown interests and the promise of a no-holds-barred campaign to defeat the initiative.

In the months since, dozens of neighborhood and taxpayers' groups have endorsed the Duskin measure, citing it as the only remaining hope for preserving San Francisco from the ravages of Manhattanization. The downtown interests, meanwhile, have remained relatively quiet. There have been only scattered outbursts from building owners, city officials and editorial writers for the Examiner/Chronicle.

But today, ten weeks before the November election, the press has been informed that the anti-Duskin campaign will explode into high gear with the introduction of a group called "Citizens for San Francisco."

Lights, silence. Municipal Judge Joseph Kennedy and architect Beverly Willis, group co-chairmen, step before the TV cameras and microphones to read a scathing prepared attack against the height limit proposal.

"Mr. Duskin and his followers have shown a total disregard for reason and facts," charges Miss Willis, announcing her own study of the effects of highrise buildings on the city's economy. The Willis report purports to show that restricting growth of the forest of downtown skyscrapers would plunge the city into fiscal disaster (the report actually shows nothing of the sort — see p164).

Judge Kennedy seconds Miss Willis' remarks and portrays "Citizens" as a "bi-partisan" group of civic-minded residents out to "save our beloved San Francisco" from "catastrophe."

Finally, during the question period, Andy Gollan of the Progress asks the crucial question: "Judge, can you tell us where your financial support will be coming from?"

Kennedy assures the press that "Citizens" is a "financially independent" organization. "We expect our support from the neighborhood people," he says. But, "We're not concerned where the dollars come from."

Gollan persists: "Are you being financed by the Chamber of Commerce?"

"At this point," Kennedy says, "we have no funds at all."

Fifteen minutes after the conference breaks up, I stand at the entrance to the Chamber's plush offices at 400 Montgomery St. and watch several familiar faces — coffee girls and anonymous men in neat suits — troop in from the "Citizens" press conference.

The Chamber's receptionist identifies four: Gwen Mishizawa, Chamber secretary of public affairs; John Greenagel, Chamber public affairs director; Mark Buell, Chamber staff member; and E. Keith Thompson, Chamber member.

A word more about Thompson. The Aug. 18, 1971 edition of the Daily Pacific Builder names him as "the man who heads up the Chamber of Commerce campaign against the height limit proposal." He's an assistant to the executive vice president of Bechtel Corporation, major contractor for BART and the world's largest construction firm.

The "Citizens" press release — given prominent, uncritical display in the Examiner and Chronicle — contains no reference to the Chamber of Commerce. But it does list E. Hornsby Wasson as "finance director."

Several phone calls find Mr. Wasson "in conference," but his secretary, Mrs. Martanelli, obliges with a description of her boss. He's a former president and chairman of the board of PT&T, currently chairman of the board of Stanford Research Institute and a director of PT&T and Standard Oil.

"He's been working on 'Citizens for San Francisco' since March," says Mrs. Martanelli. "But you should talk with John Greenagel at the Chamber of Commerce. He's the one Mr. Wasson's been working with all along."

Two other tidbits: Mr. Wasson is, of course, a member (and former director) of the Chamber of Commerce. And this eminent "Citizen for San Francisco" lives in Hillsborough, a wealthy, exclusive suburb in San Mateo county.

Now a couple calls to the Chamber. First, Gwen Mishizawa explains that Mr. Wasson's job as finance director for "Citizens" is to round up money from "corporations and businesses."

And those "neighborhood groups"? Well, Miss Mishizawa says, she doesn't really know anything about that. She's been with the Chamber only six weeks "and it was all set up long before that."

Miss Mishizawa's unexpected openness stems from her newness to the job. John Greenagel, chief Chamber flack, proves much more tightlipped. He "prefers not to comment" on how long he's been working to set up "Citizens."

Greenagel does concede, however, with extreme reluctance, that the Chamber's board of directors decided to "cooperate with" "Citizens" at "our last board meeting." When was that? Greenagel has to search his memory before replying: "It usually falls on the third Friday."

That would be Aug. 20, six days before Judge Kennedy assured the press that "Citizens" was a "financially independent" group with "no funds." Of course, "Citizens'" solvency was guaranteed long before that.

Cut now to the Chamber of Commerce Board Room. It's six days after the "Citizens" press conference, and the Chamber's about to open a second front. Same large press turn-out. Also: Mishizawa, Greenagel, Buell, Thompson.

Lights, center table, Chamber spokesman Arch Monson launches an impassioned tirade against the Duskin petition ("Yes, I would say Mr. Duskin intentionally distorts the facts!") and introduces the stars of the occasion, the Chamber's "expert consultants" on highrise questions, Dr. Claude Gruen of Gruen Gruen & Associates and Dr. Gerald McCue of McCue Boone Tomsick.

The well-paid consultants ("$25,000, $27,000, right in that neighborhood," Monson admits to reporters) announce the results of their studies, commissioned by the Chamber in late April and rushed to completion by mid-August.

"The reports demonstrate conclusively," as the press release puts it, "that a mandatory six-story height limitation . . . would do serious harm to the economic and environmental well-being of San Francisco."

During the question period, Gruen and McCue both stress the "objectivity" of their studies, one of which (Gruen's) "proves" that a height limit would lead to a tax increase, while the other writhes through a series of remarkable academic contortions to "prove" that bringing more commuters into the city's downtown would actually *improve* the traffic and air-pollution situation. (See analysis, p. 164 –165)

Neither Gruen nor McCue is ruffled by questions about anti-Duskin blasts they delivered at a Chamber forum on June 1, smack in the middle of the period when both were supposedly compiling facts in the best disinterested manner of modern science.

Said McCue at that June forum: "It would be disastrous to impede growth in activity centers, like the city's Montgomery Street section." (S.F. Chronicle, June 3, 1971)

McCue, reminded of the statement, answered at the press conference (lamely): "You can't disregard 20 years of experience."

It was so obvious what McCue and Gruen's "experience" would produce in conclusions for the Chamber that, in July, Frank D. Winston, Junior Chamber of Commerce president, said, "We do not intend to be bluffed into believing that the two reports on the highrise issue which are being prepared for the Greater Chamber are the only ones that ought to be considered by the community."

"Hysterical reaction!" fumed William E. Dauer, executive vice president of the Greater Chamber and the man who gives himself credit for persuading Lamar Hunt to propose a Disneyesque "space museum" for Alcatraz Island. Dauer charged the Junior Chamber's modest proposal for a one-year moratorium ("so that we can think about what we're doing") amounted to a "surrender to Alvin Duskin and his followers" — for a Chamber man, the ultimate insult.

Interviews with two Chamber members disgusted with its highhanded tactics and growth-at-all-costs psychosis confirm the sequence of events that led up to these two press conferences — and give a picture of the virulent, well-heeled campaign the Chamber unleashed in September and October.

Both sources — one a 17-year veteran of the Chamber — asked to remain anonymous. They produced a series of "read and destroy" memos from John Greenagel to "contributors to the campaign to defeat the Duskin Initiative" to back up their statements.

In April, the sources say, filing of the Duskin petition threw downtown interests into a state of near-panic. They were embarrassed to discover, in the face of Duskin's challenge, that they had no evidence to support the dogma they had been disseminating for years—that highrises were the next best thing to municipal money trees. Worse, secret polls showed that most San Franciscans agreed with Duskin that the monster skyscrapers rising up in the downtown—and threatening neighborhoods all over the city—were destroying the San Francisco they cherished.

Worst of all, the Duskin measure called for a city-wide height limit that, once enacted into law, could not be tampered with by city politicians and their appointees to city commissions dealing with development. Under present law, the Planning Commission and the Board of Permit Appeals can, and often do, approve unlimited variances to zoning law. The Duskin petition provided that buildings taller than 72 feet could be constructed only if approved by voters.

"Before," as one source put it, "protesters might win a battle or two against individual buildings, but the overall pattern didn't change. How could it? We had all the commissions locked up. In theory, the city 'controlled' development. In practice, it was a private enterprise free-for-all, and the public be damned."

To meet this unprecedented threat to their self-proclaimed guiding philosophy — "greater profits for our businesses and industry" — the immensely powerful Chamber board of directors put Wasson in charge of fund-raising and assigned Greenagel and Thompson to engineer a campaign to smash Duskin.

Wasson came up with promises for more than $250,000, the sources said, most of it coming from giant firms like Bank of America, PG&E, PT&T and Southern Pacific (all among the top ten landholders in the city). Meanwhile, Greenagel and Thompson, working in Pentagon-like secrecy, set up "Citizens for San Francisco" as a front group to counteract the Chamber's well-deserved public image as a champion of highrises. Willis and Kennedy — not directly affiliated with the Chamber — were enlisted as co-chairmen.

Lining up political support was no problem. Mayor Alioto — elected in 1967 after a massive last-minute campaign bankrolled by the Swig/Shorenstein/Magnin/downtown bloc, up for re-election in November — and other city officials appointed or reappointed by Alioto immediately began blasting the Duskin petition at every opportunity. Also, seven Supervisors agreed to support "Citizens": John Barbagelata, James Mailliard, Peter Tamaras, Dorothy von Beroldingen, Michael Driscoll, Terry Francois and Robert Mendelsohn (the latter three up for re-election).

For those who didn't go along, there was the disturbing example of former Supervisor Bill Blake to think about. In the spring of 1969, Blake made the mistake of telling fellow Supervisors, before the press, that "the San Francisco Chamber of Commerce is running this Board and City Hall." In the elections that fall — after a vicious Chamber attack upon him in the June, 1969 edition of S.F. Business, the Chamber's house organ — Blake had difficulty raising campaign funds and lost.

Media support was easy for the Chamber to get. The Examiner and Chronicle (both with extensive downtown landholdings and highrise interests) and local television radio news stations (all members of the Chamber and all represented on a Chamber committee producing Chamber public service announcements for local broadcast) carried favorable Chamber news publicity. Some (notably KPIX, with Louis Simon of KPIX/Westinghouse on the Chamber's board of directors) chipped in with editorial support.

For "evidence" of the municipal bonanza provided by highrises, the Chamber simply created its own bull market in pro-highrise studies by announcing it would commission studies. Gruen and McCue were chosen as the most reliable from the flock of eager applicants.

Working behind a facade of secrecy through the spring and summer, the Chamber also:

* Readied vast amounts of literature (200,000 copies of a leaflet called "Alvin Duskin Says," for example, with arguments — all demonstrably false — abstracted from the Willis report and polished by Chamber flacks).

* Hired speakers and prepared a speaker's handbook teeming with distortions, myths and scare-tactic replies to possible questions.

* Sent out invitations for a series of "Citizens" dinners for leaders of neighborhood groups.

* Made up copy for a blitz October media campaign picturing economic disaster for the city if the Duskin measure passed.

* Hired a direct mail firm to prepare a letter emphasizing different

scare issues in different neighborhoods "in order to maximize the personal impact," to be sent to 250,000 San Francisco households in October.

Greenagel detailed elements of this strategy in his "read and destroy" memos sent to campaign contributors, who in late summer had become jittery over early polls predicting a Duskin victory in November. Greenagel reassured them:

> "Traditionally, campaigns do not move into high gear until after Labor Day. We have observed this tradition and hope you will not be alarmed at the low profile of the public campaign to date. There has been a deliberate effort to hold back until the vacation season is over and the voters are in a mood to think seriously about the November election . . . Again, I ask that you destroy this memorandum and keep its contents in strictest confidence."

San Francisco voters should, according to one disaffected Chamber member, take a closer look at the group that is attempting to bulldoze and bamboozle them into defeating the height limit proposal.

"It's terrible the things we're doing in the name of San Francisco business," he said. "But then, we're not really San Francisco business any more. Local businessmen don't even get a hearing. We're big-time now. With all the big firms moving in and taking over, we've become much more nationally and internationally conscious. These new people see San Francisco as a West Coast Wall Street, only bigger. There's only a couple hundred million people to sell things to in Europe. There's two billion in Asia. It's like the State Department down there now."

But support of Manhattanization is nothing new to the Chamber. They're practically the ones who dreamed it up. In the late 40's and 50's, they led the drive to create — and controlled a majority of seats on — the Bay Area Council, a kind of super-Chamber which drew up plans for regional organization envisioning San Francisco as the financial-white collar center of a 9-county megalopolis.

The Council's enormous lobbying power led to state and regional adoption of many of its proposals, none of which had been sullied by public participation or review. A massive infusion of Chamber money into the campaign for BART — the one element of the plan that finally had to be presented to the public — was instrumental in hoodwinking San Francisco voters into buying that outrageous downtown boondoggle.

In recent years, the Chamber has been flying planeloads of business and civic leaders to eastern cities — especially New York — to sell companies disenchanted with urban chaos on the advantages of locating in BART-serviced, picturesque downtown San Francisco. Until the last year or so, the

Chamber never missed a chance to crow in public about the tremendous success of this campaign.

"These big business types have already written off the old-fashioned, 'quaint' San Francisco," the Chamber critic went on. "They don't give a damn about this city except as a piece of real estate. They don't even live here. They all live in the suburbs."

Research into the Chamber's board of directors, who make all the important decisions taken by the group, bears out the substance of these contentions:

1) The board includes the names of officers and directors of some of the richest and most powerful corporations in the world (many of them presently occupying or building downtown skyscrapers). A partial list: Westinghouse, United Airlines, Standard Oil, Bechtel, Wells Fargo, Metropolitan Life, Aetna Life, Hewlett-Packard, Safeway Stores, Utah Mining and Construction, Transamerica, Foremost-McKesson, PT&T, American Express, PG&E, Del Monte, Southern Pacific, Bank of America.

2) Thirteen of the Chamber's 32 directors take their orders from firms headquartered in other cities, 4 from New York, 5 from Los Angeles.

3) Almost two-thirds of the directors don't even live in the city they claim to·be so vitally concerned about. Eighteen of the 32 directors prefer to leave urban problems in the city and live in the suburbs: Hillsborough (3), Kentfield (3), Piedmont (2), Lafayette, Belvedere, Concord, Portola Valley, Mill Valley, Alamo, Atherton, unincorporated Marin, Oakland — and one in Beverly Hills.

4) In a city whose minorities number more than 40%, among them many successful businessmen, the Chamber's board is lily-white. Nor does it include any women.

5) Director Louis J. Mulkern is president of the World Trade Association. He's a Bank of America senior vice president in charge of the Asia Division.

6) Board Chairman Louis W. Niggeman is President of Fireman's Fund, a subsidiary of American Express of New York. Niggeman lives in Hillsborough.

7) The Chamber's vice president in charge of city planning is James E. Stretch, vice president of Metropolitan Life, a New York insurance firm with the largest assets of any company in the world. Stretch currently lives in Hillsborough, has been in the Bay Area only four years, came here from Atlanta, Ga. As a former salesman who worked his way up the ladder, he has no experience whatsoever in city planning.

These men are the power-brokers behind the facade of "Citizens for San

Francisco" — the ones who would have San Franciscans "save our beloved city," as Kennedy put it, from the "catastrophe" of a highrise limit.

One Chamber source summed it up: "The issue coming up this November is very simple. It's either stop them now or San Francisco will become 46 square miles of Wall Street. There won't be a second chance. These guys mean business."

1. The Willis Report

Miss Willis, an architect, tells us that city utilities contributed a "profit" of $100 million to the city budget in fiscal 1970. If it were only so! Actually, the utilities contributed nothing in profits — they ran up a deficit of $19.2 million. Likewise, business licenses and fines didn't provide $135 million, as Miss Willis contends, but $7.4 million — a mere 1800% error.

Miss Willis goes on to suppose that these purely imaginary revenues stem solely from the presence of highrises in the city, and that the revenues would dry up completely should a 72-foot height limit be imposed. Thus without highrises, she says, we would lose $252 million annually in revenue. (The city's total of locally-generated revenues in fiscal 1970 was only $249 million.)

To make up for that $252 million in lost revenue, according to Miss Willis, the city would have to raise property taxes by 40%. This is the basis for her conclusion that a height limit would cause an increase in property taxes.

That's it. Miss Willis's efforts to analyze the costs and benefits of highrises begin and end right there.

Miss Willis is afflicted by the curse of believing everything city officials tell her, however absurd. The rest of her report is devoted to their unproven — and unprovable — assertions. In one memorable instance, she repeats with a straight face a sewage engineer's statement that highrises "lessen the load on the wet weather system" because they have "less roof space." Translation (think about it for a moment): when it rains, it rains less in highrise districts. Which would make a fitting title for this amateurish highrise glorification job.

2. The Gruen Report

Claude Gruen, of Gruen, Gruen & Assoc., is a professional your-conclusion-for-a-price consultant, but his team of economists falls into the same errors as Miss Willis does in attempting to demolish the Duskin case against highrises.

First, Gruen attributes the skyrocketing rise in municipal expenditures to increases in salaries of city workers (as if city workers didn't service highrise areas). Second, he asserts that 80% of the city's municipal costs are "people-oriented" (as if highrise buildings didn't house people or influence the patterns by which people live in the city). Third, he asserts without out evidence that even obvious services to the highrise area — such as police, fire, sewage, etc. — haven't increased in highrise areas.

All this is nonsense, of course. Gruen doesn't produce a shred of evidence to support any of these contentions. In his sole attempt to deal directly with municipal costs and benefits of highrises, Gruen "proves" highrises pay for themselves by showing that 1970 city property tax revenues would have been less if certain highrises hadn't been built. But he does this by assuming that city expenditures would have remained the same. In other words, he assumes that servicing highrises costs the city nothing — which is what he set out to prove.

Gruen's other conclusions are equally undocumented. Example: minorities would lose jobs (he can't even show that minorities get jobs in highrises). Example: there would be fewer construction jobs (he doesn't investigate whether city residents hold these jobs, whether new jobs would open up in surrounding areas, whether renovation of existing structures would produce new jobs). Finally, his argument that high-density "clustering" is economically necessary — the more of it, the better — leads to the conclusion that a city of highrises would be ideal. Compare Manhattan.

3. The McCue Report

"Tall buildings are not the cause but the result of growth," Gerald McCue, of McCue Boone Tomsick, says. This statement (which is demonstrably false: like freeways, highrises are both the cause *and* the result of growth) lies at the core of McCue's argument against a height limit.

McCue assumes that commuters will continue flocking to downtown San Francisco in ever-increasing numbers — up to an appalling 600,000 by 1990, he says. To accommodate this growth, highrises must continue to go up. It's that simple.

McCue acknowledges that jobs in highrises go to commuters. But he contends (note the contradiction with his statement about growth) that highrises "create" service jobs for city residents in small businesses near the city core. A height limit would halt expansion of this job sector, he says. But he does not consider the abundance of evidence showing that such small businesses have been leaving the city in droves since the highrise boom began.

McCue then cites studies showing that the promised influx of commuters would be more likely to leave their smog-belching cars at home and ride BART (which at peak capacity will be able to handle only 10% of the *present* commuter flow) if the downtown were highly compact — that is, if it were crammed with more high-density office buildings. This is the source of his remarkable conclusion on the environmental question: highrises actually *reduce* air pollution and congestion.

McCue exhorts us to think about all this positively — that is, think up the best architecture we can for our inevitable Manhattanization. This is scarcely surprising: McCue is an architect himself. But his critques of recent highrises amount to little more than quibbling within the profession about how such buildings should be constructed.

4. Bureau of Governmental Research

A Feb. 4, 1971 Chronicle editorial joyfully eulogized the Bureau of Governmental Research for demolishing the Alvin Duskin case against highrise.

Eight of Duskin's charges are of "dubious validity" and one is "absolutely false," the editorial quoted the bureau's director, Louis Clisbee, as saying. There were hints of massive research, by computer no less, by this "long-established and respected citizen's agency." (The bureau is largely funded by downtown interests.)

Well, we checked and found: (a) the Chronicle's editorial writer, Al Hyman, put together the demolition job from a Chronicle news story; (b) the Chronicle reporter, Bill Workman, plucked the story from a one-page bureau press hand-out; (c) the bureau's one-page handout had one line of value judgment on the Duskin case; (d) Clisbee had no study and had done no research: he said he wouldn't "dignify" Duskin's case with a study; (e) the "computer analysis" turned out to be nothing more than a total of tax revenues before and after development of four buildings, including the Bank of America, supplied by the City Assessor; (f) this information was used last fall in a "joint labor-Chamber of Commerce" statement and published in a short Nov. 11 Examiner story.

A whopper of a story. But a good example of the incest and myth-making and obeisance to cataclysmic finance that has made skyrise "the oldest established permanent floating craps game" in New York and Chicago — and now San Francisco.

— from the Bay Guardian, Feb. 26, 1971.

How to build a pyramid: a kit of pr tools helps win
San Francisco's approval for a new high rise office building
By John Krizek. From S.F. Bay Guardian, June 7, 1971

(Krizek is public relations manager of Transamerica and a judge for the 1970 SF Press Club's "Pulitzer of the West" newspaper awards contest. This piece, including the above headline, was excerpted from the December 1970 edition of Public Relations Journal, published monthly by the Public Relations Society of America.)

Construction of a major new high-rise office building presents a public relations challenge in any city, particularly in this age of expanding environmentalism. The challenge is accentuated when the building is highly unusual (a pyramid), and the city is highly sensitive about its environment (San Francisco).

Transamerica Corporation last year found itself caught in a crossfire of controversy over its plans for a dramatic new headquarters building in its home city. From the initial announcement through commencement of construction 11 months later, public relations played a major role in moving the project from plans toward reality.

Most public relations programs for new buildings begin in earnest with a triumphal groundbreaking ceremony. For Transamerica, the groundbreaking

itself, conducted under cloak-and-dagger circumstances, marked the anti-climactic end of a year-long effort, just to get the project to that point.

It was a campaign characterized by such aspects as:
- A striking design, which generated world-wide publicity;
- Sidewalk demonstrations for and against the plan;
- A complex series of steps necessary for city approval, culminating in two dozen lengthy public hearings, all well covered by the local media.

The story began with the decision by Transamerica Corporation—a multi-market service and financial organization with assets of $3.5 billion and world-wide operations—to construct a new headquarters building. Its charming four-story flatiron building had been outgrown, and various subsidiary operations in the Bay Area were experiencing growing pains of their own.

The company's executives naturally wanted to stay in San Francisco, where the company had grown up. Early in the game, the company discovered that it would need about a half-million square feet of office space, about triple its own projected needs, in order to make the project economically feasible. The San Francisco Chamber of Commerce was then waging an aggressive national campaign to attract more executive head-quarters operations to the financial district of San Francisco, so Trans-america's plans for a sizable office building met with immediate enthusiasm from that quarter.

With no small degree of hometown love and pride, Transamerica told its architect to design the most beautiful building he could. The chosen architect, William L. Pereira, a world-renowned designer and planner of cities—responsible for, among other things, Los Angeles' airport and art museum, Cape Canaveral, and the Irvine campus of the University of California—responded with a number of preliminary designs. Of these only one had universal appeal.

The pyramid design offered a graceful, soaring, and classically simple silhouette. At the same time, its sloping sides would permit more light and air to reach the streets around it, thereby helping to avoid the Manhattan-canyon effect. And its narrowness would obstruct fewer views than the customary rectangular slab design. Views, as most will agree, are especially important in San Francisco.

The corporate relations staff became involved in planning the announce-ment of the new building, even before the Board of Directors made its final decision to go ahead with the project in late December, 1968. We were well aware that the pyramid would have a startling effect and would undoubtedly generate some controversy. How much, none of us could have guessed. Like most companies putting up a new headquarters building, we were doing it for

Which building needs to be sold with a kit of pr tools? (Photo: looking down Columbus Avenue in October, 1971).

the first time. And, it had been a few thousand years since anyone tried such an unusual approach.

The plans, including a five-foot study model, were kept under tight wraps at corporate headquarters, until the necessary steps we needed to take for announcement and approval could be determined. The Mayor and his chief administrative officer were the first city officials invited in to take a look, and to advise us as to the proper steps for approval. Subsequently, other city and Chamber of Commerce officials, and the city planning director, were invited in, prior to any public announcement, but it was obvious that a project of such unusual interest would not remain secret for long. Word of something spectacular began to trickle out.

A major press conference was announced on a Friday for the following Monday, in late January, 1969. The date coincided with the annual Chamber of Commerce banquet which would enable the Chamber officials to share in the announcement, and the building to share in the exposure of the event. It also provided a week-end of relative security in which to prepare for the announcement.

In spite of security efforts, a reporter picked up enough details to run a front page story in the Sunday paper, which helped heighten interest in the Monday conference.

The morning of the press conference, at a major hotel, was used for briefing sessions for v.i.p. and neighborhood groups. Included were key city officials and representatives of the nearby Chinese and Italian communities, the Telegraph Hill Dwellers Association, and others. Those who accepted the invitation were greeted by the architect, and the chairman of the corporation. The morning briefings were followed by a special luncheon for the publishers and general managers of all the city's newspapers and TV stations.

The press conference itself, scheduled for 2:00 p.m., was just what most non-PR people imagine press conferences to be like: lots of bright lights and TV cables, and the press seated expectantly in rows. On hand were the Mayor and the president of the Chamber of Commerce, and the architect. The board chairman spoke briefly of the company's emotional ties to the city, its needs for a new office building, and its desire to create a building of unusual beauty. When he and the Mayor together pulled back the drapes to reveal the model of the pyramid, there was an audible gasp in the room.

The model was displayed that evening at a reception for the Chamber of Commerce banquet head table group, including the Governor and several high-ranking guests. The president of the Chamber lauded the project at the banquet, attended by over 1,000.

The initial reaction was nothing less than overwhelming. The pyramid was immediate front page news. Both wire services carried pictures of the model. Clippings began arriving from such far-off places as Japan and Europe. By

May, the item had appeared in 140 newspapers in the United States outside of San Francisco, and its total circulation, based just on clippings received, passed 29 million. Both San Francisco newspapers ran favorable editorials that were later to stand us in good stead.

In the weeks that followed the press conference, meetings and briefings were sought and held with virtually every group, and every city official or politician who might have anything to do with approval of the project. A special luncheon was held for the city hall department heads, including the engineering and traffic people who would be intimately involved in the detail work. The architect was on hand to describe the project and answer their questions. A special luncheon was held for labor leaders. Private briefings were held for individual members of the Board of Supervisors, reporters, etc. A few groups spurned the offer of a special briefing. But the offers were made.

It soon became apparent that many individual battles would have to be won, that a complex community relations job was needed in order to win approval for the project. A building committee was formed, headed by the vice president—corporations, whose immediate responsibilities also included public relations and advertising. Serving on the committee, which met weekly or as often as necessary to discuss strategy and coordinate progress, were: the chairman of the board; the vice president in charge of construction; the PR manager; the president of the construction firm; representatives of the corporate PR counsel, Ruder & Finn; the architect and members of his staff; a corporate attorney; and an officer of the real estate firm responsible for land acquisition and leasing of the finished building.

Problem number one was the location of the site, on the fringe of San Francisco's downtown highrise financial district, adjacent to the low-rise and historic old Jackson Square and North Beach neighborhoods. The site lay directly in the middle of a one-block-wide strip of land, vaguely designated a "transition zone," which meant that the city Planning Commission had powers of "discretionary review" over any structure going up in that zone, even though it might meet all zoning regulations.

Problem number two was that a 1,000-ft. tall pyramid (the original configuration), even though within the city zoning code, was a far cry from what the city planning director had in mind for the area. It became clear that he would not recommend approval of the design, and the city Planning Commission normally rubber-stamped whatever the planning staff recommended.

Problem number three emerged as the project moved through the phases of study. The alley bisecting the site could not be bridged over, or straddled by the building, as provided by the original model, but would have to be closed, for safety reasons. This meant Transamerica would have to buy about one-third of a block of a public street from the city. Since the narrow street was used primarily to serve small businesses in the block, and for illegal parking, this seemed to present no problem, as far as the city departments were concerned. However, only the city Board of Supervisors had authority to sell city property. And, it would be necessary for the city Planning Commission to recommend approval or disapproval of the street closure . . .

The results of the hearing had the effect of shocking the project's opponents into a loosely-organized coalition. They realized if they were going to stop Transamerica from building, they would have to stop it over the legality of the sale of the public street, or they would have to bring public pressure to bear on the corporation to change its mind . . .

Negative publicity appeared in, of all places, the Washington Post. Its architectural critic quoted his contemporary in San Francisco, as well as the planning director who opposed the plan. The article, professionally illustrated to make the pyramid look as unfavorable as possible, was syndicated around the country. Headlines began to appear, to the effect that architectural critics were quaking with rage over what was proposed in San Francisco. There were only two architectural critics quaking with rage at this point, but such is the nature of the media.

Transamerica officials were somewhat surprised and hurt by the criticism, even though it was not totally unexpected and it appeared that there was ample support at official levels.

We learned indirectly that the opposition groups planned to meet one evening in a nearby nightclub.

We attended, surreptitiously, to observe and listen. Out of this rally, attended by 100 or so, came a letter-writing campaign directed to the Board of Supervisors. We thereupon accelerated a letter-writing campaign of our own, including support from several neighbors who supposedly were to be "overwhelmed" by the project.

A second rally was called by the opposition. This meeting was attended by perhaps 125 people, but included in that total were at least 15 people, including wives, who were there representing the corporate staff, the architect's office, and other friends of the project—all incognito.

The critics hardened. The structure was far too tall, they said, and it would destroy the beauty of the surrounding area. (Research showed a similar hue and cry raised in the 1930's over the construction of Coit Tower and the Golden Gate Bridge, both regarded today as sacred elements in the cityscape.) While the aesthetic arguments were perhaps pointless after the Planning Commission decision, it was apparent that a small group—some old, some young with long hair—were determined to have their voice in controlling changes in the city environment. At the root of their dissatisfaction was an understandable fear that high-rise urbanization might overwhelm "their" city.

It was announced, at this rally, that a sidewalk demonstration would be held the following noon in front of the Transamerica building. All opponents of the plan were urged to make their feelings known there. This left us little time to prepare for a demonstration—and the anticipated press coverage.

Our strategy was not to lock ourselves up in our corporate fortress, and thereby lend credence to the charges of corporate arrogance and insensitivity. And we did not want to expose our officers to a dialogue with highly emotional demonstrators, in front of the TV cameras. Therefore it was the public relations manager who greeted the leaders of the demonstration, as they came through the door, followed by the TV cameras. After promising to deliver their petition to the chairman of the board, he led a covey of attractive corporate secretaries out on the sidewalk to serve iced tea to the demonstrators, with news cameras as witnesses.

There were only about 30 participants in the demonstration, but the Pyramid was now a public issue in San Francisco.

The next showdown came before the three-man Streets & Transportation Committee of the Board of Supervisors, whose duty it was to study the matter, and recommend to the full board whether to vacate the street or not. While most such committee hearings are held in virtual isolation, this one had to be moved into board chambers, because of the size of the crowd, and to accommodate the news cameras. The four-hour hearing was highlighted by a surprise visit by the Mayor, who showed up to testify on behalf of the project. As a result, the news was dominated by the Mayor's praise of the project. The committee voted 2-1 to pass the matter on to the full board, with a recommendation for approval.

By this time, the corporate public relations strategy was to maintain as low a profile as possible with such a high-profile project. In a city where publicists outdo themselves to get client mentions in Herb Caen's column, we lost track of how many times the running debate over the Transamerica project was mentioned by accident—pro and con. When politicians, some of whom were not involved in city affairs, held press conferences, inevitably they were asked what they thought about the Transamerica building, and their responses were quoted. We read the papers not to see if we were mentioned, but how many times, by whom, and in what way.

As the initial showdown before the full Board of Supervisors approached, we learned, with less than a day's notice, of plans for a second lunchtime sidewalk demonstration. This one was summoned by what turned out to be the old coalition, under a new name: "Artists Against the Pyramid."

We felt a little like the over-popular hostess. We knew who was coming to the party, but what could we do that would be different, and still within the bounds of corporate propriety?

The demonstrators—basically the same group of 30 or so—appeared on schedule, five minutes before the TV cameras. This time they brought a three-foot pyramid of ice, to symbolically melt away under the summer sun, as they circled it, wearing cardboard dunce caps shaped like pyramids, bearing signs and literature prepared by the "Artists Against the Pyramid." The whole thing drew a pretty good lunchtime crowd.

Once again, out came the Transamerica secretaries, serving iced tea to the demonstrators and the press. This time they also served fortune cookies, which contained messages such as: "Transamerica not square outfit"; "Sphinx says: people who protest pyramid seek Cheop publicity." (When you

are next door to Chinatown, you can get fortune cookies made up in a hurry!)

The group was quickly joined by a few hippie-looking young men, brandishing an "Artists FOR the Pyramid" sign, and passing out a leaflet of their own, which included a cartoon showing two ancient Egyptians in a raging argument over the construction of pyramids along the Nile. Newsmen felt constrained to get their views of the project, as well.

No one viewing the scene was aware that the counter-demonstrators were led by two young men who comprised an ad agency, who had come to us a week earlier with the idea for a kookie advertising campaign to elicit public support for the building. We had declined, but when they learned of the second demonstration they were only too happy to join in!

In the midst of it all, the corporate relations staff distributed a question-and-answer fact sheet.

The effect of all this was to turn the whole demonstration into a party on the sidewalk, with both sides of the question apparently equally represented. Any aggressive intent the demonstrators may have come with was defused. Local press coverage of the event tended to be on the light-hearted side. However, the controversy had now achieved national media attention.

In this charged atmosphere, the whole issue rolled before the full Board of Supervisors in late August. After another tumultuous 4-hour hearing, with over 200 present, the board voted overwhelmingly to sell the little-used street to Transamerica.

And so the battle was won. Transamerica could go ahead with the project. Right? Wrong.

The architect and the chairman of the board took a long look at the design, and decided it wasn't right. We had over-compromised. Back to the drawing board, and a new design, substantially different enough to require Planning Commission approval; it would also require purchasing an additional 23 feet of the street . . .

By this time it was November, and another factor entered the picture: that of timing. It was essential that construction commence before the end of the year. For many years, California had encouraged insurance companies to locate home offices in the state by allowing them to deduct from their state premium taxes whatever they paid in local property taxes on a headquarters building. This law contributed to San Francisco's status as the financial center of the west, and the several insurance buildings in its skyline. But the law was to expire at the end of 1969, and if construction were to begin after December 31, the building, estimated to generate about $750,000 per year in property taxes, would not qualify for the deductions.

December came, with the final 23-foot piece of street yet to be formally acquired. A site permit, which would permit ground to be broken and construction thereby to commence, was yet to be issued. The die-hard opposition knew its only hope for stopping the project was to file a site permit appeal, which could immediately delay construction, until another hearing could be held after the first of the year. However, an appeal could not be made until a site permit was issued. Both sides therefore watched carefully as the paperwork at city hall progressed toward issuance of the site permit.

On the day in mid-December when the permit paperwork neared completion, a representative of the contractor went to city hall and made sure everything was in order, before calling a corporate vice president, who arrived in a pick-up truck during the lunch hour to avoid being recognized. A few minutes later, he flashed the message to the construction supervisor and public relations manager, lurking in a restaurant across the street from the site: "Have permits in hand. Get ready to move in 20 minutes."

Photographers who had been waiting in phone booths appeared on signal. The small group converged casually on the site. Out of a basement excavation, where they had been hidden all morning from street view, crawled a tractor and a truck. And to the cheers of the smallest crowd ever to conduct a major building groundbreaking in San Francisco, the tractor bit through the surface of the parking lot, and the Transamerica Pyramid was safely under construction.

An hour later, word came that a site permit appeal was being filed . . .

"A San Francisco Landmark Since 1872."

'Damned Monoliths': An Architectural Critique of Highrise
By John Kenyon

Declaring them to be the true heroic constructions of our time — as though they were the Queen Mary or the Brooklyn Bridge — is untrue and misleading. Put together with an elegance beyond that attained by even the governmental buildings of other nations, pre-empting precious blocks of downtown to turn the ground-levels into policed lobbies and useless plazas, hugging view, light and attention with 40 or 50 decks of technically superb accommodation that is utterly dead, utterly squandered after 5:30 p.m., the great towers stand as symbols of the ultimate insane split between work and life, at best as gigantic machines that will soon be redundant.

Are they architecture? Barely. They might better be defined as huge three-dimensional advertisements that people — a diminishing number — happen to work in until their particular job categories become obsolete. True, most buildings we enjoy as *architecture* now were once prime power-symbols of some ruling group, but few have been as limited, as socially non-fulfilling as these.

Notre Dame or Chartres, besides being dedicated to God, were social, theatrical and business-centers of their day. Even the sumptuous palace of the Sun King at Versailles was mostly generalized accommodation where courtiers, soldiers, artists and plotters came and went, often through the King's apartments. Compared with Wells Fargo or Aetna Insurance, the classic buildings were lessons in 'multiple-use.'

They were also lessons in participation. It took hundreds of craftsmen generations to build Amiens or Canterbury, whereas our enormous artifacts that command the captive audience of North Beach and Potrero Heights and even Berkeley, must hold the record for minimal human involvement. Erected by strictly scheduled labor, designed by a tiny team of not very free architects, they impose their repetitive detail and magazine-derived design upon millions. Often their only original feature is the tapestry or sculpture in the lobby.

Those eclectic "skyscrapers" of the 20's, like the telephone building on New Montgomery with its complex L-shaped plan and elaborate detail, were the product of cheaper labor and a more autocratic class and tax structure. In retrospect, they seem rich and expressive, but in terms of human fulfillment they were no less impoverished than the newer buildings.

Maybeck's old Christian Science Church in Berkeley or the connected levels and promenades of the Cannery afford spatial delights. Those 40 or 50 floor stacks of identical accommodation deliver at most a shock to the senses, a sort of esthetic 'kick.' Arrogantly huge, repetitive, humanly absurd, they are "interesting" *only* because of the rock-bottom impoverishment and disorder of our thrown-together environment. They are the hard drugs of architecture, giving less and less satisfaction for bigger and bigger doses — and architects have been heavy users. Working mostly in offices (note the word), denied the true satisfactions of making a personal environment (in which Simon Rodia's Watts Towers might be classed as normal), they tend to throw in a tower or two at the drop of a hat to pep up their dull elevations. Yet in a richly carved stone city like Oxford, full of turrets and gargoyles and symbolism — no 'highrise' is as *high* as a good spire! — one does not long for bigness or newness at all, or for shock.

From the vast paved spaces of the Embarcadero Plaza, near the new fountain — that monument to a fallen freeway — the colossal artifacts sail toward you down the slope like a naval flotilla sweeping all before them, so that you feel you must either turn around and flee to the Sausalito ferry or shout "Tora, Tora, Tora!," depending upon which side you take.

Still, it would be dishonest for me, another design-professional, to pretend that these great precision-built structures were all equally devoid of interest or did not manifest certain strange satisfactions. The elegant green-glass walls of Crown Zellerbach at Bush and Market, the misleadingly simple lobby lit by 15,842 plastic cylinders penetrating a ceiling of brass, the sunken garden with its olive trees and cobbles and water-sculpture—all of this, like Lever House or Seagram in New York, is an impressive demonstration of corporate noblesse oblige advised by good design that might (had Jack Kennedy not been shot, had the liberal dream of unity not been shattered) have set the pattern for a shining new standard of city-making. Crown Zellerbach, 19 floors of curtains and green glass, an exercise in weightless simplicity, and across Bush, that magnificent jazz-age Shell Building, all solid and defined from its fortress-like ground floor to its Egyptian lotus-capital top. An enjoyable bit of what the English "Architectural Review" once christened "townscape," but note, 19 floors, 24 floors. Not really much higher than the old masonry palazzos of the 1900's, and compensated, like Crown Zellerbach, by public gardens at the base.

But in the last decade the dialogue between concerned architects has become more of a shouting match. Stand in Portsmouth Square. Across Kearny the new raw-concrete Holiday Inn rises like ventilating machinery from an industrial-looking sloping base that contains the Chinese Cultural Center. Its tenuous relationship to that seedy but human park is made crashingly obvious by a cement footbridge over the street, described—reverently—by one passing lady as "Chinese Urban Renewal."

In a civilized city, the relation of much-loved local parks to new buildings around them would be the essence of public debate and the subject of architectural competitions, but here such calm thinking seems almost effete. For right behind the Inn and before we have even decided—after the fact— whether *that* is tolerable, the white obelisk of Transamerica grows daily taller, to terminate soon, not in a pyramid, but in a sort of KKK cone that will insure its being, for a time, the highest structure in town.

To the south, three structures rear up side by side beyond the old sagging properties of Clay Street — the dark brown pleated slab of the Bank of America Center, the elegant, white Hartford Tower, and in the middle, dominated by both, the civilized, almost miniature International Building. This last, the late Bob Anshen's contribution to a more intimate San Francisco, might be happier now in downtown Berkeley.

Its wide bands of green glass, its base, merging nicely with St. Mary's Square, and its playful, copper-edged "hat" at the top, make it that rare animal, a friendly-looking office building. And Skidmore, Owings and Merrill's Hartford Tower across California Street is a most interesting neighbor for it. S.O.M. has long been the master of the restrained corporate tower, and this one, its huge outer walls structural truss, window and shadowed surface all at once, is quite up to standard. That this great concrete grille makes an excellent foil for the toy Gothic Revival Church of Old St. Mary's next door, is a measure of its success, too, as civilized townscape.

Of exhibit number three, the Bank of America building set back on its new "plaza," it is hard to know what to say that isn't either esoteric or simplistic. Personally, I find the design flawed. It de-emphasizes structure in favor of

Our Urban Design Plan in action: from left, Alcoa, West Coast Life, Security Pacific, Transamerica, Holiday Inn, Mutual Benefit, Crocker, Pacific Insurance.

179

modelling 1,500,000 square feet of accommodation—by means of that faceted bay—as a giant fragment of fluted column or some found crystalline formation.

The irregular, broken-back top, the glassiness and the dark color strengthen this latter image, besides having overtones of those Jazz-Age skyscrapers of the '20's that swinging designers, working in a social vacuum, are clearly yearning to revive. The result is enormous ambivalence. From Telegraph Hill, the whole massive edifice is an image of something else, a giant sculpture rather than an all-day environment for 5,000 people. Up close, you can't see the whole for the shifting gleaming geometry of the parts. Thus designers, seduced more than a little by formalism, think it clever, while others, more taken by mood than virtuosity, call it a 'damned monolith,' and both are right.

Look at it long enough and you begin to doubt your powers of judgment, but this at least may be said: seen not as economic nor earthquake hazard nor traffic overloader, but merely as an impact on the senses, it is too big. Its funereal presence utterly dominates Giannini Plaza, which is more a flight of windswept steps than a pleasant public square.

Seen in its regional context it still seems too big. Observed from the foothills of the East Bay, it rises behind Yerba Buena Island like an affront to the landforms. Those older towers clustered on Russian Hill, while not an earthly paradise from near, seem, from 12 miles away, merely to intensify the structure of the land and bring some needed variety into the dense, low-rise habitat. But that 54 story chunk of man-made topography, and other giants like Aetna and Wells Fargo, introduce a brand new scale, an enormous new increment of accommodation that seems to weight down the earth and oppress the senses.

Scan the horizon from Point Richmond to the hills of the Peninsula, past the outline of Tamalpais, across the Gate and along the low whaleback of the Presidio, over the old city, all clustered cubes, then, like a slap across the face, an ominous cigar box 20 floors too high.

Again and again the eye is drawn back. One does not have to be an eco-radical or a seismic engineer to know that something has gone wrong. Just when changed concepts of work, electronics and autonomous transportation have diminished the need for a controlling center, when anything other than intelligent dispersal seem self-defeating, we are treated to this sudden accelleration of centrism.

Take transportation. With thousands of employees working in each giant building, and the automobile far from the end of its popularity, the street-system will become loaded beyond 'capacity.' But the one thing that makes these towers bearable—sometimes even beautiful—is space and vegetation.

The Hyatt House looms up over Union Square (top). Below, the Holiday Inn (with one floor of Chinese Cultural Center) at left, the Transamerica pyramid (center), the Alcoa Building in the rear.

Even from dingy Portsmouth Square, overbuilt with toilets and trellises, it is the pines and the poplars that soften the violent mix of low stucco facades and tall glassy towers so that the sheer variety seems an improvement over the old fabric. If only the *balance* could be kept, if only the public sector could expand with the private, one might not be so anxious.

From a very reformist viewpoint, one function of planning is to anticipate a public setting for private development, to create new parklike spaces around which builders and businessmen can "do their worst." Without it we get aberrations like Market Street, where Aetna rises behind Wells Fargo behind Mutual Benefit, etc., and more to come, all taking advantage of the bleak 'accidental open space' of the corridor of cars.

Here the architect's favorite fantasy arises—the city without automobiles. A Market Street filled with foliage like a linear Redwood forest might indeed be a gorgeous setting for 20 more glass towers. But having eliminated the access, how do you reach them, unless rapid transit were to become enormously—and frighteningly—more important than BART is designed to be. And that only shoves the question round full circle: why bring everybody HERE to work from Richmond and Oakland and Walnut Creek?

Richmond's downtown redevelopment project is crying out for an office building. Even one small San Francisco tower is more than they hope for. Such imbalance in the distribution of facilities is pathetic.

While this failure to think regionally persists, the question of good design must remain secondary. Already, San Francisco is a sort of laboratory of environmental possibilities, where enormous amounts of talent and energy are poured into one area. No elementary school in Oakland has a structure as beautiful as the Hartford Tower. No scheme for the reconstruction of Telegraph Avenue will be as lavish as the Alcoa garage roof garden. In this laboratory spirit, let's look at that large example of comprehensive design, Golden Gateway and Embarcadero Center, where the tall office-blocks are merely a part of the spatial whole.

Well worth exploring is the 'podium' of the new Security Pacific Bank at Battery and Clay. Instead of a repellent lobby patrolled by sorrowful old security guards, here is a welcoming, sheltered public domain. The swirl-patterned tile sidewalk extends under and through to the garden-court and one may ascend, either by spiral stair or escalator, past pharmacy, liquor-store, gown shops and restaurants, to the roof.

From here you can walk over a pedestrian bridge to the grassy top of the Alcoa Building's parking structure, then on, over another bridge, to the town house level of Golden Gateway. Up here, away from the fumes, among the Bufano animals and the Marini horse and the sparkling fountain, you may even enjoy the contrast of the two huge structures—Alcoa dark and somber,

X-braced, more like a bridge; and Security Pacific, white, dazzling, so refined that even the mullions are slotted with a three inch strip of glass.

It all seems almost civilized. The designers have had a good time. But up on these podiums, where the trees grow only where Sasaki and Walker put them, everything is so socially tame, so exclusively middle class that it cannot truly be regarded as public at all.

A teen-age platinum-blond poses in the hollows of the aluminum sculpture for a handsome black photographer. The athletic-looking family of a bluff executive admires the bronze horse. Two old ladies from the Golden Gateway towers walk arm in arm toward the Plaza Dining Room. It is doubtful whether a poor woman with kids from East Oakland would have the nerve to even mount the steps leading to these huge connected decks.

At the opposite pole from this controlled, sterile space is Union Square. For many years the surrounding buildings maintained a more or less uniform height of ten, or 11 stories and a more or less classical character. Timothy Pfleuger's marble-faced I. Magnin and the dark gray, rather forbidding St. Francis Hotel had at least height and dignity in common.

Suddenly, the old mood is broken. The 32 floor addition to the back of the St. Francis and the new 35 story Hyatt House Hotel completely change the scale of the square, even though both are set well back. The Hyatt building, the result of extended collaboration between Skidmore Owings and Merrill and the City Planning Department, is worth close study as an ingenious exercise in application of the downtown bonus system. Its low front structure on Post maintains continuity with the little 'Georgian' fragment next door, yet comes to a sharp corner at Stockton, angling back to allow a hotel plaza, hidden from Union Square.

Whether this eclectic maneuvering represents true conservation is doubtful. In fact, one is left wondering if the traditional concept of a square or plaza ever applied at all to Union Square, a very American open space. With its still gardens mounding over a basement garage and its hodge podge of facades all around, it is no Place Vendome. Conceivably, a more nonchalant approach to 'letting the buildings happen'—the English tradition of improvisation rather than the French tradition of control—would produce more dynamic results. Improvisation, however, demands a modicum of good manners, and just behind the Hyatt tower, on Sutter, is a prime example of the reverse.

The Westbury, a new Knott hotel—the steel frame is already complete—sits almost wall to wall against the side of Pfleuger's Medical-Dental Building at 450 Sutter. The T-shaped plan and gentle rounded corners of this minor masterpiece from 1930 emphasize it most poetically as a free-standing form. To shove a large building up against its windows is about the crudest thing that could be done.

California Street in 1934. "The Chamber of Commerce says, 'We need more high rise hotels for the tourists.' But how many tourists will come to see San Francisco when it looks like the Detroit or Newark they just left?" From Alvin Duskin's anti-high rise coloring book.

California Street in September, 1971. "The little cable cars that used to cling to the sides of sunny hills now moved through dark canyons. First on canyon left is the Hartford Building, first on canyon right is the International Building.

Where were the controls that time? And anyway, could controls even compare with the sort of positive planning—compulsory purchase of public open-space—that San Francisco badly needs? That corner, right across from the old Francis Drake, should have been snapped-up and turned into a public garden.

This balance, though, between older and newer is not always easy to achieve, even when the new is an expansion of the old building itself. Two hotel additions, the St. Francis and the Hilton, exemplify the problem. Obviously the somber, dignified St. Francis was a tough one. Had there been room at the back, a modern but discreet addition around a garden-court would have been the answer. Failing that, perhaps a pure contrast. What they *did* do, for all of its elegant bay windows and matching 'stonework,' seems merely to confuse the old solid mass, which now reads, from the square, as a giant shoe-shine stand. In contrast, the Hilton is all improvement. That chequerboard block, always too dull a form for a building lacking the surface modelling of a Florentine palace, now has a dynamic foil in the tall, silvery slab of the Annex, the old connected to the new by an extension of the hotel base—and by a breathtaking foot-bridge high in the air.

In comparison with such expressionist "pop" as Wells Fargo or such follies as Transamerica, this simple tower is almost too good to be true. Those open balconies, that glassy observation-lounge top between the simple service 'towers,' the air conditioning units "expressed" as surface pattern—all this is from a European-functional tradition associated more with Holland or Denmark, and demonstrates that one tower may be far less inhuman than another.

From Ellis and Larkin, by the Star Cafe and Bo Jangles, it almost restores one's faith in the positive virtues of height to see this simple unaffected form rising beyond the jumble of cornices and fire-escapes and signs that constitutes so much of low-rise San Francisco. Across duller areas like the Avenues, one might even welcome such a building every quarter mile or so, a small park at its foot and a friendly anarchy of low-rise blocks between. But how on earth do you achieve such a balance under "free enterprise"?

Duskin's proposal, of a 72 foot blanket height limit with exceptions approved only by the general vote, could conceivably turn extensive downtown districts into seven-story blocks built-up to grim capacity. It certainly wouldn't guarantee that sensitive variety of heights and levels that this hillside city needs, though it might act as a kind of truce, allowing time to develop more planning-refinement while effectively discouraging more Transamericas or 54-story banks. On the whole, I think, it would be a good conservative measure at this point, throwing the emphasis back on San Francisco as a place to live while distributing the burden of information-processing into the urban region.

A typical "blighted" building awaiting redevelopment in the Western Addition.
As a Wells Fargo study put it, most demolished WA buildings are old Victorians.

Highrise/Taxrise
By M. J. Kupferman. From S.F. Bay Guardian, June 7, 1971.

"If Russell Wolden were running for office today, he'd surely be elected."

This statement by a San Francisco home owner is not a call for the return of Wolden's "Last Hurrah" style in city hall. It's just a nostalgic commentary on Wolden's policy of holding the line on residential property tax assessments and taking up the slack with higher assessments on business property.

For a complex set of reasons, homeowners and renters now find themselves at the wrong end of a lopsided tax structure. Not only do they pay a much larger tax bill individually, but as a group they also contribute a substantially larger proportion of the City's total tax bill than they did in 1966. At the same time the downtown business area pays a proportionately smaller share than it did five years ago.

Why? Why are the homeowners and the renters called upon to bail the City out financially while big business and skyrise finance have been able to build 21 highrise office buildings and 10 million square feet of office space in downtown San Francisco in the past 10 years?

The single most important reason is the Petris-Knox Act (AB 80), which passed the Legislature in 1966. This bill set up the machinery for all California counties to standardize assessments at 25% of a house's full market value. Before AB 80, San Francisco policy was to tax residential property generally at 14% and business property at 25% of total market value. Thus, the bill brought a dramatic rise in residential property taxes and a decline in downtown business taxes.

To illustrate AB 80's effect, I took three typical blocks and calculated their assessments in 1966 (pre-AB 80), and again in 1967 (immediately after

The tax effect of the highrise boom

Year	Total Assessed Values ($000,000)Central Business District	Total Assessed Values City of San Fran. ($000,000)	Assessed Values of Central Dist. As % of Total
1950-1	242.5	883.4	27.5
1959-60	284.5	1,141.3	24.9
1970-I	409.9	1,974.1	20.8

These figures indicate that, despite the feverish pace of highrise construction, the downtown area has fallen in its contribution to the total of San Francisco property taxes.

The percentage contribution of the central business district, outlined on the map, has fallen 6.7% over the past two decades. The assessed values (upon which property taxes are based) have risen, but those of the rest of the City have risen at a faster rate.

This drop in the proportion paid by the business district comes despite the addition of 21 skyscrapers and 10 million square feet of office floor space to the area's tax base over the past 10 years.

Central Business District includes Assessor's Block Numbers 218-233, 234-289, 290-355, 3701-3714 as designated in map.

Source: Paul Wendt's "Dynamics of Central City Land Values," (1950-1, 1959-60) a UC Press book on SF/Oakland land values.

1970-1: Martin Kupferman-George Wylie-updating of Wendt data for corresponding blocks.

AB 80). One, in the downtown highrise area, is bounded by California-Pine and Sansome-Montgomery Streets. Its assessments, I found, fell by 20% as a result of AB 80 and the standardizing of assessments. Meanwhile, assessments in a block bounded by Broderick-Pacific and Octavia-Gough, in the wealthy residential area of Pacific Heights, rose by 82%.

Finally, on a Richmond district block of predominantly one- and two-family homes, assessments rose by 273%. This mammoth increase was reflected in varying degrees in all one- and two-family units throughout the city.

While downtown interests certainly fared well under AB 80, it was not enacted specifically on their behalf. It resulted from the Wolden bribery scandal.

The Supervisors initially supported AB 80 (later reversing themselves) and it passed the legislature virtually without opposition. Few realized that standardizing assessments was a policy decision that would redistribute large amounts of wealth to the disadvantage of the homeowner and renter.

The redistribution may have involved a good deal more than the $200-300 rise in property taxes. The prospect of having to pay the greater amount, not just once but down through the years, has discouraged prospective homeowners from buying. The decline in demand led in turn to a fall in property values.

Present San Francisco Assessor Joseph Tinney, in a recent interview, denied such a decline took place. He maintained that if this were true he would have slashed assessments, despite the politically dangerous prospect that the cut would have necessitated a higher tax rate to raise the same amount of revenue.

A doctoral thesis in economics by Roger Stafford Smith at UC Berkeley is at odds with Tinney's assertion. Smith states, for example, that houses with an average value of $30,300 lost as much as $4,478 off their expected sale price. Furthermore, each $1 rise in taxes resulted in a $19 decline in market value.

This took place, he wrote, when it became clear to those people buying homes for investment that higher taxes would reduce their future net income from the property. Single family units declined, on the average, between 14% and 15%, Smith reported.

Smith's estimates tend to be high. (A Sunset realtor estimated that somewhere between $5-$10 was lost with each $1 rise in taxes.) Yet Smith's perspective is largely accurate. The exact amount changes from case to case.

But even if no decline in actual value took place in the majority of neighborhoods, the local market for one- and two-family homes has been greatly weakened and results, certainly, in greater difficulty for those seeking to sell their houses.

This two-pronged jolt—increased tax bills and decreased property values—was felt by every residential section in San Francisco. The property tax boost was passed on to renters even though they paid no property tax directly to the City. This worked a hardship on those with incomes under $5,000, 78% of whom are renters. Those on welfare had to turn to city or state agencies for help in meeting the added cost of rent. Hardest hit of all, according to Col. Martin Fellauer of the West Twin Peaks Taxpayers Committee, were the elderly on fixed incomes who are too proud to turn to the government for assistance.

For others, the high and rising cost of owning a home has had more subtle effects. Jack Bartalini, head of Taxpayers Revolt, says: "Property taxes have eliminated the dream of a young family to ever own a home in San Francisco." Taxes for a family owning a $30,000 home will come to something over $80 per month, Bartalini estimates.

Tinney lays all blame on the legislature. "The legislature is simply not responsive to the needs of the homeowner," says Tinney. He points out that all attempts at reform benefitting the homeowner have been shunted aside. The City-State financial structure must be revised, Tinney maintains, so some rising costs of running the City will be met by the State. In addition, he feels that the City must be allowed to give homeowners a break by relaxing the AB 80 ratio.

Bartalini, however, feels the City could have done much more to ease the homeowner's burden after AB 80. He goes so far as to say: "If Wolden were still the Assessor after AB 80, I expect property assessments would largely have remained the same, outside of a reasonably inflationary rise, as before passage of the law."

In his view, assessments are merely opinions of value made by those more sympathetic to businesses than the homeowner. Bartalini points to the deductions now given to businesses (such as depreciation, second mortgages and maintenance) but not to homeowners, who are unequipped to protest high assessments.

In a 1967 letter to voters, Joseph Alioto, then a candidate for mayor, pledged to shift the tax burden back to big business. Yet it is clear that this shift has not taken place.

The City has refused to move despite the A.D. Little report on city taxes. It recommended: "The City does not have to take a passive stand in respect to these developments. The City may cushion the harsh effects of reassessment by imposing business and other non-property taxes that would divide the City's tax liability along more customary lines.

"In so doing, the City would insure that both the City's residents and business community, respectively, would continue to contribute what has traditionally been regarded as their fair share to financing City government."

One way to ease the effect of AB 80 would be to decrease the importance of property taxes as a source of revenue. The Little report went on to say that $58 million in business taxes was needed to fully shift the burden back from the resident to the businessman.

It recommended a shift of about half this amount—$29 million—so as not to strain the business community. In 1968, the city did impose a business license (gross receipts) tax. The rate was so small, however, that it raised only $5 million, a paltry 1.2% of city revenue in that year. Without the gross receipts tax, every homeowner would have paid a mere 25 cents more per $100 assessed valuation.

Evidently, the concern is that a larger business tax would deter new firms from locating in San Francisco. This fear, however, is not the only protection businesses have against shifting of the tax burden to them.

The State Constitution prevents the City from levying any non-property taxes on banks and insurance and finance companies, who are responsible for

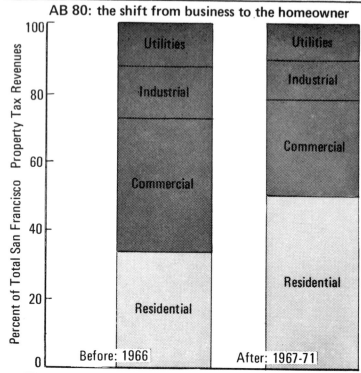

AB 80: the shift from business to the homeowner

Percent of Total San Francisco Property Tax Revenues

Before: 1966

After: 1967-71

This chart by A. D. Little & Co. shows that the old division of the property tax burden (2/3 contributed by business to 1/3 residential) became a 1/2-1/2 breakdown after AB 80.

In real figures, Little's "San Francisco Taxes" report says that business assessments shrunk by $55 million while residential assessments rose by $525 million.

Assessor Tinney denies Little's figures. He argues that single family unit assessments rose by $300 million and those of business by $240 million. Furthermore, he says the share of single family units rose from 14% to only 26%.

The difference can perhaps be explained because Tinney lumps two or more family dwelling units into the business category and thereby muddles the business-residential distinction. This distinction, Tinney maintains, is invalid because units housing more than one family are allowed at least partial depreciation and maintenance deductions and can pass the greater taxes on through higher rents.

At any rate, a shift in the tax burden from the businessman to the city resident cannot be denied. This was acknowledged by Joseph Alioto, running for mayor in Oct. 1967, in a letter he sent to all city residents. He said:

"Give me your help, Mrs. Jones, and we will put that $29 million back on big business where it was and where it belongs."

21 of the 44 skyrises already built or projected through 1972. While the State levies taxes on these institutions, it does not return any funds to the city directly related to the institutions.

The picture is startling. Citizens are told that because highrises add significantly to the tax base, they must put up with them despite their negative environmental effects. But it is clear highrise areas do not even pay their share of the city's total revenue.

Revenue analysis alone shows that the city gets merely a fraction of the revenues highrise areas are capable of providing. What's more, while the figure for property taxes paid by highrises may add up to an impressive sum, the proportion of taxes in relation to income is far less than the ratio for an individual citizen.

A business can write off or pass on to the consumer much of the property tax it pays, but a pensioner homeowner, living on under $4,000, may pay close to 10% of his income in property taxes alone.

As Bartalini puts it, "Big Business pays taxes out of profits, homeowners out of their pockets."

These facts refer only to city revenues. On the other side of the ledger, the amount highrises cost the City may be considerably more than is commonly supposed. Roger Stafford Smith points out that in the case of five cities (San Leandro, Calif.; Arlington, Va.; West Hartford, Conn.; New Rochelle, N.Y.; and Yorktown, N.Y.) the cost of police, fire, public works and sewage for an acre of commercial land runs 5.5 times higher than for a residential acre. No such studies have yet been undertaken in San Francisco.

However, there is one glaring example of preferential tax treatment for big business in San Francisco. The property tax owner finds himself saddled with repayment for bonds floated for BART. BART's rate now is about $.51 per $100 assessed valuation with varying amounts to be paid up to 1999.

For the owner of a $28,000 Richmond house, this represents nearly $40 per year (as opposed to what might have been $20 before AB 80). Obviously, BART will be of little use to him—it does not even extend to the Richmond. Rather, it will raise the value of downtown property!

It will funnel thousands of non-taxpaying commuters downtown to man the businesses and thousands of shoppers to fill the stores. They will use sewage, transportation, police and fire services, the cost of which will find its way back to SF property taxes and the BART-less owner of the Richmond house.

Tinney has referred with pride to a recent study showing San Francisco ranking well below several equivalent-sized cities in terms of property taxes. Yet, he cautioned, something must be done if San Francisco is to retain this low ranking. Many property owners agree with Tinney and the stirrings of a major taxpayers' revolt are at hand.

BART's Ride to Bankruptcy

By Burton Wolfe. From S.F. Bay Guardian, June 18, 1968.

Roger Lapham, Jr., dapper son of a former San Francisco Mayor, sat in his plush office on the 32nd floor of San Francisco's Wells Fargo Building, once called the "tallest in the West."

"The end result of BART (Bay Area Rapid Transit district) is that San Francisco will be just like Manhattan," he said, gazing past his opulent furniture and modern paintings out the window toward a stupendous view of the bay.

Lapham, president of the insurance brokerage firm of Alexander, Sexton & Carr of California, had been one of the most influential members on BART's board of directors in its formative years. He and other key movers of BART in the local business community have pushed the rail transit system as the means of transporting an ever greater number of commuters from an ever widening area to a forest of gigantic skyscrapers in San Francisco.

They formed an organization called the Downtown Advisory Committee to carry out the plan. It represented the Chamber of Commerce, the Real Estate Board, the Downtown Property Owners and Building Association, the Building Owners and Managers Association, the Bank and Clearing House Association, and the Pacific Telephone Co. and other big corporations.

The 43-story, $20 million Wells Fargo Building that Lapham's firm occupies at the corner of Market and Montgomery, key BART station stop, was the first constructed under the businessmen's plan to Manhattanize San Francisco. The Crocker Citizens Bank followed suit across the street with a $20 million, 38-story building that has, like the Wells Fargo Building, an underground concourse leading to the BART subway. The Bank of America outdid its competitors with a $92 million, 52-story world headquarters, announced in these orgiastic terms:

Up, up and away. "The architects designed an office tower building which, located as it is in the midst of San Francisco's tallest buildings, will be the apex of the visual composition of the skyline. Seen from the bay, there is a gradual buildup of forms—they grow increasingly higher as they reach the center, where the new Bank of America World Headquarters will rise to a visual climax."

Elsewhere, real estate operators, business operations and labor unions are planning to fill San Francisco full of highrise structures. Eventually, when enough of BART is completed to transport adequately the people who will commute to and from this towering mass of concrete, local businessmen plan to go all out to convert San Francisco into Manhattan.

The issue was further confused in 1968 by a fight on the Board of Supervisors over the density of buildings to be permitted under a new zoning plan. The Downtown Advisory Committee's spokesmen on the Board, James Mailliard and Dorothy von Beroldingen, thought they could engineer, without opposition, a zoning ordinance calling for the densest concrete jungle in the world. Two young supervisors, Robert Mendelsohn and Ronald Pelosi, put together the votes to beat them, and the San Francisco Examiner headlined: "Supervisors Vote Against High Density."

That was incorrect and the lead paragraph of the simplistic story was worse:

"The Supervisors have narrowly rejected a proposal to turn San Francisco's downtown into another Manhattan Island."

This is patently false. All the supervisors did was to alter a proposed building ratio (the footage of building floor space permitted for every foot of land on one's lot) from 16:1 to 14:1 in a downtown area that is right now less than 14:1. By adding concourses for the BART subway and other amenities, however, a builder can increase his ratio to 24:1—24 feet of floor space for every foot of his lot.

As City Planning Director Allan B. Jacobs told me, "The zoning plan makes it more difficult in some cases to create Manhattan, but not impossible." For example, Jacobs said, the Wells Fargo Building would have been cut down by several stories because the plot of land on which it sits would not be big enough for the ratio to add up to its present height. But the 52-story Bank of America building, Jacobs pointed out, could have been even higher than it is now under the new zoning plan.

In fact, the tallest structures in the world can and undoubtedly will be built under this new zoning plan. When they are completed, a large part of San Francisco will look and function much like Manhattan.

And it is BART that will make this more inevitable by bringing more people, much faster, into San Francisco just as the subway does into Manhattan.

This is what James Bailey, senior editor of Architectural Forum, meant when he wrote in his magazine's June 1966 issue: "BART is more than transportation—it is the largest single act of urban design currently underway in the U.S."

The design began in the early 1950's, when San Francisco business leaders started to ponder how they could expand their commerce center of the West and make more money within the confines of what is geographically a small city. They also were concerned, quite understandably, about the trend toward decentralization. More and more shopping and finance centers were being built down the peninsula and across the Bay in Alameda and Marin

"Once there was a San Francisco that was light and pastel, hilly, open and inviting," said Duskin's coloring book.

"Then rich men built tall buildings and San Francisco began to look stiff and forbidding like any other American city."

Counties, making it unnecessary for everyone to come to San Francisco to transact business.

_These San Franciscans decided to reverse that trend, to centralize shopping, finance and cultural activities in their own city, and to bring everybody from surrounding areas into the same sort of system that makes Manhattan the hub of greater New York City. So they put together a committee headed by bankers like Carl F. Wente, chairman of the board of Bank of America; Kendric B. Morrish, vice-president of Wells Fargo; and Mortimer Fleishhacker, Jr., a director of Crocker Citizens. Then they called in an outside firm to "do a study" that would conclude what they wanted concluded.

The firm was Parsons, Brinckerhoff, Quade & Douglas of New York. This firm built New York City's subway system at the turn of the century. Its management is oriented toward constructing mass rail transit systems that bring commuters into centralized areas.

In the 1953-55 study for a new San Francisco Bay Area Transportation system, Parsons-Brinckerhoff also drew up a master land-use plan. The plan—could you guess it?—was to create a much more densely populated central business district and to pack many more people into it via a mass rail transit system.

When BART was being sold to the public in 1962, the newspapers, radio and television stations made it appear that a great civic crusade was taking place to overcome the automobile, freeways, horrifying congestion and air pollution.

Anyone for BART was for progress; anyone opposed was an obstructionist. The question that the daily newspapers never allowed to be asked was: What would happen if the Bay Area followed a plan of decentralization, calling for people to live and work in the same community rather than commuting to San Francisco?

If bankers built branch finance centers around the Bay Area instead of piling more into San Francisco itself, if corporations decentralized their headquarters, if symphonies and operas were installed in other communities as they are in Europe—then no massive system like BART would be needed. Alternate systems were available that would still get rid of the automobile, freeways and air pollution.

Of course, many Bay Area citizens who worked for BART were crusading against more freeways, parking lots and air pollution—the curses of the automobile. But for campaign leaders who passed a $792 million bond issue to finance BART, it was much more than a civic crusade.

The leaders, bankers and corporate officials of San Francisco were banded together in a private organization called Citizens for Rapid Transit. It was headed by Morrish of Wells Fargo, Fleishhacker of Crocker Citizens and

A tiny patch of blue shows in this photo of the Embarcadero Freeway ramp. The Alcoa Building and the Golden Gateway are on the left.

Wente of Bank of America. And the first three highrise buildings that went up in conjunction with BART construction were the Wells Fargo, Bank of America and Crocker Citizens buildings.

As their man to head BART's board of directors, the bankers and businessmen chose Adrien Falk, retired vice-president of S & W Fine Foods and past president of the California Chamber of Commerce. (There was no provision in BART's charter to select its directors democratically. The board was appointed by local mayors and supervisors in accordance with the wishes of BART's promoters.) Falk held the position for a decade, although he was frequently ill and could not attend meetings. In 1967, at 82, he was finally unseated by the directors.

Shortly before Falk was ousted, I called on him at BART to ask him whether he thought it was desirable for San Francisco to become Manhattan.

"It's not a question of whether it's desirable," he said. "It's the only practical way. Certain finance, banking industries, want to be centralized, want to have everyone near each other. They don't want to have to go one day to Oakland, the next day to San Jose, the next day to San Francisco."

"What is this, then," I asked Falk, "a system of, by and for the banking and finance community—or the people of the Bay Area?"

"Well," he replied, "there's also a cultural aspect. You can't have the symphony, the opera, the ball park in every community. The big city is naturally a center to which everyone comes. This is the history of civilization. I believe there is a renaissance of our big cities taking place. BART will make it possible to bring all the people in here. The new construction it will generate will be a great improvement for San Francisco."

New construction number one is the Wells Fargo Building, rising into the heavens, darkening the street below, obliterating views of the bay for all but its occupants. When I visited an occupant, Roger Lapham, Jr., I found out that Bayard H. Dillingham, president of the firm that built the Wells Fargo building—the Dillingham Corporation—is on the board of directors of Lapham's firm, Alexander, Sexton & Carr. Dillingham is also taking over the management of North Waterfront Associates, headed by Lapham, to put up the blockbuster International Market Center along Telegraph Hill.

"Is it desirable that we create a city of gigantic skyscrapers like Manhattan, with an underground railroad to serve them?" I asked Lapham.

"It's not a question of whether it's desirable," he said, "but what's the practical matter. As a practical matter, you can't have 18 different banking and insurance centers. You have to concentrate them with all the various services around them. The people who run these centers want all their services, the people they work with —advertisers, attorneys, accountants— around them. It's a complete part of the way we do business in this country."

"Suppose some people in San Francisco don't want their city converted into a Manhattan?" I asked.

"Then let 'em go someplace else," Lapham replied. "But don't keep complaining about it, because that's what is GOING to happen, and nobody can stop it."

That need not be so. A new concept in urban planning, called the "satellite city," abandons the idea of trying to squeeze more business and people into one centralized area, and relocates them instead to new communities.

In these new communities, the emphasis is on total land planning. Residential areas are split up by trees, parks and recreation areas so that you don't have to travel long distances to get back to nature or enjoy some outdoor relaxation. A cultural center is built into the community; you do not have to depend on Falk's concept that only one city can have a symphony and opera so that everybody must come to that city for his "culture."

Finally, industries—although separated from residential areas by a green belt—are just a short hop away from home. You get to your job in five or ten minutes. Many people can even walk or ride a bicycle to work. The need for mass transit is eliminated.

This is a completely individualized system, with no congestion, no freeways, no air and water pollution.

The first of the satellite cities—Reston, Va., 18 miles south of Washington, D.C.—was created by a millionaire real estate genius from New York, Robert Simon, who became fed up with commuting from Long Island to his Manhattan office.

BART, on the other hand, is taking us on an expensive ride to Manhattan. And there are two majestic ironies:

First, the builder of the biggest blockbuster now planned is Manhattanite David Rockefeller who evidently wants to spread New York's misery. His "Rockefeller Center West," a labyrinth of theaters, television studios, retail stores, office buildings that look like inverted ice cube trays and underground passages and shopping arcades hooked up to BART, alone will add 50,000 people, all jammed into one concrete mass, to San Francisco's weekday population. Office space alone will produce 15,000 new jobs.

Nobody seems to dare to argue against job-creating. It's humanitarian. But nobody stops to ponder what will happen when you keep pouring additional souls in one given area—the pushing and shoving mobs that are created as in Manhattan, satellite ghettos and the loss of all individuality as people turn into numbers in cells with huge skyscrapers. Nobody stops to think of what Manhattan is like—only the additional commerce and money it will produce.

And that leads to the second irony. While San Francisco fumbles toward Manhattan West, many giant corporations headquartered in New York's

201

skyscrapers now are fleeing the scene. Pepsi-Cola is moving from Park Avenue in mid-Manhattan to a 112-acre polo club grounds in suburban Westchester County.

American Can Co. is shifting its 1,300 employees at international headquarters in Manhattan to a 141-acre tract in Greenwich, Conn. Olin Mathieson Chemical Corporation is leaving for 60 acres in Stamford, Conn. Altogether, seven of the nation's largest companies are getting out of Fun City.

Board Chairman Leonard C. Yaseen of the Fantus Company, largest location consultant in the world, says 14 more corporations are seriously considering moving. The reason: problems such as "commuting, the rising crime rate, swollen welfare rolls and the subway strike." Yaseen concludes: "New York is not a happy place to be."

The main reason, however, as American Can Co. officials explained, is that there simply is no more room to "live and breathe in New York City." The city has become so big, so overpopulated, that it is totally, perhaps irrevocably, unmanageable.

Now San Francisco, refusing to heed the lessons of New York, is headed on the same course toward unmanageable bigness. Instead of altering this lemminglike march, the new zoning plan just passed by the supervisors makes it a continuing possibility. The argument is that the new highrise structures will not be as close together as they are in Manhattan.

Perhaps, perhaps not. But the system will be the same: people commuting from suburban areas via a 50-year-old train and subway system into a centralized business district that every day grows more congested, more uncivilized. That is the Manhattan system.

When it is fully operating here, San Francisco no longer will be "the last big city worth living in." It'll only be a place to work in. As Herb Caen, San Francisco's greatest glorifier, puts it:

"I don't know how much longer we can maintain the myth of San Francisco."

As long as it takes to construct BART and the new highrises?

Redevelopment: Bulldozers for the Poor, Welfare for the Rich
By Marsha Berzon. From S.F. Bay Guardian, April 17, 1970.

About one hundred San Francisco businessmen, architects, land developers, financiers and public officials gathered on the morning of Mar. 23 to spar verbally before the Redevelopment Agency Board. The prize: this year's biggest real estate bonanza, the chance to develop the $200 million Central Blocks of Redevelopment's South of Market Yerba Buena Center. As

Redevelopment: Bulldozers for the Poor, Welfare for the Rich

Clement Chen, head of one of the four competing developer groups, candidly admitted, contestants were "attracted to it (YBC) by its profit potential."

The meeting of opponent developer groups was convivial and clubby. Almost every person in the room managed a hearty handshake and friendly greeting for every other during the breaks which punctuated the three-hour meeting. In the role of benign coach was M. Justin Herman, Executive Director of Redevelopment, who carefully elicited information he and the contestants had already had many "private conversations" about.

The session's amiability was a fitting climax to the 20 years of maneuvering which had completely transformed the federally subsidized project to include all sorts of goodies, inside the project and out, for the benefit of a section of the city's power elite. What had been a small scale, light industrial, spot clearance, downtown support project on 19 blocks full of heavily blighted buildings, many of them family residences, is now a giant imitation of New York's Rockefeller Center to be built in a gerrymandered area of residential hotels and substantial industrial buildings.

Once the project outlines were finally established, it didn't matter much who got the Central Blocks award. (See postscript.) The real issues were never visibly in debate.

What were the goals of this downtown redevelopment? Who should benefit? What about the people living and working and owning buildings there? How does Yerba Buena square with other blockbuster downtown developments, say on the waterfront and adjacent to Telegraph Hill? Why is San Francisco proceeding with Yerba Buena now that this kind of remove-it-all-clear-it-away renewal has been discredited, according to the Wall Street Journal, even in Philadelphia, the citadel of urban redevelopment?

The strategic deficiencies in Yerba Buena were summed up recently when the Department of Housing and Urban Development (HUD) rightly rejected San Francisco's "Workable Program" for redevelopment.

HUD said the city's plan failed to expand low and moderate income housing, failed to replace housing units demolished by urban renewal on a one to one basis and failed to encourage citizen involvement by denying Yerba Buena residents the right to negotiate.

Indeed, the Yerba Buena story is a case study of how redevelopment funds and eminent domain powers can be used by a section of the city's power elite and turned to what Lewis Mumford has called "cataclysmic finance and the Zeckendorf building syndrome."

As the San Francisco Labor Council put it in a 1965 news letter, "Speculative real estate operators seem to have taken over the planning functions of our City. As projects develop, it becomes obvious that the needs of our people become secondary to the interests of speculators."

Yerba Buena started in the early 1950s as a 19-block industrial, spot clearance renewal project in a heavily blighted section. At the request of Ben Swig, owner of the Fairmont Hotel and one of the city's most powerful Democrats, the Supervisors added in 1955 four blocks to Redevelopment Area D, first designated in 1953, despite Planning's findings that most of the four blocks were not blighted. (See map 1.)

Swig explained his plan in 1955 to the Commonwealth Club:

"God gave us here in San Francisco everything that he could bestow on any community. . . . we have not capitalized on these great assets . . . Here is a great opportunity to help this wonderful city of ours."

But in the same speech Swig revealed the myopic vision of what makes a great city which motivated his interest in a huge commercial and convention project South of Market—and which continues to motivate Redevelopment and its business allies.

San Francisco, he said, "is primarily a financial and residential city. It depends to a great extent upon its convention and tourist business . . ."

If a convention and shopping center, complete with a sports arena, shopping center and 1,000-room hotel is built South of Market, he claimed, "Every single store—every downtown restaurant and hotel—every theater and moving picture house is going to benefit . . . Their business will prosper and when their business prospers, values of real estate must go up . . . If Houston can do it, so can we. Land in San Francisco can become worth $2,000 per square foot."

Swig was furious when, the following year, the Supervisors reconsidered their unorthodox addition in the face of a memorandum from Redevelopment and Planning saying that Swig's plan "perverted" the whole point of redeveloping South of Market. His answer to the de-designation of the two and two-thirds non-blighted blocks was blunt:

"Private capital knows a great deal better than city planners. I say to the city fathers, stop planning, stop thinking but go out and do something."

A SPUR committee, headed initially by the late Jerd Sullivan, helped pressure Redevelopment in 1961 into re-designing a redevelopment area South of Market. The earlier designation had been rescinded because of a delay in federal funds and intense pressure from area property owners.

(Sullivan was vice-president and director of Swig's Fairmont Hotel; he was also a director of Crocker Citizens National Bank. Crocker Citizens was one of the first three corporations to benefit from the Yerba Buena project by acquiring written-down land from Redevelopment. Crocker Citizens is a corporate member of SPUR.)

The newly designated area included all the Swig blocks and very little else of the original area. Not one square inch of Section II of the original area,

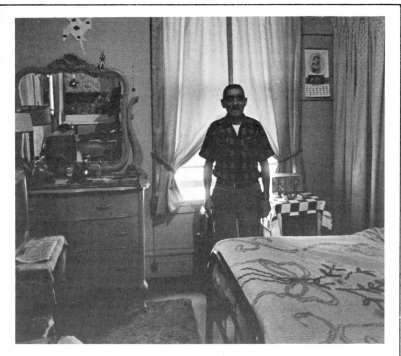

Eddie Hider — 64 . . . resident of the South of Market for 14 years . . . relocated from the Argus Hotel to the Tenderloin, August, 1970 . . . former prizefighter, stevedore, warehouseman, night-watchman . . .

"Finally we got to the critical point: 'Everyone's got to move out of here.' And I says I haven't got anyplace to go yet. 'You've got to get out, or we're going to get the sheriff to put you out. If you don't get out, I'm going to put a padlock on your door.'

Pope, he's the head guy down there. He says, don't worry about nothing. We'll find you a place, just sign the papers. What a fool I was. I never had to sign papers in my life, not even when I was fighting.

I signed my life away. They promised me $1,000 lump sum and $80 moving expenses. But they violated the contract, now they give me $41 a month. You know what the alibi was: you don't know how to manage money. Like I'm a little kid. And I only got six more checks and then all I'll get is $54 social security.

When the checks disappear, then what? I pay $100 a month here. My buddy was to leave, and I expect him to leave, how am I going to manage? Got to go live under the bridge. Well, there it is. That's the injustice they're doing to the people."

which Planning found most blighted, was included. (See Maps 1 & 2.)

Redevelopment tried, and succeeded, in covering up this acquiescence to the plans of empire builders. It issued statements indicating the 1961 area was essentially the same as the 1953 and 1957 areas. And it used the exact language that described the 1957 area to describe the later, very different one, changing only the figures.

Thus, Herman wrote the Supervisors in 1961: "The blighted nature of the South of Market Area D was first officially recognized by the Board of Supervisors in 1953 and the area was again the subject of a careful analysis in 1957. The area has been restudied by the Redevelopment Agency and the Department of City Planning and the condition of blight South of Market has remained unameliorated and indeed worsened." The implication Area D was the same all along is obvious, but entirely untrue.

A less obvious example: the 1957 application claims "The area now encompassed includes the greater part of the dwelling units in the vicinity as well as a substantial portion of the skid row element." In 1961, Redevelopment reproduced essentially the same statement in its federal application: "The area encompassed includes a substantial portion of the housing units in the vicinity as well as the skid row area."

While the 1957 Area D included the blocks around Sixth and Mission (which is full of resident hotels for single men—skid row hotels), this area was left out of both Area D and Project Area D-1 in 1961. And many of the hotels in the 1961 Area D—mostly those on Howard St.—had in fact been knocked down by the time the application was submitted.

So "skid row" type hotels are much more prevalent OUTSIDE the renewal area than in it.

Redevelopment's deception continued after the boundaries were approved. The 1964 Tentative Proposal gives this history of South of Market development:

"Original designation of Redevelopment Area D 4/1/53

De-designation of Redevelopment Area D 9/24/58

Re-designation of Redevelopment Area D 12/11/61."

But the original 19-block area was not the area which was de-designated. Nor was the de-designated area the same as the area that was re-designated.

The Chronicle; the Examiner and the now defunct News Call Bulletin; all with offices in the renewal area or nearby, played along with Herman's word game. The Chronicle, in 1961, claimed that the redevelopment area had been called "the most exaggerated type of slum anywhere in the West." But that statement, of course, referred to the 1957 area. And the Examiner claimed that most of the 1961 area was included in the earlier plans—an obvious misstatement.

Pete Mendelsohn — 64 . . . retired merchant seaman . . . long-time union organizer . . . resident of Yerba Buena area 40 years, living in the Westchester Hotel.

"I think it's a criminal thing to take and go up and tear all this housing down and tell the people who been living in this area for all these years that they have to go and move to another city or out of this city.

Which is what they really want to do. They want to drive all the working class and all the lower-middle-class out of the city. They got a book that tells you the whole shebang. You can buy the book.

I spent 30 years in one block there, between Market and Mission on Third Street. And naturally we make a lot of friends, and we usually can help each other in a lot of different ways. But if we were to be taken out of here and had to go even five blocks away to a different area, it would be the same as going to another country. We'd have to start all over again and try to make friends, and these days you can't make friends like you did in those days.

We had Governor Brown come in here and investigate the whole matter, and he told the judge that he thought it was a crime to move the people out. Because all the places left in the city are inferior to the places we're already living."

Redevelopment assured the Supervisors in 1961 that South of Market renewal would be of a spot clearance and industrial nature. Only about 25 per cent of the buildings would have to be razed, Herman claimed, and he cautioned Supervisors against thinking of redevelopment as vast, cleared blocks. Businesses in the area wouldn't be disturbed, he promised: "We will keep what's good, redevelop what's rehabilitable and raze the rest."

Herman even mentioned it might be possible to retain some small residential hotels, although he warned against including such retention in the federal application.

However, Herman's final plan presented to the Supervisors in 1966—the next time Supervisors had to pass on Yerba Buena except for the Market Street Breakthrough—advocated abolishing 85 per cent of the buildings in the project area. Two and one-half blocks were to be cleared (the Central Blocks now up for grabs). And not a single hotel was retained.

San Francisco businessmen accept credit for the massive switch. Melvin Swig, Ben Swig's son, says he "was after Justin to get something going arenawise and conventionwise." And Albert Schlesinger, a former head of the San Francisco Convention and Visitors Bureau and the Parking Commission and presently a member of one of the development groups interested in the Central Blocks, says he and the Convention Bureau got after Redevelopment because they were convinced the city needed a convention center and South of Market was the only place for it.

In fact, according to Schlesinger, he and the younger Swig co-chaired the Mayor's Committee on South of Market Development which first announced

---

Harry Boisen — retired newspaper reporter . . . 74 . . . based in San Francisco since World War II . . . living in present room in Jessie Hotel for 7 years.

"To get to Redevelopment, here's the way I look at it: the theory's right. I think that a lot of people here, that if they'd been convinced that a really genuine effort was being made to provide buildings, what you might call industry of a sort, I think the whole attitude would have been different.

This Redevelopment here's been nothing but a real estate grab. Some of this space has been vacant for 11 years. Redevelopment's got the best attorneys in the world, and they've been well-schooled. Some of them come out of Boston like Justin Herman. You know what I call him — Old Injustice.

The people here have no place to go, nothing's been provided."

the new plans—and came up with the Yerba Buena name—in early 1964.

(Redevelopment Agency records show the Mayor's Committee was officially headed by Sup. Roger Boas and that Swig and Schlesinger chaired a sub-division concerned with the sports arena and convention center. Both Swig and Schlesinger had financial interests in the San Francisco Seals, the hockey team and the Warriors.)

John Dykstra, Assistant Director of Redevelopment, contends the real reason for the change in plans was that economic studies of the area indicated light industry couldn't afford land prices so close to downtown.

Redevelopment, in official documents supporting Dykstra's point, uses the enormous vacant land rate in the project area—variously quoted as 40, 44 and 26 per cent of the land—to show the area is economically not viable as the service and industrial area it has traditionally been. But the vacancy rate was a result of the confusion Redevelopment created South of Market.

When the blight designation was lifted in 1958, a group calling itself the Associated Investors of Northern California began buying up land in the area in hopes of developing it themselves. They bought most of the Howard Street block between Third and Fourth and had knocked down the buildings on their land when re-designation came in 1961. So the vacant land, used as parking lots while redevelopment decides what to do next, demonstrates investors' confidence in the area, not the economic uselessness of the area.

(Note also: two main consulting firms Redevelopment used in its economic and planning studies are corporate members of SPUR: Livingston and Blayney and the Real Estate Research Corporation.)

The Department of Planning is, according to California law, directed to decide project boundaries and devise a Preliminary Plan once the area is declared "blighted."

But it was kept in the wings during the second round of South of Market redevelopment. Its Preliminary Plan came out late in 1964—after much play had been given to the Mayor's Committee plan and Redevelopment's version of it. The plan consisted of a map and four pages of writing based on Redevelopment's plans. Earlier, Planning had approved the project area designation, but it claims no part in drawing the boundaries.

No one interested in pushing redevelopment in Swig's old area wanted to involve Planning. For the department had already given its stamp to much of the area: not blighted.

Anyway, Dykstra says, Planning's blight studies should not be taken too seriously. "They just looked at the outside of buildings," he said.

In fact, the 1955 study of the two blocks between Mission and Folsom and Third and Fourth surveyed each piece of property quite carefully.

Redevelopment and its business allies were promoting a version of the present Yerba Buena plan, complete with theaters, museum, sports arena and convention center, throughout 1964 and 1965. Yet, the "final plan" approved by Planning and the Supervisors spoke of two plans: "A" would include "special uses" on the Central Blocks and "B" would include only parking garages and commercial buildings.

Plan B was "simply a device for beginning demolition immediately after the Loan and Grant Contract is executed," according to the South of Market Improvement Association which, headed by maverick land owner Lou Silver, has fought Redevelopment all the way. Silver and his lawyers claim there was never any intention to build solely a commercial project. But if only Plan A had been approved, then land activity could not begin until plans for "special uses" were set, including the passage of necessary bond issues.

Besides playing these tricks with the law, Redevelopment also played tricks on other public agencies.

Planning balked for a while before approving the "final plan." In fact, it was sent to the Supervisors without Planning's approval. But when Planning finally okayed the plan, it thought the special uses it was approving were only the sports arena and convention center.

City Planning rightly objected to building highrise offices, theaters and hotels South of Market. It contended these uses competed with other sections of the city. .

Yet, when Herman presented the plan to the Supervisors a few months later, he included the whole plan, with theaters and museum.

HUD had quashed plans to include a hotel the summer before. The final plan includes no provisions for a hotel. Yet, a hotel appears in the current model displayed in Redevelopment headquarters. Redevelopment's rationale: the hotel is not yet officially approved, but we will get it approved if we go ahead with it.

Planning also noted the contradiction between the finding of Redevelopment's consultant on the demand for office space and the amount of space of various kinds shown in the plan: there was too much highrise office space, Planning Director McCarthy noted, and too little service and light industry space in the plan.

Planning hasn't taken any action on Yerba Buena since the 1966 "final plan" was approved. But the final plan now contemplated is actually—if not legally—different from the one popularly promoted in 1964-65 and also from the one Planning thought it approved. (The Del Monte building, for example, exceeds the 25 story height limitation in the final plan by almost one-half—it will be 35 stories.)

Redevelopment played a numbers game to go along with its word games. It came up with the figures needed to justify approval to the federal government via ingenious statistical manipulation.

Redevelopment: Bulldozers for the Poor, Welfare for the Rich

First, Redevelopment devised a checklist of building deficiencies and sent an inspector around to most of the buildings in the area—those "obviously" in good condition were left out. The list included such frivolous problems as inadequate drainage on porches and improper light sources. The language was vague: "inadequate," "deficient," "not satisfactory." On the basis of the findings, the buildings were divided into five categories. Category 5 included perfect buildings, 4 included buildings with a few minor problems and 1, 2 and 3 included buildings with various degrees of more serious difficulties.

One criterion for categories 1, 2 and 3 was an estimate of how much it would cost to fix up the deficiencies in relation to the worth of the building when rehabilitated. Since no actual cost estimates were made, local landowners claim that factor was entirely subjective.

Opponents of the project also insist most of the buildings in category 3 actually had very minor deficiencies and that, in fact, most of the buildings in the city would have been in categories 1, 2 or 3.

But the numbers game wasn't over when the categories were completed. Since 1, 2 and 3 were considered "substandard to a degree warranting clearance"—a vague criterion anyway—Redevelopment pushed some category 4 buildings into category 3 by changing the standards a bit.

But it still couldn't come up with the federal and state requirements to justify clearance in the Central Blocks: 20 per cent of the buildings in the whole area and in any sizable portion must be "substandard to a degree warranting clearance" and another 30 per cent must represent a "blighting influence" ("skid row" hotels and bars and all pawnshops were considered "blighting influences" per se).

On the Mission-Third-Howard-Fourth block, for example, only nine of the 48 buildings were substandard to a degree warranting clearance. But that block was slated to be one of the Central Blocks.

So Redevelopment dragged out the plan itself to justify knocking down the rest of the buildings: 23 would not be accessible, according to the plan, and 16 were on land slated for new rights of way. Because the plan said so—not because there was anything wrong with the blocks or the buildings—39 good buildings, over 80 per cent of the buildings on the block, must go!

At the 1966 hearings the Supervisors delayed approving the "final plan" for two months. The reasons: they wanted assurance from Herman—in the form of an amendment to the plan—that developers wouldn't be able to come in from "Texas or Oklahoma or somewhere," as Supervisor William Blake put it, and buy up whole blocks for renewal.

(They were also queasy about Herman's vague relocation plan and insisted on certain provisions to protect the area's relocatees. These provisions were, however, like most of the Board's attempts to control Herman, too vaguely worded to have any real effect.)

The Golden Gateway and Western Addition, Supervisors complained, had been bought up extensively by out-of-town interests—and the Redevelopment Agency had not sought local investors. Only San Franciscans, the Supervisors contended, know what the city needs and have a sense of responsibility toward it.

A vaguely worded statement was added to the plan requiring every effort to sell land in individual parcels and to local people. Herman also promised no huge parcels would be sold off.

But three years later, Redevelopment published an elaborate booklet offering two and a half blocks—25 acres—to developers as a package. And the designer of the project now up for auction is Kenzo Tange of Japan—as the ad in Fortune, a decidedly national publication, trumpets proudly.

Various participants and on-lookers draw different morals from this long sorry saga.

To Sidney Wolinsky of San Francisco Neighborhood Legal Services, the story shows how a small group of businessmen wield enormous power in this city, ignoring the poor in particular and the resident public in general.

To Redevelopment, Yerba Buena remains a triumph of enlightened urban renewal. To some officials involved in the project's early stages, it developed because of the conventional wisdom at the time that anyone putting obstacles in the path of Redevelopment was backward. Now these people see that bulldozer projects don't make for effective renewal of cities.

To other observers, like the Guardian, the Yerba Buena tale calls into question the redevelopment law itself. Despite attempts by Congress to tighten it, it does not assure adequate attention to housing and other needs of people living in redevelopment areas.

Most important: by defining "blight" vaguely, the law facilitates exactly what happened here. Land speculators and developers come in, decide what piece of property they'd like to have but can't afford to pay for and then get together in "civic" groups and power blocs to see that it is declared "blighted" and designated for redevelopment. As Ben Swig said, "If Houston can do it, so can we."

Postscript The award went to Schlesinger-Arcon-Pacific in November of 1970. SAP was a combine formed by original bidder Arcon-Pacific, headed by Berkeley architect Lyman Jee and promoter Albert Schlesinger, who was originally affiliated with the Dillingham Corporation bid.

However, a year later, the death of Herman and internal squabbling among principals and beneficiaries of the project made it appear as if Yerba Buena wouldn't come to pass and much of the clearance was for naught.

Redevelopment: Bulldozers for the Poor, Welfare for the Rich

People like Eddie Hider, Pete Mendelsohn and Harry Boisen used to live here. Now this site off Clementina Alley awaits Yerba Buena development.

Redevelopment — Who Gains

A. The sleight of hand with redevelopment boundaries South of Market will certainly benefit those who own adjacent land. When the area is developed, these land values will skyrocket, retail establishments can expect much more volume. Biggest adjacent owners and their locations:

The Emporium .... 1 & 2 (see map 2)
Hearst (3rd and Market) 3
Hearst/Chronicle buildings (804 Howard and Fifth and Mission) ... 4
Benjamin Swig and Eugenia Hayme 5
Pacific Telephone 6

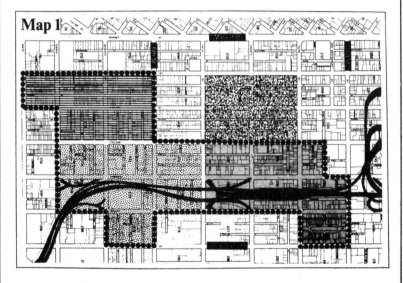

Map 1

●●●●● *1953 South of Market Redevelopment Area D*

▤ *Section I: Largely residential. Should be developed SECOND, according to Department of Planning.*

▦ *Section II: Industrial. Some residential. Most blighted. Should be developed FIRST, according to Planning.*

■ *Section III: Largely non-residential. Industrial buildings good. Relocation problems with elderly men. Should be developed LAST, according to Planning.*

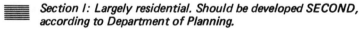 *At the request of Ben Swig, Fairmont Hotel Owner, Supervisors added this four block area to Area D in 1955.*

     B. Several companies have built or are building new structures on
land they acquired privately while land in the area was still inexpensive.
If the area becomes a commercial center, they will have quite a bargain.
They are:
- continued next page

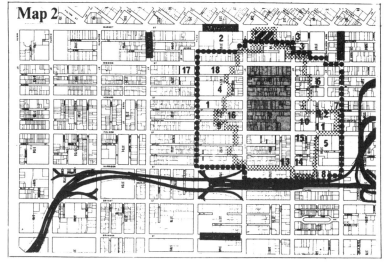

Map 2

●●●●● *Redevelopment Area D (1961)*

▨▨▨ *"Market Street Breakthrough": Added to Area D in 1963*

░░░ *Project Area D-1 (1963 to the present)*

■ *Central Blocks*

C. Redevelopment is beginning to sell land to companies for office buildings. These companies must pay fair market value for the land, but they save the cost of buying the original buildings, demolishing them and preparing the land for construction. Three companies have acquired cheap redevelopment land:

Crocker Citizens National Bank 13
Del Monte 14
Taylor-Woodrow (England) 15

The Housing Authority will operate housing for 300 single men on the fourth piece sold so far (16).

*Significantly, the Fifth and Mission city parking garage (18) has built an extension at the corner of Fourth and Mission—an obvious case of gerrymandering. Walter Kaplan, Chairman of the Board of the Redevelopment Agency, is President of the "non-profit" Fifth and Mission garage Corporation and Secretary and Treasurer of the Emporium (1 and 2) which relies heavily on the garage for customer parking.

More: The examiner and Chronicle/KRON have all loudly supported Yerba Buena and concealed its strategic shift in character and geography. Redevelopment is one of the most sensitive beats on both papers. One reason, perhaps, is that Hearst owns two buildings, (3rd and Market and Fifth and Mission), the Chronicle one (Fifth and Mission) and Hearst/Chron together one (804 Howard) next to the project area.

Perhaps this is why they are as interested in the editorial care and cultivation of Redevelopment and Redevelopment's M. Justin Herman (who can make their property values rise astronomically) as they once were in the care and cultivation of Assessor Russell Wolden (who saved Ex/Chron millions of dollars in personal property taxes by allowing them to underreport their assets for years).

Wolden was eventually convicted on bribery and conspiracy charges and the Ex and Chron were found, according to a new audit by the new assessor, Joseph Tinney, to have escaped paying some $250,000 in personal property in 1964 and 1965 alone. (See Sept. 25, 1967 Guardian.)

Also: The specially favored Fifth and Mission garage is across the street from the Examiner and Chronicle buildings and across the alley west from the Ex/Chron merger headquarters in the old News-Call-Bulletin building.

The High Cost of Ugliness

By Michael Stephen Metcalf. From S.F. Bay Guardian, Feb. 26, 1971.

"New York's failure is in human arrangements, a failure with many sources. It can be traced to the apathy and venality of the city's politicians; to the remoteness and indifference of the city's business and financial leaders, to the selfishness of competing groups and interests whose actions take little account of the general welfare."

— *R.J. Whalen: A City Destroying Itself*

Proponents of U.S. Steel's proposed waterfront project like to claim it will "widen the tax base" through increased property tax payments to the city. But experience with other building projects suggests this may not be so at all. There is evidence, in fact, that projects of the sort proposed by U.S. Steel actually add more to city costs than they provide in new taxes.

The Bank of America building, for instance, is often cited as a prime example of "widening the tax base" because, while the same location yielded $280,742 in property taxes before construction of the building, it now yields $3,193,495.

The contention is that the city services required by the new building could not cost nearly as much as this increase in tax revenue. But city services are provided for people, not buildings.

The Bank of America building houses approximately 5,000 people during the day, as compared with roughly 425 in the 11 buildings that were there before. Thus, the property tax per occupant is less in the new building than in the old: $638.70 for the Bank of American building, $660.57 for the buildings it replaced or a decline of 3.3 per cent.

It seems safe to say, then, that no substantial increase in per capita revenue has resulted from the replacement of low density development with high density development.

And the per capita revenue will probably drop lower when the building is at its full capacity of 7,500. The present low occupancy appears to be caused by the "prestige" nature of the building—tenants currently allocate an unusual amount of space to each employee, many of whom are presumably senior executives.

As the "prestige" of the building declines, and as its views are destroyed by the erection of other tall buildings nearby (ironically stimulated by the Bank of America building itself), senior executives will move on to new "prestige" locations. They will be replaced by other employees requiring less space.

Moreover, property tax revenues are based upon the market value of the building, and, as the building ages and thus depreciates, the taxes will decline.

How a city's per capita costs increase with density and size*

Size of city (thousands)	Expenditure per person			
	Hospital	Police	Fire	Sanitation
100-199	$ 8.60	14.60	13.03	16.76
300-499	5.12	18.33	13.80	25.59
500-999	12.54	21.88	13.88	22.12
New York	55.19	39.83	18.22	24.41

*1969 Study by the League for Industrial Democracy for the Stern Family Fund

This combination of depreciation and greater occupancy should significantly reduce per capita property tax revenues.

It also is questionable whether the concentration of people in highrise/high density developments would effectively lower the cost of providing municipal services to building occupants.

While it is clearly more efficient to provide certain services, such as police protection, to highrise occupants, the cost of other services (such as the city pound or the municipal court) has little relationship to the distribution of population. The significant factor in determining costs for departments like the latter is population size, not density.

Thus, the example of the Bank of America building indicates that, on a per capita basis, replacement of low density development with high density development does nothing to "widen the tax base." It probably will, in fact, reduce tax revenues.

Of course, the total economic effect of a single tall building is difficult to separate from the general economic activity in its immediate area. The construction of high density buildings inalterably changes the characteristics of a neighborhood and consequently exerts tremendous pressure for the construction of more high density buildings in the same area.

These tall building zones could be compared to automobiles en masse. While one automobile provides cheap, flexible and efficient transportation, 25,000 automobiles on a freeway constitute not only a highly inefficient system of transporting people, but also smog, noise, urban sprawl, traffic deaths and fantastically expensive freeway systems, all of which would have been difficult to extrapolate from a single automobile.

Similarly, a single tall building may indeed enhance a community, but 200 tall buildings result in noise, congestion and higher costs for municipal services, as New York demonstrates.

The net effect of many tall buildings in close proximity to one another is high density population, which, says Mayor John Lindsay of New York, "is responsible for inevitably higher costs for every conceivable service."

**Before and after the Bank of America:
How the per occupant property tax revenue goes down**

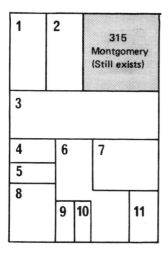

Pre B of A structures	Est. number of occupants
1. Cluny Bldg.	116
2. Pacific Nat'l. Bank Bldg.	232
3. Bohemian garage	15
4. Retail store	5
5. Retail store	5
6. Vacant	-
7. Hotel	42
8. Vacant	-
9. Retail store	5
10. Retail store	5
11. Retail store	5
Total occupants	425

Total tax revenue from 11 buildings $280,742

Previous development:

$$\frac{\$280,742 \text{ (tax revenues)}}{425 \text{ former occupants}} = \$660.57 \text{ per occupant before Bank of America}$$

Bank of America Building:

$$\frac{\$3,193,495}{5,000 \text{ present occupants}} = \$638.70 \text{ present B of A per occupant tax}$$

$$\frac{\$3,193,495}{7,500 \text{ eventual occupants}} = \$425.80 \text{ eventual B of A per occupant tax}$$

Conclusion: the B of A now requires city services for 5,000 persons (eventually, 7,500 persons) instead of 425 persons working in 11 small pre-B of A buildings. Yet, the city gets much less now in property tax revenue per occupant than it did before the B of A. Apply this analogy of diminishing per occupant taxes for each highrise building and you can see why they become so explosively expensive.

The population of San Francisco's downtown area is already very dense, yet the density of the downtown area could increase by 276 percent. According to the Downtown Zoning Study, which explains city policies for highrise construction, the city would permit 400,000 more office workers occupying 82,448,000 square feet of new office space—the equivalent of 66 Bank of America buildings.

The study continues: "Such figures would represent an increase to nearly five times the present floor space and employment in offices.

"The transportation facilities needed to carry that number of people into or out of the downtown area in one hour would be extensive: either 110 lanes of new freeways, or five new rapid transit systems with a capacity equal to that of BART, or some combination of the two; in addition, pedestrian and vehicular congestion would require increases in sidewalk capacities and possibly a complete separation of pedestrian and vehicle movement."

It would be optimistic indeed to believe that the transportation needs predicted by the Downtown Zoning Study could be provided without substantial increases in property tax rates. If freeways are decided on, revenues lost from homes and businesses displaced by rights of way could only be regained by raising tax rates. If mass transit subways are chosen, they probably would be financed with general obligation bonds and Federal aid, which is provided, of course, by taxpayers. It should be noted that property tax support of BART will continue until 1999, that the cost of BART has risen 18.8% in 8 years, and that this increase is financed with a regressive sales tax.

There is evidence that the high density of the Downtown area already forces the existing public transit system to operate below maximum efficiency, costing city taxpayers money.

First we took a San Francisco tradition

Bay windows have been a feature of San
San Francisco architecture from the
earliest days. They enlarged upon our
lovely views and allowed more natural light
to brighten interiors. You'll find them
in the Mission District. On Twin Peaks.
Marching up Potrero Hill. And along
Pacific Heights. Now we've brought bay
windows downtown to help create a bold
new look in the Financial District.

From a Bank of America advertising section in the Sunday supplement

The High Cost of Ugliness

It costs $15 per hour to operate a Muni Bus, and at 5 mph. or 15 mph. 4700 Muni buses enter and leave the downtown area every weekday between the hours of 7 AM and 7 PM.

Given the congestion in the downtown area created by automobiles, jaywalking pedestrians, double parked delivery trucks, construction, etc., it is reasonable to assume that each bus averages a 15-minute delay, or $3.75 lost per trip.

The yearly cost to Muni is thus $3,727,750, and that sum can only increase as downtown congestion rises with the construction of more tall buildings.

As size and density increase, the per capita cost of running a city goes up, not down. "Density makes for frictions that demand expensive social lubricants," as Gus Tyler wrote in the Saturday Review.

A 1969 study by the League for Industrial Democracy for the Stern Family Fund showed that municipalities with populations between 100,000 and 299,000 spent $14.60 per person on police. Those of 300,000 to 499,000 spent $18.33; those, like San Francisco, of 500,000 to one million spent $21.88. New York spent $39.83.

and created a beautiful modern version.

The 3,268 bronze-tinted bay windows in our building add interest to every floor. A delight to see, they're also functional for the thousands of San Franciscans who work in this striking new building. Through the bay windows, they enjoy views of the city, the bridges and the bay never possible before.

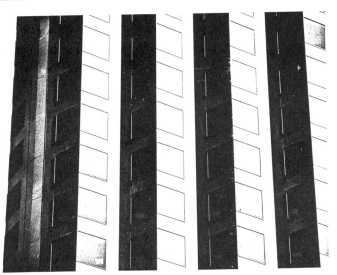

of the San Francisco Examiner/Chronicle on October 26, 1969.

The issue then, is not whether to approve the U.S. Steel proposal. The real issue is whether to allow the consummation of the Downtown Zoning Study; whether to permit the construction of any building higher than eight or ten stories.

Another important aspect of continued highrise development is the cost of displacing people now living in the Tenderloin and South of Market areas where new office buildings will go up. The downtown Zoning Study deals with the problem with typical inadequacy:

". . . Some downtown areas also have concentrations of social problems, including poverty, alcoholism, vice and drug addiction . . . it has not been, nor could it be, a function of this zoning study to deal with these problems."

But where will these people live when they are displaced by 400,000 office workers?

Not in other existing low income housing areas in the city, because they're already full.

Not in the suburbs, because low income housing does not exist there.

Most likely, they will move within the city, into the "nice," stable, middle income, middle class neighborhoods, a process well documented in the experience of Urban Renewal Projects in Oakland.

They will take with them their Tenderloin/South of Market value systems and behavior patterns, and middle class families now living in northern and western San Francisco, fearful of crime and drug abuse and unwilling to cope with problems in the schools, will move to the suburbs in the familiar pattern of urban decay.

The net effect will be the gradual decline of the middle class residential and commercial areas which are the backbone of the "tax base."

There will be a gradual erosion of property values in these areas, a resulting loss of tax revenue and an increase in property tax rates for the remaining middle class neighborhoods to offset the loss.

It would be unwise to allow the aged and deteriorated buildings in these areas to remain indefinitely, however, so the fairest policy would be to replace existing low-income housing with new low-income housing (for which Federal funds are available), instead of new highrise office buildings.

Another probable result of runaway highrise would be a decline in tourism. Vancouver, Seattle, Portland and San Diego are all Western cities that can offer alternatives to tourists seeking scenic yet cosmopolitan relief from the urban crises of Los Angeles and San Francisco.

Any decline of tourism because of ugly development, or even because of a failure to take complete advantage of the increasing numbers of American and foreign tourists, would not only reduce the tax income to the city but also the direct income of thousands of San Franciscans.

Highrise Headstones
By J. Cockwold. From Program Guide No. 82, KTAO, Los Gatos.

"Someday, when they write the history of the destruction of the Americas, they will have to give a whole chapter to the banishment of 'the eyes of the city'[Jane Jacobs' phrase—not my own].They will have to see the tall dark buildings as what they really are: stakes driven into the heart and life of the once lively urban areas.

"Walk through Chinatown in San Francisco. The streets are filled with commerce, and foot traffic: there is noise and excitement and life. Shops are filled with mysterious smells — and people. Visitors come from all over the world to participate in the life of a hundred small shops and restaurants.

"Then walk down to 750 Kearny, at the corner of Washington. There is a new gravestone set over the now dead part of the city. Where there were once shops, and tourists, and a thousand curios spilling out onto the curb, now stands — a bloody Holiday Inn, 27 stories up. And, its base, a parking garage. Where the citizenry walked, and wondered at the mysterious life in a mysterious street — there are now a few angry ruffians, hiding menacingly in the shadows of this concrete rocket. No one will venture a half a block to see a monument to the automobile.

"The man who designed that concrete dragon should be tied to one of the concrete pillars for a few weeks to live in the destruction he has created. The president of Holiday Inns, Inc., and the Chairman of the Board, and the Vice-President in charge of Expansion should be chained up there with that blind and foolish architect: chained up there at the corner of Kearny and Washington for six weeks, a year, so they can witness the decay that they have brought to a once meaningful, alive corner of the city . . .

"Perhaps then they would repent, and realize the wickedness of their ways . . . " — J. Cockwold, *The Profit Motive and the Dildo.*

Some Medical Advice
By Jon Carroll, H.S.D.

Being a Guide to sundry New Diseases frequently contracted by Persons in close and/or prolonged contact with Extremely Tall Buildings:

Skyscraper Neck Symptoms: Muscular pains in the neck, shoulder and back area, occasionally accompanied by disorientation and vertigo. Cause: Subject repeatedly attempts to find the sky, certain that it "must be up there somewhere." Treatment: Remember that a desire to orient your soul to the sun and sky is purely psychological. Skyscrapers, on the other hand, are an Economic Necessity. Would you stand in the way of progress just to preserve a few self-indulgent pleasures?

Brown Lung Disease Symptoms: Coughing, gasping, occasional blackouts. In terminal cases, subjects have been known to challenge automobiles to hand-to-hand combat. Cause: Subjects breathe large amounts of noxious chemicals brought into the area by commuters and others who must work in or service tall buildings. Treatment: Breathe as little as possible. Try exhaling three times for every time you inhale.

Earthquake Nerves Symptoms: Severe tremors in the extremities, profuse sweating, loss of appetite, general irritability. Cause: The certain knowledge that, should an earthquake strike, subject would be buried under 11 million tons of glass and cement. Treatment: There is no known cure, although the prophylactic effects of alcohol and other drugs are unquestioned. Try repeating the words: "There probably won't be a quake this year, and by next year I'll be in Omaha."

Elevator Shoulder Symptoms: Shooting pains in the shoulder and back area. Cause: Twofold. First, strain on the muscles caused by pushing the "Down" button 37 times with ever-increasing amounts of force. Second, pressure on the affected area caused by leaning against the wall of the elevator for up to 45 minutes waiting for your floor to arrive. Treatment: Stand erect and be patient. Don't try to walk away from it, lest you contract the equally virulent, but far less common, **High Density Feet.**

Flickhammer's Syndrome (Named after Jack L. Flickhammer, who, on July 17, 1971, attempted to destroy, or at least modify, the Bank of America building by completely covering it with whipped cream and chocolate pudding.) Symptoms: Unreasoning hatred of every building over five stories tall. Cause: Lots and lots of tall buildings in a relatively small area. Treatment: Move to Montana, or find someone both willing and able to supply you with 71 tons of pudding.

Quotes from Caen, McCabe, Nolan and Wright

San Francisco Examiner and Chronicle editorials on highrise often read as if they come directly from the Chamber of Commerce mimeograph. But some of their columnists feel differently. Some excerpts:

Herb Caen Chronicle (3/28/71) A Vision of Battlements

... The Mayor's Chief Administrative Officer, Tom Mellon, a splendid chap with a shock of honest white hair, compared opponents of highrise building with early-day San Franciscans "who opposed the development of Golden Gate Park, insisting it should be kept in its natural state of sand dunes."

That's rich, that is. If Golden Gate Park weren't there already, do you think the manic-progressives would be clamoring to create it? Are you mad? It would be covered with supermarkets, service stations, lookalike houses and wall-to-wall concrete — another Doelgerville . . .

But as long as we have Manhattan-minded Mayors, politically powerful real estaters and wheeler-dealer architectural firms like Skidmore Owings & Merrill ("The three blind Mies," as the architects' joke goes), San Francisco is in constant danger of turning into something quite different from "the city everybody loves."

Broaden the tax base, narrow the vision. This is not to say that people who like highrises are more un-American than those who don't, and it's pointless to try to blame this group or that. Call it a failure of the imagination, a pellmell helter-skelter willingness to trade the God-given beauties of San Francisco for a mess of blottage . . .

The irony is that these build-and-be-damned (the public be jammed) types think of themselves as hard-nosed businessmen. Since tourism is our No. 1 industry, do they ever stop to consider what visitors come here to see? You can bet your bottom that it isn't more tall buildings and traffic jams. They come here for what San Francisco has always been famous for and what is now being threatened: exhilarating vistas, good food in a variety of little eating places, a way of life that is "different," a bit more free and open than their own. Parks, not parking lots. Even topless dancers in preference to topless buildings.

It's instructive to read the ads published elsewhere in the country by the S.F. Convention & Visitors Bureau. They extol the cable cars, Fisherman's Wharf, Bay cruises, Ghirardelli Square and the Cannery, the Lombard St. curly-cue, the bridges, even the street musicians.

Amazing. No mention of Bank of America World Headquarters and its "amenities" — that icy, windswept plaza you hurry across as fast as you can. Not a word about the new Holiday Inn and its ridiculous $500,000 bridge across Kearny St., stealing yet a few more precious feet from Portsmouth Square. No glowing words about the structure that just misses being noble, St. Mary's Cathedral. Certainly we have some handsome new buildings, but the Convention Bureau seems to sense that the potential tourist wouldn't be interested.

When it needs an illustration, it turns to the flower stands.

IT IS too late? When you see the plans for the rest of Embarcadero Center, a few yards from the waterfront, the question may be academic. But if you love a city, you go on butting your head against the walls that grow higher and higher and will eventually encircle the last of the best we have.

Dick Nolan   Examiner (5/27/71)   Tourist Troubles

The prime directive here has been Manhattanization: dense office and ᴄsidential construction in complement ... creation of a white collar city with an army of white collar employees working in hygienic file cabinets by day and filed away in hygienic high-risers by night.

This grand design has completely overlooked the facts of population. San Francisco has been filling with urban immigrants not only lacking in white collar skills but also in trade skills.

Quite systematically, factories, warehouses, and even the old produce market have been driven out of town. The market site is given over to a high rising development. The mattress factory becomes a stores-restaurant-apartment development. The printing industry is scattered. And so on. The jobs go where the people are not, and the people teem where there are no jobs. Welfare costs go through the roof.

Ah, but there's the tourist trade. Restaurant workers press for higher wages and benefits they need to live in a high priced town like this. Restaurant owners boost the menu prices. The result is that probably nowhere else in the world except our model, Manhattan, are restaurant prices as high. The words gets out, and family type tourists are properly appalled.

At the same time hotel space expands. Construction workers in an unsteady market and a high priced town press hard for the higher wages and benefits they need. Costs spiral. In some hotel developments and expansions the simple arithmetic requires a $50-per-unit-per-night room tab to amortize construction investments. Tourists are appalled ...

All the time we were making all these planning errors, we were adjusting the San Francisco economy so that it depended more and more on the tourist dollar. For some reason, perhaps the glamor of the cable cars, the people in charge have always felt that tourists will fight their way past all obstacles and camp in the park, if necessary, to see San Francisco . . .

The hellish part of all this is that tourism can't suddenly be abandoned as a civic enterprise. We can't put the factories back and re-balance the economy. We have to live with the Manhattan we have created, at best seeing that it develops no farther in that insane direction.

Guy Wright Examiner (3/7/71) Height of Foolishness

Views are precious in San Francisco, and every politician has pledged in some way to preserve them.

Yet, if we turn our backs for half a minute, someone starts building another view-blocker, with the sotto voce blessings of the City Hall chameleons and the battle of the vista must be fought all over again . . .

Somewhere, properly pickled and preserved for the bemusement of posterity, San Francisco has a master plan that sets height limits. But it doesn't mean much.

If you are influential, shrewd or guileful enough, you can build whatever you please anywhere in this town. The sky is literally the limit.

The quiet wink, the understood nod, the consenting gesture that only an auctioneer would catch, and the rules are suspended.

The rule on building heights in San Francisco is simply this: Try it and see if you can get away with it.

Only if someone kicks up a fuss and the politicians start to fear they may lose more votes than the favor is worth are the rules enforced.

Charles McCabe Chronicle (4/23/71) Is Growth Good?

That our civilization in general, and our cities in particular are living far beyond their income, is no longer a speculation or a whimsicality. It is an indisputable fact.

It is hard to equate progress, which is largely the sale and development of real estate, with the consequences of progress: crowding, dirty water, dirty air. You can put a dollar and cents label on a skyscraper. You cannot do it with air so dirty that children are kept from school on account of it . . .

The choice between economic growth, which has been our national aim and deeply-entrenched ideal, and the cleanliness of the air and water envelope in which we spend our days, is surely going to be a desperate one. It's hard to tell a man who's making a million bucks a year that he must take a cut to half a million because the thing he makes hurts the air and water, and consequently the people, of his country. Greed is the most tenaciously-held emotion of man . . .

The message is clear: Economic growth has made us live beyond our means as human beings. That growth, it is becoming apparent, is not all that great.

How to make a city Beautiful.

FIRST, TAKE AN ORDINARY UGLY AREA, WITH ORDINARY, UGLY, SMALL BUILDINGS AND HOUSES, AND UGLY OPEN SPACE AND UGLY TREES

AND MAKE EVERYBODY MOVE OUT

AND CLEAR THE AREA

AND BUILD A COUPLE OF TALL BUILDINGS

AND FILL THEM UP WITH PEOPLE FOR A FEW HOURS EACH DAY, MONDAY THROUGH FRIDAY

WHICH MEANS A FREEWAY TO
BRING THE PEOPLE INTO THE CITY

AND THEN BUILD MORE TALL BUILDINGS
(AND A FEW MORE FREEWAYS)

AND BEFORE YOU KNOW IT, YOU HAVE A PERFECTLY *Beautiful* CITY!

If You Like New York and Chicago, You're Gonna Love San Francisco

Compiled by Marilyn Morgan

Compl. Date	Building	Stories	Gross floor area in sq. ft. (in thousands, rounded off)	Floor area ratio 9 (rounded off)
New York				
1931	Empire State	102	2,074	25:1
1932-40	Rockefeller Center (group of buildings)	6-70	6,056	12:1
1961	Chase Manhattan Bank	60	1,860	16:1
1964	Pan Am	59	3,000	19:1
1970	World Trade Center (group of buildings)	5-110	12,000	17:1
Chicago				
1969	First National Bank	60	2,000	18:1
1929-30	Merchandise Mart	22	4,000	15:1
1955	Prudential	41	1,763	10:1
1965	Civic Center	31	1,166	10:1

Selected Tall Buildings, San Francisco

#	Compl. Date	Building	Stories	Gross floor area	Floor area ratio
1.	1921, 1948	Standard Oil	22	632	17:1
2.	1926	Russ	31	632	16:1
3.	1929	450 Sutter	26	289	12:1
4.	1930	Shell	30	316	18:1
5.	1892, 1930	Mills Bldg.	22	486	10:1
6.	1955	Equitable	25	430	18:1
7.	1958	Jack Tar (office)	11	175	3:1
8.	1959	Crown Zellerbach	20	341	6:1
9.	1959	John Hancock	15	189	7:1
10.	1959	550 California	13	206	8:1
11.	1959	Insurance Securities	14	283	7:1
12.	1961	Fairmont Tower	29	193	5:1
13.	1963	Hilton	17	676	8:1
14.	1963	Federal Bldg.	20	1,219	11:1
15.	1964	Pacific Telephone	13	628	9:1
16.	1964	Standard Oil-Chevron	22	283	7:1
17.	1964	Hartford	33	467	18:1
18.	1965	Hong Kong Bank	19	119	12:1
19.	1966	Wells Fargo	43	717	24:1
20.	1966	Fox Plaza (office)	29	310	10:1
21.	1959, 1967	Pacific Telephone	16	432	9:1
22.	1967	Insurance Center	16	137	13:1
23.	1967	Bank of California	21	300	13:1
24.	1967	Alcoa	27	590	5:1

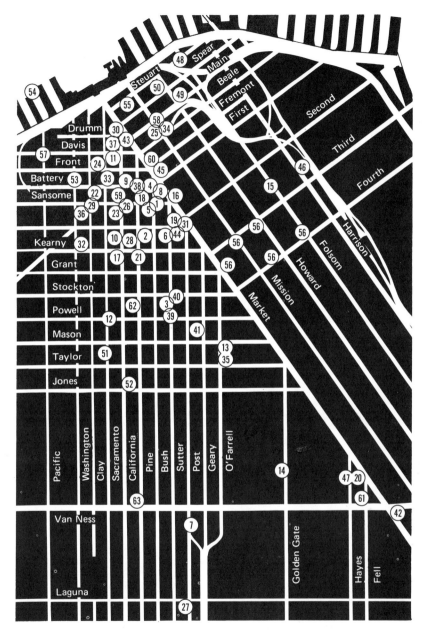

Only New York and Chicago have more skyscrapers than San Francisco.
Selected downtown highrise: numbers on map correspond to numbers on
chart.

25.	1967	Bechtel	23	706	14:1
26.	1968	First Savings	26	186	20:1
27.	1968	Miyako Hotel	15	50	2:1
28.	1969	Bank of America	52	1,771	18:1
29.	1969	Wells Fargo Annex	20	379	17:1
30.	1969	Mutual Benefit Life	32	568	13:1
31.	1969	Aetna	38	455	20:1
32.	1970	Holiday Inn (Chinese Cultural Center)	26	316	9:1
33.	1970	Security Pacific Bank (Embarcadero #1)	45	946	13:1
34.	1971	PG&E	34	907	11:1
35.	1971	Hilton Tower	46	372 (tower) 1,048 (total)	12:1 (total)
36.	1972	Transamerica	48	535	13:1
37.	1972	West Coast Life	37	738	19:1
38.	1972	Pacific Insurance	33	416	17:1
39.	1972	Westbury Hotel (Knott)	29	276	14:1
40.	1972	Hyatt House (Union Square)	30	505	14:1
41.	1972	St. Francis Hotel (tower)	31	1,025 (total)	13:1 (total)
42.	1972	Howard Johnson Hotel	n.a.	n.a.	n.a.
43.	1973	Embarcadero Center Hotel	20	772	n.a.
44.	1976 (?)	Crocker-Citizens	n.a.	n.a.	n.a.
45.	n.a.	Tishman Cahill	38	1,041	24:1
46.	n.a.	Del Monte	25-30	600-900	n.a.
47.	n.a.	Fox Plaza Addition	13	n.a.	n.a.
48.	n.a.	Blake Building	11	165	12:1
49.	n.a.	Folger Building (addition)	17	353	9:1
50.	n.a.	Spear Streets (2)	13	250	10:1
			13	186	10:1
51.	n.a.	Princess Hotel	29	214	9:1
52.	n.a.	Hyatt House (Nob Hill)	15	245	7:1
53.	n.a.	Embarcadero Center #2, 3, 4	31, 31, 60	n.a.	10:1
54.	n.a.	Ferry Port Plaza	10	1,140	2:1
55.	n.a.	Southern Pacific (2 towers)	27	n.a.	n.a.
			43	n.a.	n.a.
56.	n.a.	Yerba Buena Complexes			
		#1	37	760	n.a.
		#2	13	273	n.a.
		#3	13	273	n.a.
		#4	13	273	n.a.
		Hotel	16	n.a.	n.a.
57.	n.a.	Golden Gateway Apts.	n.a.	1,000	4:1
58.	n.a.	Gateway Plaza	36	859	12:1
59.	n.a.	Bank of Tokyo	n.a.	n.a.	n.a.
60.	n.a.	Metropolitan Life	38	950	20:1
61.	n.a.	Calif. State Automobile Assn.	29	427	12:1
62.	n.a.	Pierre Hotel (2 bldgs.)	15	n.a.	n.a.
			12	n.a.	n.a.
63.	n.a.	Holiday Inn (Van Ness)	25	n.a.	n.a.

How to Sniff Out, Then Snuff Out Highrises

1. Demolition of a Building
How to find out

a. Call the Central Permit Bureau (558-3294) and ask if an application for a demolition permit has been filed to demolish a specific building at a specific address. Note: Sometimes, to lay down a smokescreen, the owner will file an application for the same building at two addresses.

b. Plug into the neighborhood grapevine (realtor, merchants' association, local businessmen) or local neighborhood conservation group (some check demolition and site permits regularly). If you suspect a building may soon be demolished, write Alfred Goldberg, Superintendent of the Bureau of Building Inspection, Room 202, 450 McAllister St., and ask to be notified in writing when a demolition application is filed for a specific building at a specific address. Follow up with phone calls.

What you can do

a. Request the Planning Department, Building Inspector and Bureau of Engineering not to issue a demolition permit on specific grounds that the demolition will adversely effect the neighborhood and adjoining property. Notify the news media and kick up a storm.

b. If the permit is approved, you have 10 days to file a written appeal ($10 filing fee) with the Board of Permit Appeals. Meets every Monday at 2 p.m. in Room 228 in City Hall.

c. This board approves one monstrosity after another without flinching ("they're businessmen on that board, they know the value of investments and they're not about to turn down a developer on a whim," a man in the building inspector's office summed up approvingly). So: you should work with an attorney, a neighborhood group, with maximum publicity to be effective.

d. An outside chance: if the building is of historical or architectural value, you may be able to delay for months and possibly halt demolition by persuading the Planning Commission and Supervisors to declare it a city landmark. Start with the Landmarks Preservation Advisory Board, which meets every first and third Wednesday at 2:30 p.m. at the Planning Department. Don Stover, an architect with Wurster, Bernardi and Emmons, is the chairman and Mrs. Peter Platt, who surveyed landmarks for a Junior League book of historical residences, the most active member. Other members: Dr. Charles Albert Shumate, the Rev. John D. McGloin, Charles Fracchia, Francis L. Whisler, Mrs. John W. Mailliard III and W. Stanley Whitaker. (Incidental note: Shumate was a member of Citizens for San Francisco, the Chamber of Commerce front group fighting the Duskin initiative.)

2. Zoning Variance or Conditional Use Permit for New Building
How you find out

a. Call the cases section in the Planning Department (Dan Sullivan, KL 8-3056) and ask to be placed on the notification list for zoning changes in your neighborhood. Plug into your neighborhood grapevine and neighborhood groups. Watch city legal notices in the Examiner.

b. The city must notify everyone by mail who lives within 300 feet of the place where the rezoning would occur.

What you can do

a. The moment you hear of a variance or rezoning coming up, press the zoning administrator for an administrative hearing and then testify. The crucial question: does the variance involve a 10 per cent deviation from the codes? If it does, then you can request public hearing and you have an immensely stronger case.

b. Good strategy: whenever your early warning system tells you of coming demolition, a new building, a tricky variance, plunge ahead and ask for a rezoning to protect the site. If nothing else, as the Mis-

oplop

San Francisco

sion Coalition and other groups have found, this smokes out the owner/developer and forces him to fight you and openly declare his intention for the property.

b. If you lose, appeal to the Board of Permit Appeals, then if necessary to the courts.

3. Site Permit
How you find out

a. Call the Central Permit Bureau (558-3294) and ask if a site permit has been filed for a specific address. Owner/developer must file by street address.

b. Sometimes, you can check the property records (as shown in Bolton power structure research, p.241) and get a hint if a developer is assembling parcels for the possibility of a big project (example: Transamerica/Divisadero in the South Park area).

What you can do

a. Ask the president of the planning commission for a discretionary review of the project. Make critical internal comments to the planning staff and building inspectors. Notify the media (start with Herb Caen on the Chronicle, Andy Gollan on the Progress, Tom DeVries on Newsroom), shake the grapevine of neighborhood groups and kick up the dust.

b. If you lose, appeal to the Board of Permit Appeals, then if necessary to the courts.

Manhattan

The Most Active Neighborhood and Conservation Associations †

*76. Alcatraz Heights Improvement Club
Jack E. Early, Pres.
134 Pfeiffer St., SF 94133, 781-1950

71. Alta Plaza Improvement Association
D.C. Lundy, Pres.
2210 Broderick St., SF 94115, 346-7743

12. Anza Vista Civic Improvement Assn.
Mrs. Lee Dolson, Vice Pres.
85 Fortuna Ave., SF 94115, 346-3553

27. Balboa Terrace Homes Association
Fred W. Wentker Jr., Pres.
650 Upland Dr., SF 94127, 587-9210

Bayview-Hunters Point Joint Housing Committee
Elouise Westbrook Dent, Chairman
223 Southridge Rd., SF 94124, 648-7793

Bernal Heights Association
Ralph Larson, Pres.
158 Bocana, SF 94110, 648-6036

59. Buena Vista Neighborhood Assn.
Wesley L. Dawe, Pres.
79 Buena Vista Terrace, SF 94117, 556-5908 Work, 431-1991 Home

32. Cayuga Improvement Association
Ashod Mirigian, Pres.
198 Seneca Ave., SF 94112, 587-1224

Citizens Planning Committee
693 Mission St., SF, 861-4569

Citizens Waterfront Committee
Mimi Lurie
1 Maritime Plaza, SF, 362-4195

Coalition for Responsible Inner Sunset Planning
Tom Rickert
1329 7th Ave., SF 731-0123

Committee for a Vote on High-Rise (Duskin)
Tom Lea
520 3rd St., SF, 397-9220

† Complete list available from SPUR for $3.

* Numerals shown before many of the groups listed correspond to a boundary map on file with the Zoning Division, Department of City Planning. Neighborhood organizations shown without a numeral and who wish written notice of proposed zoning changes within their areas should send a written request to Zoning Division, Department of City Planning, Attention: Miss Marilyne Labagh, 100 Larkin St., SF 94102. Include an ordinary gas station map with the association's boundaries marked in crayon.

5. Cow Hollow Improvement Club
    Raymond P. Haas, Pres.
    650 California St., Suite 2920, SF 94108, 434-1600 Work, 567-1311 Home
    Crestlake Property Owners Assn.
    George H. Koster, Pres.
    317 Crestlake Dr., SF 94132, 564-4716
58. Crocker-Amazon Improvement Assn.
    W.A. Angeloni, Pres.
    1356 Geneva Ave., SF 94112, 556-0620 Work, 585-7173 Home
102. Diamond Heights Neighborhood Assn.
    Peggy Graves, Chairman
    108 Turquoise Way, SF 94131, 826-0955
    Divisadero Area Assn.
    Everett Pugh, Pres.
    650 Divisadero St., SF 94117, 346-2155
18. Dolores Heights Improvement Club
    Donald S. Quick, Chairman
    385 Cumberland St., SF 94114, 863-6093
43. East & West of Castro Improv. Club
    Harry Small, Pres.
    866 Foerster St., SF 94127
19. East Mission Improvement Assn.
    Donald A. Ramacciotti, Pres.
    1426 Florida St., SF 94110, 824-9505
    Ecology Center
    Gil Bailie
    13 Columbus Ave., SF, 391-6307
    Environmental Workshop
    David Gast
    135 Greenwich St., SF
47. Excelsior District Improv. Assn.
    Mark C. Tasovaz, Pres.
    25 Santa Rosa Ave., SF 94112, 585-1360
89. Friends of Noe Valley
    Claire Pilcher
    471 Hoffman Ave., SF 94114, 282-1587
68. Francisco Heights Civic Club
    Mitchell Cutler, Pres.
    2942 Turk St., SF 94115, 221-1009 Home, 221-3012 Work
80. Geneva Terrace Property Owners Assn.
    Ralph Fong, Sec.
    421 Argonaut, SF 94134, 333-6928
40. Glen Park Property Owners Assn.
    Velma Rae Scripps, Pres.
    42A Lippard St., SF 94131, 585-8247
16. Grand View Neighbors
    Elsa J. Strait, Sec.
    204 Grand View Ave., SF 94114, 647-4916

38. Haight-Ashbury Neighborhood Council
   Raymond R. Waller, Pres.
   1525 Waller St., SF 94117, 661-1870
   Inner Sunset Action Committee
   Douglas W. Weddell, Chairman
   329 Irving St., SF 94122, 564-6046 Home, 362-1834 Work
10. Jordan Park Improvement Association
   Stuart Kuhn, Pres.
   91 Commonwealth Ave., SF 94118, 752-5265
82. Judah Street Improvement Assn.
   William A. Blanck, Pres.
   1399 46th Ave., SF 94122, 681-8722
56. Lakeshore Acres Improvement Club
   James A. Tufo, Pres.
   87 Lakeshore Dr., SF 94132, 564-2880
26. Lakeside Home Owners Association
   Edward J. Reidy, Pres.
   64 Woodacre Dr., SF 94132, 587-0956 Home, 474-6655 Work
29. Lakeside Property Owners Assn.
   Abbe A. Vederoff, Pres.
   101 Stratford Dr., SF 94132, 333-9651
11. Laurel Heights Improvement Assn.
   Grace G. Goldberg, Pres.
   65 Lupine St., SF 94118, 751-6959
1. Marina Civic Improvement & Property Owners Assn., Inc.
   Wm. F. Train, Pres.
   2435 Bay St., SF 94123, 561-5090 Work, 567-7493 Home
2. Marina Home Owners Protective Assn.
   John Battaglia, Pres.
   3731 Divisadero St., SF 94123, 931-9174
85. Market-Castro-Duboce Property Owners Assn.
   Eugene K. Mayo, Pres.
   182 Noe St., SF 94114, 431-2532
25. Merced Manor Property Owners Assn.
   J. William Conroy, Pres.
   650 Eucalyptus Dr., SF 94132, 664-0153
   Midtown Terrace Home Owners Assn.
   Ernest Marx, Pres.
   661 Panorama Dr., SF 94131, 824-2762 Home, 664-6760 Work
60. Miraloma Park Improvement Assn.
   Mary Joe Pandolfi, Pres.
   151 Molimo Dr., SF 94127, 334-3057
86. Mission Coalition Organization
   Larry Del Carlo, Pres.
   2707 Folsom St., SF 94110, 647-3140
1B. Mission Neighborhood Centers, Inc.
   Harvey E. Gabler, Exec. Dir.
   2588 Mission St., Room 224, SF 94110, 285-3400

88. New Mission Terrace Improvement Association
   Rose M. White, Pres.
   306 Delano Ave., SF 94112, 587-5398
101. Outer Richmond Neighborhood Assn.
   R.H. LaRue, Co-Chairman
   5021 Anza St., SF 94121, 386-1547
69. Pacific Heights Neighborhood Council
   Edgar S. Bissinger, Pres.
   2199 Jackson St., SF 94115, 346-0312
21. Parkside District Improvement Club
   Joseph Balanesi Jr., Pres.
   924 Taraval St., SF 94116, 731-7900 Work, 681-2711 Home
94. Peralta Heights Improvement Assn.
   Harold F. Gilbert, Pres.
   135 Holladay Ave., SF 94110, 661-3325
   Planning Assn. For The Richmond
   Richard I. Klein, Pres.
   633 Clement St., SF 94118, 751-2053
33. Portola & McLaren Park Assn.
   Neil Wallace, Pres.
   1830 Burrows St., SF 94134, 587-1650
51. Potrero Hill Homeowners' & Residents Council
   Anna I. Buck, Pres.
   690 DeHaro St., SF 94107, 282-1904
73. Potrero Hill Neighborhood House Committee
   of Community Concern
   Mrs. Carl Sundahl, Chairman
   1230 19th St., SF 94107, 282-4113
62. Presidio Heights Assn. of Neighbors
   Robert P. Lilienthal
   One Spruce St., SF 94118, 221-0770, 221-4327
   Property Owners Association of North Beach
   John P. Figone, Pres.
   550 Columbus Ave., SF 94133, 397-0698
   Richmond Environment Action
   Kathryn Beebe, Sec.
   2118 Anza St., SF 94118, 751-0210
   Richmond District Community Council
   Natalie White, Pres.
   360 18th Ave., SF 94121, 752-3557
   Richmond Renewal Association
   Mikio M. Fujimoto, Pres.
   606 Third Ave., SF 94118, 386-7962
   Rossi Park Protective Assn., Inc.
   Patrick J. Walsh, Pres.
   524 Fourth Ave., SF 94118, 751-3860 Home, 553-9111 Work
3. Russian Hill Improvement Assn.
   Frank Hinman, Jr., Pres.
   1000 Francisco St., SF 94109, 421-4338 Work, 673-5553 Home

San Francisco Beautiful
Mrs. Hans Klussman
260 Green St., SF, 421-2608

52. St. Mary's Park Improvement Club
Tom Cotter, Pres.
65 Genebern Way, SF 94112, 585-2710

SF Tomorrow
Michael Doyle
693 Mission, SF, 861-4569

Sierra Club
Dan Rosenberg
220 Bush St., SF, 981-8634, Ext. 27

34. Silver Terrace Improvement Club
Mario D. Giampaoli
40 Santa Fe Ave., SF 94124, 467-1178

SPEAK (Sunset-Parkside Education & Action Committee)
Thomas E. Rickert, Coordinator
1329 Seventh Ave., SF 94122, 731-0123

Sunnyside Improvement Club
Lillian Perinoni, Sec.
44 Hearst Ave., SF 94131, 587-8429

13. Sunset Heights Improvement Club
Charles A. Walworth
1975 Funston Ave., SF 94116, 397-0100 Work, 731-7423 Home

4. Telegraph Hill Dwellers
Curtis J. Baldwin, Pres.
370 Chestnut St., SF 94133, 781-8534

74. The Telegraph Hill Survival Assn.
Gene Morzenti, Pres.
350 Green St., SF 94133, 362-3059

39. Twin Peaks Improvement Association
Mrs. Albert W. Long, Trea.
90 Mountain Spring Ave., SF 94114, 566-5317

63. Union Street Association
Robert Moor, Pres.
1800 Union St., SF 94123, 563-8767

Upper Market Planning Association
Arthur H. Middleton, Jr., Exec. Sec.
160 Grand View Ave., SF 94114, 282-8805

36. Upper Noe Valley Neighborhood Council
Barbara Schipper, Sec.
105 Chenery St., SF 94131, 647-3622

Van Ness-Polk Civic Council, Inc.
Ernest A. Hanni, Pres.
1641 Jackson ST., SF 94109, 673-0727 Work, 681-9721 Home

Visitacion Valley Community Center
William Smith, Exec. Dir.
50 Raymond Ave., SF 94134, 467-6400

22. West Portal Home Owners Association
1410 Portola Dr., SF 94127, 392-1314 Work, 664-3823 Home

A Citizen's Guide to Land/Power Structure Research

Written and compiled by Charles Bolton

IF YOU WANT TO KNOW:
Who owns the land and the building?

GO TO:
Tax Assessor's Office
Rm. 101, City Hall

WHAT YOU WANT:
Realty Index

WHERE:
Red book located on the counter

YOU CAN FIND OUT:
1. The name of the owner
2. The block/lot number

HOW IT WORKS:
Realty Index lists entry alphabetically by street names. Numbered streets/avenues are in front of the books.

NOTE:
Block/lot number is another way to identify property aside from the street address. In this system, each lot on a block is numbered, and every block in the city is numbered. Remember to write down the block/lot number! It is necessary when you need to look up other information on a piece of property.

WHAT YOU WANT:
Sales ledger

WHERE:
Located on shelves next to counter

YOU CAN FIND OUT:
The Sales Ledger covers all property transactions for a lot on a particular block from 1906 to the present.
It tells you:
1. Who sold the property
2. Who bought it

3. Date of the transaction
4. Block and page number of the Property Deed in the Recorder's Office (only in the newer books)

HOW IT WORKS:
1. Get block/lot number from realty index.
2. Turn to page number that corresponds to block number.
3. Look down the column marked "lot" to find the transaction(s) affecting this particular lot. In these books, a block number corresponds to a page number.

NOTE:
Write down the old survey block number at the top of the page. It will be necessary to identify the property if you look up the property deed.

WHAT YOU WANT:
Also in this office:
1. Duplicate Assessor's Roll (useful to look up value of property). Entries listed by block/lot number
2. Block Map Books—maps of lots on block showing lot numbers and physical dimensions. Page numbers correspond to block numbers
3. Duplicate alphabetical index to Secured Assessment Roll (see Tax Collector's Office in "What property does he own?" on how to use)
4. Polk's City Directory (see "Who is he?" on how to use)
5. Edward's Abstracts of daily records
6. Giant city map showing the numbers of all the blocks in the city

IF YOU WANT TO KNOW:
What property does he own?

WHAT YOU WANT:
Alphabetical Index to the secured property rolls

WHERE:
Blue books with red binding on counter in right rear section of office

YOU CAN FIND OUT:
The index lists block/lot number of each piece of property owned by an individual

HOW IT WORKS:
Index is alphabetical by name of owner

GO TO:
Tax Collector's Office
Rm. 107, City Hall

WHAT YOU WANT:
Secured Assessment rolls

WHERE:
Large grey books located on counter in middle of the floor

YOU CAN FIND OUT:
1. The address of property
2. The worth of the land and the building on it
3. The address to which the property tax bill is sent (This address may be a clue to where he lives, his business address, or his business associates.)

HOW IT WORKS:
Entries are arranged by block lot numbers.

Each entry in the assessment rolls gives:
1. The name of the owner
2. The address of the property
3. The address to which the tax statement is mailed
4. The value of the land
(The "C" in the left hand margin indicates the "cash or market" value of the land and building. The "A" in the margin equals the assessed value which is 25% of the cash or market value. The "A" value is the base that the actual property tax is computed from.)
5. The value of the building (called "improvements")
6. The type of tax exemption
7. The amount of taxes
8. The dates that the taxes were paid

NOTE:
1. Check addresses of property in Polk's to see who lives there
2. Check tax mailing address in Polk's to see who occupies that address

WHAT YOU WANT:
Also in this office:
1. Realty Index (see Who Owns It)
2. City Directory
3. Owners' mailing address index, arranged by block/lot number. Gives tax statement mailing address only.

IF YOU WANT TO KNOW:
Who was involved in the sale of property?
How much was paid?
Where was the money borrowed?

WHAT YOU WANT:
Grantor/Grantee Index
WHERE:
Current books are located on counters. To find volumes covering previous years, ask the clerk to assist you.

YOU CAN FIND OUT:

1. The date a deed was recorded

2. The names of the grantors and grantees

3. The deed book and page number (necessary when looking up the deed)

HOW IT WORKS:

Grantor Index—lists person(s) who granted or sold property alphabetically by last name. Grantee Index lists person(s) who received or bought property alphabetically by last name.

NOTE:

1. Corporations are listed in separate indexes right after the sur-name index of both the Grantor/Grantee Indexes.

2. Deed book and page numbers can also be found in the sales ledger, located in the Assessor's Office.

GO TO:

Recorder's Office
Rm. 167, City Hall

WHAT YOU WANT:

Property/Trust Deeds and other land records

WHERE:

1. Microfilm reels (pre-1959) are in room in back of office. Ask the attendant to locate the document number.

2. Microfilm cards (post-1959) are located in grey metal cabinets to left of main counters.

YOU CAN FIND:

Deeds are usually either Grant Deeds or Deeds of Trust. A Grant Deed records the transaction of the property from one person (grantor) to another (grantee). A

Deed of Trust indicates that a mortgage is on the property. If the right to sell the property is involved, it is a first mortgage. If the top of the deed says "Deed of Trust and Assignment of Rents" or the text uses the phrase: "assignment of rents " it usually indicates a second mortgage. You can also find out:

1. Where the deed is to be mailed after recording

2. The names of other individuals involved in the transaction (useful clues to other connections)

3. The approximate amount of the sales, indicated by the amount of the transfer tax (paid at the rate of 55¢ per $100)

4. The amount listed in the Deeds of Trust

HOW IT WORKS:

Microfilm cards are arranged in numerical sequence. Each microfilm card contains 50 page numbers. Mark the location of the card you remove from the file with a green plastic tab. Take the card over to a microfilm viewer. Near the top on the right side of the viewer is a small flipper which is pressed down to raise the viewer head for inserting the microfilm card. On the left side is the on-off switch; on the top, the focusing knob.

WHAT YOU WANT:

Also in this office:

1. Individual block charts of every block in the city showing the configuration of the lots

2. Old block charts for the city, going back to 1913. These charts are useful for translating old block numbers into the current block number system.

3. Edward's Abstracts of daily records

IF YOU WANT TO KNOW:
All about a corporation

GO TO:
County Clerk's Office
Rm. 325, City Hall

WHAT YOU WANT:
Index to Corporations

WHERE:
On far rear counter, towards the back of the room

YOU CAN FIND OUT:
Who owns a firm or company

HOW IT WORKS:
Names of corporations or businesses are listed alphabetically. Use the chart in the front of the book to find the page number. Names are grouped alphabetically and entries are by date. Index gives file number. Use file number to find file.

WHAT YOU WANT:
Corporation filing papers

WHERE:
Back of room, to right of desk where indexes are located

HOW IT WORKS:
Look up file number. Pull out file and examine.

YOU CAN FIND OUT:
Names of directors and their addresses for corporations, whether or not stock has been issued, who owns the stock, the purpose for which the corporation was created, and the merger history

NOTE:
Often the people listed as directors are the incorporators—the people who signed the incorporation papers. They are not the directors and often serve to shield the real people who control the company. Check to see if incorporators are lawyers.

WHAT YOU WANT:
Index to Businesses with Fictitious Names

WHERE:
On far rear counter, towards the back of the room

YOU CAN FIND OUT:
The name of the owners and home addresses for businesses with fictious names

HOW IT WORKS:
Names of businesses are listed alphabetically. Use the chart in the front of the book to find the page number. Names are grouped alphabetically and entries are by date. It will also often list the owner's name in the index. Use file number to find file.

WHAT YOU WANT:
Fictious name filing papers

WHERE:
Back of room, to right of desk where indexes are located

HOW IT WORKS:
Look up file number, pull out file and examine

GO TO:
Assessor's Office
Rm. 101, City Hall

WHAT YOU WANT:
Polk's City Directory

WHERE:
Under the counter

YOU CAN FIND OUT:
1. Names of partners, officers or

directors of a business (white section)

2. Look up the address of the firm in the green section to see who else occupies the same building.

HOW IT WORKS:
See "Who is He?" Assessor's Office

GO TO:
Main Library

WHERE:
History-Social Science Room

WHAT YOU WANT:
Moody's Manuals-Industrials, Bank and Finance

YOU CAN FIND OUT:
Background on:
1. Corporations' history, major acquisitions and mergers
2. Major executive officers and the directors of the company
3. Its major subsidiaries, properties, plants, etc.
4. Financial accounting data on the company's performance

HOW IT WORKS:
Look up page number in green, alphabetical index in the front of the book

WHAT YOU WANT:
Contacts Influential

YOU CAN FIND OUT:
Each volume lists all the businesses and non-profit organizations in a designated area (separate directories for San Francisco, Peninsula and East Bay).
All listings (except "Key Man" listings) give:
1. Name of the company or corporation
2. Names of key officers, executives, directors, partners and owners

3. Address of each facility and whether it's a home office, branch office or local business
4. Number of employees
5. The SIC code of the company

HOW IT WORKS:
Each volume is organized into an alphabetical listing section (white pages) by zip code area, by standard industrial classification code (activity type) and by the name of the owner, key executives, directors and managers. The "Key Man" section (yellow pages) lists each person's name alphabetically and states his position and the name of the company or organization.

NOTE:
This source is excellent for tracking down middle-sized or local businesses. However, information should be verified to insure accuracy.

WHAT YOU WANT:
Walker's Manual of Far Western Corporations

YOU CAN FIND OUT:
Each entry gives the corporate address (home office), where first incorporated, date of incorporation, type of business, list of directors and the amount of corporate stock they own, and abbreviated financial and stock data.

HOW IT WORKS:
Find corporate name and page number in the green index in the front of the book.

WHERE:
History-Social Science Room

WHAT YOU WANT:
Polk's City Directory

YOU CAN FIND OUT:
See "Assessor's Office" above.

WHAT YOU WANT:
Standard and Poor's Corporation Records

YOU CAN FIND OUT:
Background on the major U.S. corporations. Usually used as a secondary source to Moody's.

HOW IT WORKS:
Listings alphabetically by corporation name

WHERE:
History-Social Science Room

WHAT YOU WANT:
Standard and Poor's Listed Stock Reports

YOU CAN FIND OUT:
Financial data related to corporate growth as an investment indicator

HOW IT WORKS:
Listings alphabetical by corporation name

WHERE:
History-Social Science Room

ALSO WHAT YOU WANT:
1. Dunn & Bradstreet's Reference Book of Corporate Managers, Standard and Poor's Corporation Records, Studley Shupert's Analysis of Corporate Securities, The Insurance Almanac, The Petroleum Register, Rubber Red Book, reports by the Federal Trade Commission and Senate Judiciary Committee (located by referring to index of government documents.)

2. Directory of Shopping Centers (lists owners, developers and leasers)

3. Poor's Security Dealers of North America (for stock dealers and investment bankers)

4. Martindale-Hubbell Law Directory (lists major clients of law firms)

5. Standard Directory of Advertisers (who advertises with whom)
6. Official Summary of Security Transactions (lists stock transfers and total stock holdings any time corporate officers or major stockholders purchase or sell stock)
7. If you are unable to obtain above, refer to the Value Line Investment Survey Special Report on Officer-Director Transactions (a quarterly investment guide available from business libraries).
8. Vicker's Guide to Investment Company Portfolios (to determine stock holdings in a corporation held by an investment company)
9. Commercial Banks and Their Trust Activites: Emerging Influence in the American Economy (to determine amount of stock controlled by a commercial bank in a corporation: available from government printing office for $7.50 or libraries carrying government documents)
10. Sources of Business Information (book by Edwin R. Corman, which gives a complete analysis of corporate research)
11. Trade journals and house organs (available at SF Business Branch library on Kearny St.)

GO TO:
State of California, Dept. of Corporations, 600 California, S.F.

WHAT YOU WANT:
Corporation reports

YOU CAN FIND OUT:
Corporation reports provide valuable data on the financial health of the corporation. The reports are required by law to be filed each year when the corporation issues stock.

HOW IT WORKS:
To get the file index number for a corporation, call Central Index—557-3812. Then, give that file number to the clerks at the counter and they will bring the file out. Files not in San Francisco can be ordered from other locations.

NOTE:
There is a coin operated xerox machine in the office.

GO TO:
California Dept. of Real Estate, S.F. Office — 350 McAllister, Sacramento phone — 916-445-5741

WHAT YOU WANT:
Real estate information

YOU CAN FIND OUT:
Records tell when license expires, where a realtor is located, etc.

NOTE:
San Francisco office gives out no information on realtors. Call the Sacramento number for this information.

GO TO:
Insurance Commissioner's Office of the State of Calif., 1470 Market St., S.F.

WHAT YOU WANT:
The yearly report to the Governor on insurance companies operating in California

YOU CAN FIND OUT:
1. Insurance rates
2. Agents and broker's license data

GO TO:
Savings and Loan Commissioner's Office of the State of California, 111 Pine St., S.F.

WHAT YOU WANT:
Reports filed every three months by state chartered savings and loan associations

YOU CAN FIND OUT:
Statement of financial condition, the profit and loss statement, the branch savings statement, and in some cases, the audit report

HOW IT WORKS:
EDP printout in Commissioner's office

WHAT YOU WANT:
Commissioner's yearly report to the Governor

YOU CAN FIND OUT:
Year-end balance sheet on each savings and loan association

GO TO:
S.F. Chamber of Commerce, 400 Montgomery

WHAT YOU WANT:
S.F. Chamber of Commerce 700 Largest Corporations in the San Francisco Area

YOU CAN FIND:
Name of corporation, address, name of principle officers or owner, annual sales range, and number of employees

HOW IT WORKS:
Corporations listed by location, alphabetically

GO TO:
Stanford Business Library, Palo Alto

WHAT YOU WANT:
Corporate Prospecti

YOU CAN FIND OUT:
Plenty of valuable information including lists of amount of stock controlled by each director in the company

HOW IT WORKS:
On microfilm cards, filed alphabetically

NOTE:
Prospecti for new stock offerings also available from stock brokers

IF YOU WANT TO KNOW:
Who is he?

GO TO:
Assessor's Office, Rm. 101, City Hall

WHAT YOU WANT:
Polk's City Directory

WHERE:
Under the counter

YOU CAN FIND OUT:
1. Where he lives and where he does business (white and green sections)
2. The name of his wife (white)
3. What he does for a living (white)
4. Any businesses he might be connected with (white)
5. Who else is involved with him (white)
6. Who owns the phone (blue)

HOW IT WORKS:
Polk's has three main sections:
1. White section—lists individual or business alphabetically by last name or business name
2. Green section—lists streets by name alphabetically with who lives or does business at a particular address
3. Blue section—lists phone numbers by exchange (first three numbers) and then by following four numbers

NOTE:
Information in Polk's should be verified to check accuracy. Some simple ways are:
1. Call information to see if the phone number and address are still correct.

2. Call the party and ask him for his name.

GO TO:
Voter Registrar's Office, Rm. 164, City Hall

WHAT YOU WANT:
List of registered voters and voter registration affidavits

YOU CAN FIND OUT:
1. His full name and address
2. Occupation and social security number
3. Date and place of birth
4. Party affiliation
5. The assembly and precinct in which he lives and is registered to vote (SF is divided into four assembly districts, 18, 19, 20 and 23.)
6. Which elections he voted in
7. Which petitions he signed

HOW IT WORKS:
Ask the clerk to see the voter registration lists. They are on computer print-outs in brown folders and are in alphabetical order by name.
The voter registration affidavits are in books on shelves numbered by assembly district. Column on right gives the elections the voter has voted in; column on left, the petitions he has signed.

NOTE:
Key petitions that may indicate political ideology:
54 Proposition 14 against fair housing

70 Proposition P Ceasefire and withdrawal from Vietnam
72 Restricted busing proposition
75 18-year-old vote initiative
77 Recall Reagan initiative
80 McCarthy for President
89 Proposition I—police reorganization
92 Vietnam ceasefire declaration
93 Pollution-clean environment act

GO TO:
Recorder's Office, Rm. 167, City Hall

WHAT YOU WANT:
1. Records of marriage licenses. Listed by date, husband's last name, wife's maiden name.
2. Recorded military discharges

GO TO:
Main Library, S.F.

WHAT YOU WANT:
Biographical index (card file)

WHERE:
Special collections department (3rd floor open from 1 to 6 p.m. M—F, all day Saturday)

YOU CAN FIND OUT:
Lists major newspaper articles, magazine articles on the major business, political and social influentials of S.F.

HOW IT WORKS:
Ask attendant to bring you all index cards on a particular person. Each entry gives story headline, publication in which article appeared, date and page number.
Check publication in periodical room (3rd floor).
Check newspaper (on microfilm: Examiner, Chronicle, News-Call-Bulletin, NY Times, Wall Street Journal, Christian Science Monitor) in newspaper room (3rd floor).

NOTE:
Best clip files are in Examiner and Chronicle morgues, but they are not open to the public. You can often get information by calling their morgues with short, specific questions but it's better to make a written request. At the library, you can often call and get information from the proper room librarian. Usual rule: they'll look up three corporations/names for you.

WHAT YOU WANT:
Poor's Register of Corporations, Directors and Executives

WHERE:
History-Social Science Room

YOU CAN FIND OUT:
Lists most of the major corporate officers and directors of major U.S. corporations and subsidiaries.
Each biographical listing gives:
1. Residential and business address
2. Major position in home corporation
3. Those corporations in which the person is also a director
4. Public or civic offices held

HOW IT WORKS:
First half lists corporations alphabetically and lists chief executives and directors. Second half has biographical data on each director/executive. Listings are alphabetical.

WHAT YOU WANT:
Who's Who in Finance and Industry.
Also: Who's Who: in the West, International, America, California, Public Relations, Banking, American Politics, of American Women, in World Jewry, in Colored America, American Catholic Who's Who, Italian Catholic Who's Who, Who Was Who.

YOU CAN FIND OUT:
1. Residential and business addresses
2. Capsule career history
3. Names of companies in which directorships are held
4. Names of public, private, professional and civic organizations he's connected with
5. Club, political and religious affiliations

HOW IT WORKS:
Listings are alphabetical by last name

ALSO:
Current Biography, Biography Index, New York Times Index, National Encyclopedia of American Biography, Dictionary of American Biography, Social Register for SF, Scott's Blue Book (blacks)

NOTE:
To see what political campaigns he's contributed to, check campaign contribution lists in city clerk's office.

WHERE:
Main reference room

WHAT YOU WANT:
Polk's City Directory

YOU CAN FIND OUT:
See "Assessor's Office, City Hall" above

IF YOU WANT TO KNOW:
What condition is the building in?

GO TO:
Bureau of Building Inspection, Division of Apartment and Hotel Inspection, Rm. 205, 450 McAllister St.

WHAT YOU WANT:
Building File

WHAT YOU CAN FIND:
For any building with more than three units:
1. Name of owners or controlling parties
2. The original building permit

3. Permits for alterations and repairs
4. Past and current building code violations against the building and actions taken
5. Building inspectors' reports
6. Number of units and rooms in building
7. Year built and type of construction

HOW:
Request clerk to see file for the building located at a specific address.

The last lovely city under siege.

Additional Reading

Indispensable: copies of the three glossy & free components of San Francisco's "Comprehensive Plan": Urban Design Plan, Improvement Plan for Residence, Improvement Plan for Transportation. Be prepared for vast deserts of planner's jargon & miraculous city-beautiful mirages: skip all that, read the fine print and the outlines of Manhattan by the Bay will clearly emerge. Available from the Planning Department, 100 Larkin.

San Francisco/Bay Area/California Books

OPEN SPACE: CHOICES BEFORE CALIFORNIA
Williams, Edward A.   Diablo Press   . . . . $ 4.95
BIG BUSINESS & URBAN STAGNATION
Pacific Studies Center   Pacific Studies Center, Palo Alto. 50
EARTHQUAKE COUNTRY
Iacopi, Robert   Sunset Books 2.95
EARTHQUAKE HAZARD IN THE SAN FRANCISCO BAY AREA
Steinbrugge, Karl   UC Institute of Government Studies. 1.50
FRANKLIN K. LANE MONOGRAPHS - CITY AND REGIONAL PLANNING
    FOR THE METROPOLITAN SAN FRANCISCO BAY AREA
Kent, P.J., Jr.   UC Institute of Government Studies
                                    (2 Vol. Series) 1.50
HERE TODAY - SAN FRANCISCO'S ARCHITECTURAL HERITAGE
SF Junior League   Chronicle Books 14.95
POWER AND LAND IN CALIFORNIA
Nader Task Force   Center for the Study of Responsive Law . . .   30.00

Sociological

DEATH & LIFE OF GREAT AMERICAN CITIES
Jacobs, Jane   Vintage Random (V241) 1.95
ECONOMY OF CITIES
Jacobs, Jane   Vintage Random (V584) 1.95
THE CITY IN HISTORY: ITS ORIGINS, ITS TRANSFORMATIONS
    & ITS PROSPECTS
Mumford, Louis   Harcourt Brace 4.95
CULTURE OF CITIES
Mumford, Louis   Harcourt Brace 4.95
URBAN PROSPECT
Mumford, Louis   Harcourt Brace 2.45
HIGHWAY & THE CITY
Mumford, Louis   New American Library. 75
MYTH OF THE MACHINE: THE PENTAGON OF POWER
Mumford, Louis   Harcourt Brace 9.50
THE HIDDEN DIMENSION
Hall, Edward   Doubleday/Anchor 1.45
COMMUNITAS
Goodman, Percival & Paul Vintage Random 1.65

Architecture/Planning

ARCHITECTURE WITHOUT ARCHITECTS
Rudofsky, Bernard   Doubleday 3.95

Additional Reading

CITIES
Halprin, Lawrence   Van Nostrand-Reinhold 15.00
THE IMAGE OF THE CITY
Lynch, Kevin   MIT 2.95
TOWNSCAPE
Cullen, Gordon   Van Nostrand-Reinhold 15.00
BEYOND HABITAT
Safdie, Moshe   MIT 10.00
REPORT ON DEVELOPMENT OF PALO ALTO FOOTHILLS
Livingston/Blayney   Livingston/Blayney . . . .   Available at UC
                                                                    Main Library

Citizen Organizing

RULES FOR RADICALS
Alinsky, Saul   Random House 6.95
THE ORGANIZER'S MANUAL
Organizer's Manual Collective   Bantam 1.25
ECOTACTICS: THE SIERRA CLUB HANDBOOK FOR ENVIRONMENTAL
    ACTIVISTS
Mitchell, John G. w/ Constance L. Stallings   Pocket Books 95

Coit Tower Preserved

Writers and researchers by chapter
52 arch skyscraper foes

Neighborhoods: Charles Bolton, Michael Cussen, Martin Kupferman, Greggar Sletteland.

Economics: Project Director - Tom Lehner, Research Chief - Rich Hayes. Cesare Ades, Al Averbach, Jerry Berkman, Robert Berry, Richard Burke, Mike Cussen, Alec Dubro, Dave Harrington, John Jekabson, Martin Kupferman, A.P. Margaronis, Michael Miller, Marilyn Morgan, Ann Nicks, Peter Owens, Peter Petrakis, Katie Rice, Jane Silverman, Greggar Sletteland, Rose-Marie Turko, Tim Ward.

Politics: Project Director - Charles Bolton, Research Chiefs - A.P. Margaronis, Michael Miller. Joe Bowles, Bruce Brugmann, Dave Harrington, Rich Hayes, Sue Hestor, Roger Newman, Ann Nicks, Peter Petrakis, John Rogers, Linda Prock, Leslie Waddell.

On the Waterfront: Project Director - Richard Reinhardt. Robert Jones, Marilyn Morgan, Katie Rice, Dale Rosen.

Highrise Miscellany: Marcia Berzon, Charles Bolton, Bruce Brugmann, Jon Carroll, Mike Cussen, Jane Galblum, John Kenyon, Martin Kupferman, Michael Metcalf, Peter Owens, Greggar Sletteland, Burton Wolfe.

Graphics: Dennis Barloga, Michael Bry, Marion Dibble, Louis Dunn, Mick Stevens.

Production: Alston Dutton, Barbara Furrer, Ellinor Gordon, Dennis Linden, Robert Menendez, Sandra Payne, Katherine Reifenberg, Wendy Tanowitz.

Managing Director: Jean Dibble

Editing: Bruce Brugmann, Jon Carroll, Marion Dibble, Greggar Sletteland.

Graphics Credits

CARTOONS
Louis Dunn - FRONT & BACK COVERS, pgs. 29, 40, 54, 65, 67, 95, 120, 121, 152, 163, 188, 223, 228, 229, 234, 235, 253
Mick Stevens - pgs. 167, 174, 176
MAPS
Marion Dibble - pgs. 24, 25, 68, 129, 135, 140 (adapted from a U.S. Geological Survey Map), 141 (adapted from a study by the State Earthquake Investigation Commission - 1908), 197 (building adaptations), 214, 215, 231
PHOTOGRAPHY
Bancroft Library, University of Calif. - Berkeley - pgs. 146, 155
Dennis Barloga - pgs. 2, 15, 22, 23, 146, 169, 179, 181, 185, 213, 235
Stewart H. Bloom, Faulkner Photography; Courtesy of Edward F. Bielski - pg. 184
Michael Bry - pgs. 32, 117, 199, 205, 207
Pacific Resources, Inc.; Oakland - pgs. 196, 197
William L. Pereira - pg. 251
Robert Reinhardt - pg. 13
SF Opposition - pg. 109
SF Port Authority - pg. 97
Lloyd Ullberg - pg. 187
US Geological Survey - pg. 129

Printed by The Rip Off Press, San Francisco

Upper level (l to r): Greggar Sletteland, Marion Dibble, Peter Owens, Leslie Waddell, Bruce Brugmann, Dave Harrington

Ground level (l to r): Louis Dunn, Jean Dibble, Rich Hayes, John Kenyon, Charles Bolton, Dan Brugmann, Katrina Brugmann, Sue Hestor, Mike Cussen, Peter Petrakis, Sparky. (Complete list of credits on opposite page.)